D1137349

THE REAL CHARLES

Alan Hamilton has been staff correspondent on *The Times* of London since 1970, covering the world from the Falkland Islands to Tibet. He has been the newspaper's observer of royal events for nearly a decade, ever since the wedding of the Prince and Princess of Wales, and has travelled extensively with many members of the Royal Family, observing them at first hand.

Born in Edinburgh in 1943, Alan Hamilton is the author of *Essential Edinburgh*, *The Royal Handbook* and *The Royal 100*.

The Real
CHARLES

Alan Hamilton

FONTANA/COLLINS

First published in 1988 by
William Collins Sons & Co. Ltd

This edition published in 1989 by
Fontana Paperbacks
8 Grafton Street, London W1X 3LA

Copyright © Alan Hamilton/Antler Books 1988

Printed and bound in Great Britain by
William Collins Sons & Co. Ltd, Glasgow

CONTENTS

ACKNOWLEDGEMENTS

This book would have been impossible without Charles, Prince of Wales, but it is in no way an authorized or approved biography. Its subject nowadays takes the same view as his mother, that the life stories of royalty are best left unwritten during their lives. Nor is it a revelation of the kiss-and-tell variety winnowed from below-stairs gossip. Rather it is the fruit of the last seven years on *The Times* newspaper acting as a regular Boswell to a royal Johnson, and trying to separate facts from unproven innuendo. I am grateful to very many people in Britain and around the world, from members of the Royal Household to British ambassadors abroad, who have submitted to questioning and interview during the royal progress, and to colleagues from the greatly maligned royal ratpack whose company I have enjoyed and whose brains I have mercilessly picked, particularly Victoria Austin, Harry Arnold, Richard Kray, Stephen Lynas, Andrew Morton, Ashley Walton and James Whitaker. My thanks too to John Stidolph of Antler Books and Caroline White for guidance and encouragement. I offer my apologies to the subject for having the temerity to write about him at all, and plead the defence of legitimate fascination. From the dungeons of the Tower I shall continue to insist that the opinions expressed herein are entirely my own.

1

Introduction – A Singular Man

A WEALTHY American Republican attending a charity dinner at the White House gazed in fascinated admiration at the guests of honour, the Prince and Princess of Wales. He was dazzled by the glamour of the one, and struck by the way the other fiddled with his cufflinks and darted nervous glances around the room as though unsure whether he should really be there at all. 'His mother's got the throne and his wife's got the media,' observed the Republican. 'What's left for that poor guy?'

What is left for Charles Philip Arthur George, Prince of Wales, Duke of Cornwall, Duke of Rothesay, Earl of Chester, Earl of Carrick, Baron Renfrew, Lord of the Isles and Prince and Great Steward of Scotland, is to be the sixty-third occupant of the throne of England since the Saxon Egbert of Wessex defeated the Mercians on a Wiltshire hill in AD 825 and began the welding of a tribal island into a single nation under one king. The poor guy's problem is the waiting.

Yet he is in no hurry to claim his inheritance, for any eagerness to hasten on his destiny is tantamount to wishing his mother dead. And he knows as well as anyone that when he finally assumes what outwardly appears one of the most potent offices created by man, he will be all but powerless. He will never be as free to speak and to act as he is now.

He now faces being forty, that supposedly menopausal milestone at which men are told – mainly by their wives who fear a straining at the leash before it is too late – that the final curtain is rung down on youth, and that a man should be set fair in his life and work ready for the long downhill coast to the seventh age of mere oblivion. Not many men have to wait until their fifties or sixties or even later to occupy the first proper job of their lives.

Bernard Shaw, in *Man and Superman*, thought every man over the age of forty a scoundrel, while his dramatist contemporary Sir Arthur Pinero has *The Second Mrs Tanqueray* declaring that from forty to fifty a man is at heart either a stoic or a satyr. Oliver Wendell Holmes, addressing the birthday of the septuagenarian Julia Ward Howe, lyricist of *The Battle Hymn of the Republic*, thought to be seventy years young sometimes far more hopeful than to be forty years old.

As Prince Charles approaches the plateau of his life between the old age of youth and the youth of old age, he shows not the slightest inclination to become a scoundrel, for it is simply not in his nature. No satyr he; training and circumstance have instilled into him a stoicism just sufficient to hold at bay any innermost desire to be somebody and something else. As for reaching the age of forty, he has at times in those past years appeared sewn into a hair shirt of gravity and solemn awareness of his lot which suggests that, even as a child, he was never really young.

He is no revolutionist, for revolution is anathema to an institution whose primary modern purpose is to represent stability and continuity beyond the span of governments, and he knows only too well that two of the previous three Princes of Wales in their different ways rattled the rafters of the royal house in a disturbing manner. Rather he is an evolutionist, well schooled in the Windsor theory of survival, postulating that the rare species he represents must adapt to the times it lives in; otherwise it will go the way of the dinosaur and the woolly mammoth.

The dinosaur's well-known deficiency was to have a body the size of a railway carriage and a brain the size of an egg. The late Earl Mountbatten believed, although not in so many words, that the old Hanoverian royal line was becoming so weak in the genes that it was going the way of the Jurassic Diplodocus, and that Charles was the living proof of its rescue by an injection of fresh blood – especially Mountbatten blood.

There is a good deal more than Mountbatten blood in his veins. When, in 1986, his mother paid her historic state visit to the People's Republic of China, the British Ambassador in Beijing, Sir Richard Evans, posted up on the Embassy gates a genealogical chart showing her descent from the ninth-century kings of Scotland and England, a cunning public relations wheeze in a land that so reveres ancestry. Among the more direct forebears of Elizabeth II's son and heir are the royal houses of England, Scotland, France, Germany, Austria, Denmark, Sweden, Norway, Spain, Portugal, Imperial Russia and the Netherlands.

He can trace a connection to Alfred the Great, Hereward the Wake, William the Conqueror and every English monarch since (but not, apparently, to Oliver Cromwell). He is descended no fewer than twenty-two times over from Mary, Queen of Scots, and at least once from the Welsh prince Owen Glendower, the Irish high king Brian Boru, Robert the Bruce of Scotland, Sven Forkbeard the Viking, Catherine the Great of Russia, Good King Wenceslas of Bohemia, Vlad the Impaler of Transylvania, the emperors Charlemagne and Frederick Barbarossa, Frederick the Great of Prussia, Pope Nicholas II, and, last but far from least among mere commoners, George Washington.

'Prince of Wales' has been the title given to the monarch's eldest son ever since Edward I, having routed the last of the native Welsh princes Llewelyn ap Gruffydd ap Llewelyn in 1282, held up his infant son, the future Edward II, from the ramparts of his new Caernarfon Castle and presented him to the Welsh people as a sop to their subjugation. The young Edward was not formally invested with his new title until some years later and that event, it must be said, took place far from Wales, at Lincoln. Only in the present century have Princes of Wales paid much heed to their principality.

Charles is the twenty-first Prince of Wales, yet strangely only thirteen of the previous holders of the title ever became king, and one of those was Edward VIII, who did not stay at his post long enough for his coronation. The previous line of Welsh princes stretches backwards from Llewelyn to Rhodri the Great in the ninth century, when the fierce Welsh tribes of ancient British stock had little truck with the Saxon English.

Princess Elizabeth, in 1948, was only the fourth Heiress Presumptive in British history to give birth to a male child, and so far only one of those children has become king, as Henry II. Charles was the first born in direct line of succession to the throne since the future Edward VIII, eldest son of George V, fifty-four years earlier.

It is strange how rarely the first rule of succession, that the departed monarch is followed by the eldest son, has applied since the beginning of the nineteenth century. George IV followed his father George III, but he in turn was followed by his brother William IV. William outlived all his heirs, and was succeeded by his niece Victoria. Conventional to the last, Victoria was followed by her eldest son Edward VII, but Edward's eldest son Albert Duke of Clarence predeceased him, leaving the throne for the second son George V. George's eldest son Edward VIII abandoned the throne to his younger brother George VI, who in turn had no sons at all, leaving the succession to his elder daughter Elizabeth. His impressive pedigree notwithstanding, the historical odds are one way and another stacked against Charles rather more than might be imagined.

He is the inheritor of the premier office on earth still attained by birthright and not by election, subterfuge, ability or force. Almost from birth he has been trained and moulded towards acceptance of a fate which no sensitive, intelligent and socially conscious man would ever choose of his own free will. People might envy the material wealth, the exotic foreign travel and the generously long vacations that go with the job of monarchy. But do they also envy the hideous restrictions on personal freedom – the diary booked solidly for months in advance, the inability to walk down a street without the accompaniment of detectives, crowds and weeks of planning, the convention that you never utter a contentious word in public, and no retirement, only death as a release from the harness?

It is a curious fact that some of the most successful and popular of recent monarchs have been those who did not have the benefit of a lifetime's preparation. Victoria was only eighteen when the death of her uncle thrust her to greatness. The future George V was twenty-seven and a professional sailor when the death of his elder brother put him in line for the throne and gave him only nine years in the wings. George VI was forty-one and enjoying a life of relative obscurity when the abdication of his brother dragged him, stammering and protesting that he was nothing more than a naval officer, to high office. At that time his daughter Elizabeth was ten years old, and she was still an inexperienced young woman of twenty-five when his premature death forced her in her turn to accept the destiny for which she too felt far from ready.

If there is any lesson in those precedents, it may be that the only way to learn the job of kingship is to do it, and that however careful the syllabus of preparation it is at best an uncertain course. Victoria and Albert resolved from the outset to mould their son into the very paragon of a modern monarch, and although his brief nine-year reign was popular and perfectly stable, he spent most of his life in rebellion against the excessively rigorous induction course his parents had designed for him.

The only previous member of the Windsor dynasty to be trained for the crown from the day of his birth was the future Edward VIII, and the memory of his desertion still bears heavily on his successors. In the lives of the young Edward and the young Charles there are occasionally parallels: both in their own way the darlings of their generation, and both exhibiting varying degrees of social concern. But there is little parallel in their characters.

Possibly one of the best qualifications that an heir to the throne can have is a degree of boneheadedness, which will allow an unquestioning acceptance of his awful lot, and enable the crown prince to enjoy a painless wait in the wings pursuing a life of hedonism mixed with sport that is the hallmark of the talentless rich. Unfortunately for Charles, he has no such qualification.

He has been a pioneer, both conscious and unwitting, from the day of his birth. He was the first heir to the throne to be born without the presence of the Home Secretary of the day at the confinement bedside to guard against changelings; Charles's facial features are an assurance that he is no one other than who he claims to be. He was the first heir to go to school, and the first to gain a university degree, proof enough against Mountbatten's assertion that the Hanoverians had become so dim they could no longer pass their exams.

He is the first modern Heir Apparent to have married outside the interbred circle of European royalty; the future George VI was mere Duke of York with no thoughts of kingship when he married the remarkable Elizabeth Bowes-Lyon, daughter of a Scottish earl, in 1923. He is a pioneer in the sheer number of his future subjects he has met, and the degree of familiarity he has enjoyed with them, whether sharing a Cambridge college stair with the Marxist son of a Welsh Nonconformist minister, or mucking out the cowshed with one of his Duchy of Cornwall tenant farmers. But most significantly, he is a pioneer in being something of an aesthete and an intellectual, a self-doubting introvert, a lover of books, Italian opera, classical architecture and scholarship, in a family of philistines who have made a virtue of being distinctly middlebrow. Since the death of the clever Prince Albert the Crown has shirked from bestowing much patronage, or setting many trends, in any creative endeavour, preferring to court public approval by reflecting public ordinariness.

Intellect and sensitivity are not essential qualifications for this job; indeed they may even be a danger if they cause the king-in-waiting to question why he cannot choose his own life. The political far right may see Charles as a danger, the far left may see him as a hope. Danger and hope could have identical results; a questioning, insecure candidate might permit the destabilization and eventual demolition of an institution which one side sees as a monstrosity on the face of a modern, democratic, technological society, the other as the best hope for the preservation of its own secure and privileged lifestyle.

But to ascertain such hopes or fears is to ignore the blatantly obvious fact that for all his pioneering ways, for all his appearance of self-doubt, Charles is at heart an out-and-out traditionalist, both by upbringing and by inclination. He expects, and accepts, the inevitability of the throne, and has never said or done anything to suggest otherwise.

For much of his very young life he knew as much of royal nannies as he did of his parents. His education was a departure from tradition, but the tradition was that of private tutors teaching in a hermetic atmosphere of stuffy unreality that could not seriously be contemplated in the second half of the twentieth century. His own schooling was hardly that of the majority of his subjects; all calls for him to spend at least some time at a State school were firmly rejected, and amid the prison-camp rigours of Gordonstoun he met few classmates who would develop into lifelong friends. Yet far from rebelling, and in spite of his unhappiness at the time, he has swallowed wholeheartedly, and frequently regurgitates, the Gordonstoun ethic of character-building through deep discomfort. The first eighteen years of his life were unashamedly elitist. The next ten, at university and in the Navy, were rather more egalitarian, but in dress, manners, attitudes and choice of acquaintances he showed himself to be more at home with the safely conventional rather than the dangerously experimental.

He still prefers tradition to innovation. He is intensely loyal to his mother and family, and willingly and respectfully follows them on their annual pre-ordained progress to Windsor, Sandringham and Balmoral, not only out of duty but because he enjoys it. He is stubbornly conventional, even old-fashioned, in his dress in spite of the best efforts at modernization by his wife. His sense of humour is anachronistic, belonging more to the Fifties than to his own formative decade of the Sixties. And in his present-day pronouncements on architecture, the environment and urban social problems, his call is more for a return to old values than a search for new ones.

He has never exhibited any self-doubt about his eventual role, however much he may dread his destiny in his own mind, and however much he may fret about his function as king-in-waiting. Nor has he, it must be said, shown any serious disinclination to enjoy the privilege and comfort that come with being Prince of Wales and Duke of Cornwall. He relishes, and takes seriously, his occasional dressings-up in full ceremonial military gear, joining his mother at the Trooping the Colour parade or visiting one of the several regiments of which he is colonel-in-chief. He embraces enthusiastically, in his polo, foxhunting and skiing, the sporting passions of the talentless rich – although without much taste for their attendant hedonism – until the inevitable consequence of high sporting risk finally caught up with him at Klosters in March 1988. In pursuit of his passion for physical challenge he led his skiing party to a precipitous mountainside away from the well-used runs. That the party ignored the day's avalanche warnings was their undoing; a huge wall of snow descended the mountain above them, killing Major Hugh Lindsay and seriously injuring Pattie Palmer-Tomkinson, both experienced skiers.

It was perhaps the most dreadful moment in Charles's life since the killing of Mountbatten. When he returned to Klosters the following week to visit Pattie, her legs badly broken, in Davos Hospital, his face was gaunt and ashen with grief and guilt. For years he had, against much well-meaning advice, courted physical danger as a safety valve to a life hidebound by protocol and rigid timetables. It caught up with him in the most tragic way, and has weighed heavily ever since on a man already too much given to introspection and self-doubt. Even before the accident he was a serious man, not lonely but solitary, enjoying his own company as would anyone who spends so much of his life gazed at by millions, his hand shaken by thousands, with a permanently full diary that rarely permits spur-of-the moment desires.

What racks his conscience is a need to justify his existence, to himself as much as to his public, and an awareness that his long wait for the Crown must be put to some good and positive use rather than be frittered away in pointless pleasure.

It is that traditional upbringing, in which a sense of duty and responsibility was drummed into him from his earliest years, that is the springboard for his present-day concerns. For all the eclectic collection of alternative thought that has been poured into his adult ear, the major influence on his life and thinking remains his immediate family.

The life of the young Charles was short on the company of other children, and dominated by adults, which has always given him a gravity beyond his years. The adults were predominantly women – his nannies, governesses, mother and grandmother, even his great-grandmother Queen Mary for a brief spell – which gave him a perception and sensitivity that he would not have so readily acquired in rough, bluff male company. One result has been his tendency to treat his women with more respect and with more understanding than is usual.

His father has been a major influence on his life, although not always a happy one. The two are of entirely different temperaments; Charles was raised in secure and loving family surroundings, while the young Prince Philip was exiled from his native Greece before he was a year old, saw his parents' marriage crumble soon afterwards, and was left largely to fend for himself wherever he could find a bunk among a motley collection of European relatives. But from his father Charles inherits a strong streak of physical courage and a desire, now slightly abated, to push himself to extremes on the sports field and occasionally off it.

In his desire to mould a son of a different mental outlook into his own image, Philip sometimes did little more than undermine Charles's shakily emerging self-confidence, and made him that much more determined to be his own man. A natural talent for music was never much encouraged; natural shyness and reticence were left to Charles to conquer for himself, against the odds of school classmates who tended to treat him as a thing apart. He never acquired his father's taste for hearty team games, and was put off sailing as much by the hectoring of the parental skipper as by his own capacity for seasickness. The gulf between them has been much exaggerated, but there is still a distance; Philip does not often drop in for tea.

Charles grew up fully aware that he was privileged, insulated and different. In adulthood one of his greatest assets has been an insatiable curiosity about the world beyond his immediate horizons, and about the daily lives of those in it. He is still a man apart, and always will be, but his interest is perfectly genuine, and anyone who meets him perceives at once that his questioning is no mere royal platitude of the 'Have you been waiting here long?' school of conversational art.

To meet Prince Charles is to be charmed, flattered, and not a little surprised. He is of average height, but the frame is unexpectedly small and is unencumbered by a single obvious pound of spare flesh. He is not a muscular man, but he looks alarmingly fit. The hair, brown and luxuriant elsewhere, is thinning rather seriously on the crown, but as he is never the one who does the bowing it is noticeable only to spectators and television cameras positioned on balconies above his head. His handshake is brief and not too tight – he has to preserve his palm through a lifetime of greeting – but it is more than merely perfunctory. His gaze is direct, and his whole attention is engaged. He is *interested*, and manages to show it. He exudes the benignly quizzical, faintly puzzled air of a bishop in a betting shop. Yet his manner is easy, chatty, and friendly enough without being over-familiar for even the most deprived, cynical and street-wise youth from a black ghetto to come away feeling that the most privileged young man in the land is on his side.

He laughs readily, and parries joke with joke. He will banter happily in private even with one of his least favourite classes of men, the press. Meeting this writer in some foreign part, he engaged in long and earnest debate on why *The Times* had become so difficult to read. (We agreed that it was the narrower columns rather than the content.) Turning to a colleague from the *News of the World*, he asked with a disarming grin: 'Do you have to go to a special school to unlearn English before you can write that sort of stuff?'

Yet the barriers never come down completely; there is never quite a sense of talk between equals. You can get so close, and no closer. This man is like a visitor from a far country, friendly and inquisitive, who has taken the trouble to learn the language and customs, who would never think of immigrating, but who remains wide-eyed with curiosity, and sometimes with astonishment, at what he sees.

He has a scholar's love of books and study, a side of his character that was encouraged and developed, to his delight, under the wise tuition of the late Lord Butler at Trinity College, Cambridge. He would enjoy being a don, but the other pressures and duties that compete for his time make it difficult for him to be more than a voyeur on the edge of scholarship, and his natural intelligence and abilities would seem to a professional scholar wastefully dissipated and fragmented over a wide spectrum of disciplines, from community architecture to parapsychology. Still, he has managed some worthy writing on the subject of his favourite, and in his view seriously maligned, ancestor King George III.

At Cambridge he read history and anthropology, two subjects of some relevance to a future monarch. To the study of history he brought the unique perspective of his own position, and learned in return that monarchy through the ages has not been particularly noted for being a secure job. Anthropology formed in his mind the impression that people of whatever race and whatever era are really all much the same; from ancient Indian writings on kingship and from his own immediate experience he was intrigued how monarchy

11

through the ages had the power to stir a kind of spiritual appeal in its subjects. He believes in constitutional monarchy as a worthwhile and useful institution, but his study of history has surely given him few illusions, showing the ease with which public adoration can turn to disaffection.

When Prince Charles left the Navy at the age of twenty-eight he had to embark on a different kind of voyage, one of self-discovery and exploration of his new-found position as a full-time Prince of Wales, an ocean of uncertainty for which there is no published chart. Some immediate work awaited him, helping to administer the charitable trusts set up to mark his mother's Silver Jubilee, and it brought him into early contact with two areas of interest which have grown into major concerns: the deprivation of inner cities and the alienation of black people in Britain.

During his voyage he tragically lost his compass with the assassination of Earl Mountbatten, who had been perhaps his closest mentor and had to a great extent assumed the role of father. The event turned Charles in on himself in search of some spiritual comfort. His religious faith has always been simple and strong, as befits a future Head of the Church of England, but his questioning nature nonetheless sought to rationalize his great-uncle's death and to seek some justification for it. Steered by his other philosophical guiding light, Sir Laurens van der Post, he emerged from his mourning more convinced of the need for a spiritual dimension to life, although in his expression of it he seemed sometimes to drift into obscure backwaters and get himself lost in the ill-charted everglades of alternative philosophies.

Marriage settled him, and put him back on course. It gave him a secure base and a much stronger *persona* of his own, reducing his dependence on the attitudes and opinions of his own family, particularly of his father with whom he had long been out of intellectual sympathy. But it too brought its problems, as he found himself overshadowed by his wife's glamour and an obsession with her fashions which quite eclipsed anything of interest or importance that he might have to say. He has learned to overcome that disability by ensuring that he and his wife lead largely separate public lives.

After more than a decade of full-blown public life and no clearly defined role to play, Charles's many and often fragile strands of thought show some signs of being spun into a common thread. It has taken him a long time to form a coherent view of the world and his place in it; the average undergraduate untroubled by the interruptions of royal business, and with well-defined work awaiting his graduation, would probably have formed at university all the perceptions that it has taken Charles until middle life to sort out.

Cambridge University unlocked many of the shackles placed upon his mind by his background and by a public school education, which still does more to perpetuate class divisions than almost any other element in British society. The receptive void that was opened up as a result has since been filled by a vast kaleidoscope of ideas and opinions, and in the confusion his own thoughts have sometimes come stumbling out without proper preparation. Opinions embraced enthusiastically, even impetuously, he has occasionally aired too quickly and without proper research.

Recently, however, his thoughts have become more coherent, his researches more thorough, and he speaks with increasing confidence and conviction. On his favourite subject of architecture, he has become almost withering in his denunciation of the enemy.

A pattern begins to emerge to all his public thoughts, woven from a clearer understanding of his own position, and especially his limitations. He perceives that as heir to the throne he carries no formal authority, power or position, and that anything he does or says he does as an individual. Although without power, he is an individual who, simply because of who he is, has the ability to command attention. Few ever refuse his summons to dinner or discussion. He also has the potential to command respect; respect has to be earned, but being closely associated with the much respected institution of monarchy, he is off to a head start. He can therefore have influence, but only of a limited kind; his position precludes him from having direct influence on the workaday decisions of government, either national or local. That leaves him with the ability to influence people's attitudes and values, and he attempts to do so with increasing vigour.

As a mere individual himself, representing no public body, corporation or arm of government, Prince Charles has become deeply concerned with the importance of the individual against bureaucracy and big institutions. In that he is a disciple of Kurt Hahn, who believed in development through individual effort rather than team sports, of Laurens van der Post, who is much concerned with the inner self, and of E.F. Schumacher, who argued that small-scale community projects were of much greater benefit to the Third World than vast foreign aid projects with their attendant bureaucracy and remoteness from the people ultimately supposed to benefit.

He supports community architecture because it permits tenants to live in the kind of houses they want, and is a bulwark against city authorities and their love of 'comprehensive development'. His ideas for inner city regeneration rely heavily on the creation of new employment through very small businesses; it is one of the few areas where his thinking coincides with that of Mrs Margaret Thatcher.

He approves of big business provided it respects the individuality of those it employs, and he admires some British firms, particularly some well-known High Street retailers, who pursue an active policy of making their workers feel involved in the business. He firmly believes that employers should pay far greater heed to the science of psychology.

He believes too in one nation, which considering that he will reign over it one day displays a degree of self-interest. He abhors the thought of ghettoes in the big cities, being well aware of the American experience in that area which he does not wish repeated in his own country. He does not necessarily argue on behalf of ethnic groups, but he goes out of his way to encourage Asians and blacks as individuals. He believes in one world too, and accepts the hopeful doctrine of United World Colleges that the wars of the future will be avoided only by a better understanding between nations at the level of the individual.

He is a firm believer in the Commonwealth, which encompasses one quarter of the earth's population, as a contributor to one world, and prefers to travel inside rather than outside it, always making a point of visiting member schools of United World Colleges or gatherings of old boys, and inspecting the work of the Commonwealth Development Corporation, on whose board he sits. The Commonwealth is a frail club held together largely through the personality and dedication of its present Head, the Queen. Whether Charles will succeed as Head of the Commonwealth is one of the less clear aspects of his future reign; there might be a move to rotate the headship around member countries to kill off finally its remaining whiff of British Empire. But if it still exists, Charles will undoubtedly support it.

Overriding and governing his belief in the importance of the individual is his conviction that modern capitalism, in its inherent greed, race for profit and preoccupation with materialism, is in danger of making people forget that there is any deeper, more spiritual meaning to life. By that he does not necessarily mean a search for God through organized religion, more a search for the inner self through a better quality of individual life in a world less despoiled by human greed.

Prince Charles is extremely modest in what he thinks he can achieve, but still feels frustrated and occasionally angry that he can achieve so little. He retains an endearing belief that he can accomplish much simply by banging heads together, which is his own vision of his everyday purpose. He becomes easily angered if thwarted; he has inherited a streak – but only a streak – of his father's legendary intolerance. For one born to take an overview, he can also at times be fussy and precise, a legacy of a family background in which everything had its season, there was an exact time to every purpose, and everything was done correctly or not at all.

15

He is a good man, and a patently honest one, whose mental luggage has sometimes seemed weighed down with a feeling of guilt about who he is. He has at times seemed faltering and uncertain, as though in need of someone to pat him on the back and encourage him to go on. He has occasionally displayed a naivety about the world beyond his immediate horizons, which is at once touching to his multitude of fans and worrying to those who wonder if he will be adept enough to steer the Crown safely through hurricanes as yet unblown.

Prince Charles's greatest asset is his openness of mind, set in a foundation of belief in the institution he will eventually represent. He told the author Anthony Sampson, in *The Changing Anatomy of Britain*: 'Something as curious as the monarchy won't survive unless you take account of people's attitudes. I think it can be a kind of elective institution. After all, if people don't want it, they won't have it.'

2

The First Post-War Prince

THE GREAT BRITAIN of 1948 was a land of grimness and tribulation, in which the brighter new world of prosperity and hope that should have succeeded the dangers, toils and sacrifices of a six-year world war still seemed a long way off. The Russians were blockading Berlin and threatening the outbreak of another massive conflict. Britain was in economic crisis after the withdrawal of American lend-lease, and it was almost impossible to lay hands on a pair of nylons. Only the previous year King George VI had written to his mother: 'I do wish one could see a glimmer of a bright spot anywhere in world affairs. Never in the whole history of mankind have things looked gloomier than they do now, and one feels so powerless to do anything to help.'

It was the year that a depressingly wet summer followed the worst winter for a century with trains and traffic snowbound, coal imprisoned at the pitheads, and 800,000 men thrown into temporary unemployment as a result. Petrol and meat rations were cut. And yet, amid such a catalogue of trials, the shape of the new world to come was indeed being drawn. It was the year of the assassination of Mahatma Gandhi, of the election of the first Nationalist South African government on an apartheid ticket, of the invention of the transistor and the long-playing record, and of the dropping of the words 'British' and 'Dominion' from documents relating to the Commonwealth. The coinage of 1948 was the first to omit from the legend encircling the King's head the words 'Ind. Imp.' – 'Indiae Imperator' (Emperor of India). The British Crown no longer bestrode one quarter of the earth.

Political events in Great Britain ought to have dictated a decline in the popularity and relevance of the monarchy. Clement Attlee's Labour Government had won an entirely unexpected landslide victory over Churchill the war hero in 1945, on a ticket that amounted to little short of revolution. They promised – and to a limited extent achieved – a new social order in which public ownership would guarantee a hitherto unknown equality for all. In addition, the millions who had served in the war, at home and abroad, had had their horizons widened and their expectations raised by their experience. In such a brave new world, where every man could give his children secondary education and hope to own a car, a traditional hereditary monarchy might have seemed to sit uneasily.

If anything, the reverse proved true; it was as though the British were quite willing to embrace social revolution provided they could always look to one constant, unchanging institution for reassurance. The standing of the monarchy in the immediate post-war years was high; the British looked to their wartime King, who had been a shy, stammering figure when dragged unwillingly to the throne in 1936, and saw a man who had grown in stature to lead his people through the dark vale of war with a dignity and courage which was never seen to waver. They had begun by feeling sorry for him; now they loved him. A great mutual respect developed between George VI, the often tongue-tied aristocrat, and his prime minister Attlee, the monosyllabic lawyer from Harrow. The King also had a high regard for some of the brilliant working-class boys that Attlee brought into his Cabinet, like Ernest Bevin, Herbert Morrison and Aneurin Bevan.

The monarchy's own public relations machine had also been hard at work. When Princess Elizabeth announced her intention to marry Lieutenant Philip Mountbatten in 1947, the King thought that any display of opulence in these times of austerity would only alienate the population. But Attlee persuaded him that a dazzling display was exactly what the public wanted to lift their spirits in those grey days, and the wedding in Westminster Abbey on 20 November, 1947 was conducted to great popular curiosity and acclaim. Brides throughout the land were fascinated to know that the Princess, like them, had had to save up her clothing ration coupons for her wedding dress.

There was great good will towards the couple. The King's daughter, already a familiar figure in her Auxiliary Territorial Service uniform maintaining military trucks in the last days of the war, had matured into an exceptionally attractive young woman, as Cecil Beaton's photographs of the period show. Her fiancé, although described by the historian Philip Ziegler as 'amiable but dim', cut something of a dash in his Royal Navy uniform, and besides, he had seen a good deal of wartime action. The wedding caught the public imagination, and on that grey November day the streets of London were packed with sightseers hungry for a dash of colour in the era of austerity.

The marriage was followed by a number of other events which bolstered public good will towards the monarchy. In April 1948 King George VI and Queen Elizabeth celebrated their silver wedding anniversary with a service in St Paul's Cathedral and a 22-mile (35-kilometre) drive through the streets of London, including the East End that had borne the brunt of Hitler's Blitz. The following month Princess Elizabeth and her new husband, now sporting the title His Royal Highness the Duke of Edinburgh, paid a well-publicized official visit to Paris. And, as the year wore on, the King revived the splendid ceremonial, missing for ten drab years since the war clouds had begun to gather, of the State Opening of Parliament, despite the fact that the Attlee Government was busy limiting the powers of Parliament's Upper House.

It was no surprise, therefore, when it became known that Princess Elizabeth was expecting her first child, that the public responded with warmth and insatiable curiosity. On the cold, raw, moonless evening of Sunday, 14 November, 1948, a crowd of thousands gathered in The Mall, alerted by BBC radio news bulletins reporting the increasingly frequent comings and goings of eminent physicians at Buckingham Palace. At 11 p.m. the official announcement was posted on the Palace railings and, by tradition, on the door of the Lord Mayor of London's official residence at the Mansion House: 'The Princess Elizabeth, Duchess of Edinburgh, was safely delivered of a Prince at 9.14 p.m. today. Her Royal Highness and her son are both doing well.'

Princess Elizabeth had enjoyed a perfectly normal and healthy pregnancy and, as was the fashion of the time, continued with all but the most strenuous of her normal activities – except horse riding – until almost the last moment. Forty-eight hours before the birth, she was out dining with her friends the Brabournes; not for her a long Victorian *accouchement*. For her delivery the Princess was given pain-killing anaesthesia, which in the post-war years was being administered to 90 per cent of all British women in labour, a medical fashion which has since mercifully declined; that the Princess used it was a great comfort to the thousands of other expectant mothers who were wary of the procedure. She was unconscious for just under an hour, during which a healthy boy of 7 pounds 6 ounces (3.34 kilograms) was delivered by forceps.

King George had no sons, and his elder daughter was therefore the Heiress Presumptive, the presumption being that the King would continue to have no sons; so the new baby was a potential future heir to the throne. As befitted the first Prince born into the new world of the post-war age, traditions were already being broken at his very arrival. James Chuter Ede, a grizzled ex-schoolmaster, was the first Home Secretary for over a century to be spared the duty of attending the birth of a potential heir. Instead he waited by his telephone in Whitehall to receive the news on trust from Buckingham Palace, and to sign the typewritten formal announcement.

William Joynson-Hicks, Home Secretary in 1926, had waited dutifully downstairs while the new baby's mother was born at the Strathmore family home at 17 Bruton Street, London. The custom was of unknown antiquity, but is generally ascribed to the so-called 'warming-pan incident' when Mary of Modena, wife of James II, was suspected of producing a changeling as heir to the throne in 1688, despite the fact that the Lord Chancellor and a substantial body of Privy Councillors were gathered at the foot of her bed. George VI, shortly before his daughter's baby was due, decided to dispense with the custom, describing it as 'neither a statutory requirement nor a constitutional necessity'.

The birth of Prince Charles was celebrated by the King's Troop, Royal Horse Artillery, firing a 41-gun salute, the bell-ringers of Westminster Abbey ringing a peal of 5,000 changes, the fountains of Trafalgar Square running blue – for a boy – for a week, the British fleet being dressed overall, and the Poet Laureate, John Masefield, proving as Poets Laureate usually do, on the occasions of state at which they are required to perform, that verse written to order tends more to the deadly than the deathless:

> May destiny, allotting what befalls,
> Grant to the newly-born this saving grace,
> A guard more sure than ships and fortress-walls,
> The loyal love and service of a race.

Genealogists consulted their learned charts to determine the significance of the birth. He was the first royal baby to be born at Buckingham Palace since the daughter of Arthur, Duke of Connaught, sixty-two years earlier. He was the first born in direct succession to the throne since the future Edward VIII in 1894. And Princess Elizabeth was only the fourth Heiress Presumptive in British history to give birth to a male child. A potential problem over the child's title had been corrected by the King less than a week before the birth, when he decreed that any child of the Duke and Duchess of Edinburgh would have the title Prince or Princess and the appellation Royal Highness. The decree was necessary, because in granting the Duke of Edinburgh the title His Royal Highness the day before his wedding, the King had omitted to specify the further title of Prince, apparently assuming that it was automatic. But beyond the genealogical niceties there was a far greater and more sombre coincidence in the precise location of the infant Prince's birth.

He was born in the Buhl Room on the first floor of Buckingham Palace, normally part of the royal children's apartments, which had, a short time previously, been fitted out as a fully equipped operating theatre for the King, whose health had begun to deteriorate markedly after the immense strains of the war. Two days before the birth, in the same room, surgeons had diagnosed arteriosclerosis in the King's leg, but on his express instructions his daughter had not been told. His health continued to fail, and a little over three years later he was dead from cancer of the lung at the age of fifty-six.

For the moment, however, all attention was on the baby. He was provided with a hand-me-down cot 100 years old, a miniature four-poster with safety rails on the sides, last used for George V's son the Duke of Kent. It was cleaned up, repainted and reupholstered in white satin. He could, of course, have had a new one, but the House of Windsor has long been noted for its thrift and careful housekeeping which to outsiders appears sometimes to border on meanness. His pram too was secondhand, the same one that had borne his infant mother in 1926 and his aunt Margaret in 1930; it was sent to a specialist baby carriage manufacturer and given a smart respray and reupholster. It was a very large pram, and the earliest memory that Charles says he now has is lying there in its vastness.

Gifts for the baby poured in: innumerable bootees and matinee jackets knitted by an adoring nation; a ton(ne) and a half of nappies from a donor in the United States who clearly had an exaggerated idea of the baby's requirements. In this time of shortages and clothing coupons, even Prince Philip managed to unearth some of his own baby clothes. However elevated a personage, this was the first prince to be born into the Welfare State, and he duly received his ration card, free milk allowance, Ministry of Food orange juice (one of the century's greatest contributors to tooth decay) and cod liver oil. He was inoculated against diphtheria, and circumcised, not for any reason of religion but because many doctors at the time regarded it as good hygienic practice.

Charles was attended by two nannies who were, naturally, Scottish; Scots were the favoured breed of nanny among an earlier generation, presumably from a belief in the value of a certain Calvinistic sternness and unimpeachable rectitude. Helen Lightbody, a spinster but by a curious aristocratic tradition awarded the courtesy title 'Mrs' as senior nanny, had brought up the Duke of Gloucester's children and was already well known to Princess Elizabeth. Mrs Lightbody died at her home in the Scottish borders in 1987, and at her graveside was a wreath from her former charge. She was assisted in her nanny's duties by Mabel Anderson, who subsequently stayed on to look after all four of the Queen's children. The young Charles, deprived as he was soon to be of much contact with his parents, grew deeply attached to his nannies, Mrs Lightbody in particular.

An eager public clamoured for any scrap of information about the new baby. Countess Granville, sister of the infant's grandmother Queen Elizabeth, told a group of Ulster Girl Guides: 'He could not be more angelic-looking. He is golden haired and has the most beautiful complexion, as well as amazingly delicate features for so young a baby.' His mother, writing to her former music teacher Mabel Lander, commented on the size of his hands and the length of his fingers, 'quite unlike mine and certainly unlike his father's'.

On 15 December, 1948, the baby was christened. The Buckingham Palace chapel, destroyed by a particularly daredevil Luftwaffe pilot who flew down The Mall in 1940, was still out of action, so the Lily Font made for the baptism of Queen Victoria's first child, Princess Victoria, was brought from Windsor and set up in the Music Room of the Palace, to be filled with River Jordan water from a Hebron phial, a custom dating back to the Crusades. He was wrapped in a shawl of Honiton lace that has been used for the christening of all royal babies since Princess Victoria. His godparents were the King and Queen, Princess Margaret, King Haakon of Norway, the Queen's brother David Bowes-Lyon, the Duke of Edinburgh's grandmother the Dowager Marchioness of Milford Haven, his uncle Prince George of Greece, and his cousin Lady Brabourne, daughter of Earl Mountbatten. King Haakon and Prince George, both very elderly, were represented by proxies.

Dr Geoffrey Fisher, Archbishop of Canterbury, baptized the child into the Church of England, a prerequisite for a future monarch under the Act of Settlement of 1701. Mr John Clare, register of births, marriage and deaths at Caxton Hall, Westminster, arrived with his large bound register to record the names Charles Philip Arthur George. The name of Charles appeared to be a return to favour of the ill-omened Stuart dynasty, although the Queen later let it be known that no such considerations were in mind; she and her husband had simply liked the name. He was christened Philip, naturally, after his father; Arthur for tradition, both royal and ancient Celtic (Henry VII, the first Welsh King of England, named his eldest son Arthur, and Victoria gave the name to her third); and George after his grandfather, great-grandfather, and a whole line of Hanoverian ancestors. His father and mother were Duke and Duchess of Edinburgh, so the child was known formally as Prince Charles of Edinburgh.

Charles was eight months old when the conversion of Clarence House, next door to St James's Palace, was finally completed to give the Edinburghs a home of their own. Built in 1829 by John Nash for the third son of George III, the Duke of Clarence, it had been occupied for decades by Victoria's son Arthur, Duke of Connaught, and modernization had completely passed it by. On Arthur's death in 1942 it had been requisitioned as the British headquarters of the Red Cross. The £55,000 conversion, in which the Duke of Edinburgh took a particularly close interest, to the irritation of the professional

architects, included the installation of two vital amenities –
electricity and a bathroom.

It was in the day nursery at Clarence House that Charles
learned to crawl. His nannies would wheel him in his huge
pram to take the air in St James's Park, accompanied even
at that early age by a detective, a shadow that has continued
to tail him wherever he goes. Sometimes he would be taken
a little way along The Mall to Marlborough House to see his
great-grandmother Queen Mary, then into her eighties but
still ramrod erect as she sat with her legs on a footstool,
surrounded by cabinets full of her priceless jade and other
precious objects.

As children, Elizabeth and Margaret had never been allowed
to handle the collection, but the old Queen Dowager indulged
Charles and permitted him to play with anything he liked; the
small boy at her feet was, after all, the future of the dynasty.

Even at such an early age, Charles began to pay one of
the penalties of his high birth, which was considerable separation from his parents. His father was a serving naval officer,
stationed for a good part of his son's earliest years in Malta,
and his mother became increasingly pressured into official
engagements as her father's health continued inexorably to
fail. Worry about her father was in itself a considerable drain
on her attentions and energies. During enforced separations
the young Charles was shipped off to stay with the King and
Queen at Sandringham, where he began to develop a strong
bond with his grandmother Queen Elizabeth that has continued ever since. King George wrote to his daughter in Malta:
'Charles is too sweet, stumping around the room. We shall
love having him at Sandringham. He is the fifth generation to
live there and I hope he will get to love the place.' Charles in
later years never quite developed the same attachment to the
Norfolk country estate that his grandfather had.

Charles, aged three, stayed at Sandringham while his parents toured Canada, and it is from that time that he retains
his only memory of King George VI: that of someone much
bigger sitting on the sofa beside him. A contemporary and

much-published photograph of the two of them from that time remains one of the Queen's favourites, and still sits on her desk at Buckingham Palace.

Apart from the enforced separations when both his parents were abroad, Charles probably saw as much of them as any child brought up by nannies in the fashion of those times. His mother, when at home, religiously reserved half an hour every morning, and an hour and a half in the evening, when she played with Charles, and Anne after her birth in 1950, bathed them herself, and put them to bed. Bathtimes were shared with Philip, when he was at home, Lord Mountbatten, who was a regular visitor to Clarence House, and any other member of the extended royal family who happened to be passing the bathroom door at the time.

The rest of the day was strictly regimented, as might be expected in a family with such a strong naval tradition. The children were woken at 7.00 sharp and given breakfast by the nannies, followed by play in the nursery until the 9.00 visit by their mother. Next, they were dressed for their hour and a half walk; lunch was at 1.00 p.m. (Charles became utterly devoted to boiled chicken and rice) followed by a well-dressed afternoon visit with the nannies to Queen Elizabeth or Queen Mary, or play in the Clarence House garden. Tea was at 4.30, followed by games with mother, bath and bed. When, in subsequent years, Charles had children of his own, he did his best to follow a determinedly less formal routine. Yet he has imposed on his children one of the same penalties that he himself had to suffer – long periods without their father, sometimes apparently out of choice rather than necessity.

There seems to be a belief among the upper-class English, which the rest of the world can never understand, that provided the financial means are there, children can get along perfectly well without seeing much of their parents, especially their fathers.

One element of which the young Charles's life was pointedly short was the company of other children. His world was dominated by adults: his extended family – in which there were few, if any, other children of his own age – his nannies, and his parents' staff. On the nursery floor his mother taught him the rudiments of learning, with ABC bricks and a bead frame for counting. But she never used baby talk; trains were never 'puff-puffs' nor horses 'gee-gees'. He was taught from the earliest age to bow to Queen Mary, and never to remain seated when his grandfather the King entered the room; but by those around him, family, staff and friends, he himself was treated with a relatively informal ease, with no bowing or curtseying.

As an infant he was a happy and contented child who slept well at nights, unlike his sister who had a clear will of her own and was often fractious and tearful. But from a very early age Charles's parents, relatives and staff observed him to be thoughtful, serious, patient, obstinate even, a little grave, and definitely dignified. He was immensely considerate towards his baby sister, taking a watchful, protective interest in her from the moment he was allowed to get down from the lunch table to take his first look at her.

Despite his serious bearing, he was anything but withdrawn. His favourite occupation was a healthy desire to make a very loud noise, shouting 'bang' with a popgun, blowing a raucous tin trumpet, or beating an old saucepan with a wooden spoon. *Babar the Elephant* was his favourite story, *Pop goes the Weasel* his favourite nursery rhyme, *Listen with Mother* his favourite radio programme. His favourite toys came to be a powder-blue Austin pedal car, still sitting in a corridor at Buckingham Palace to this day, and a train set given to him by Gibraltar which his father, when at home, played with as much as he did. There was, however, another deprivation in comparison with other children; he very rarely went to the seaside, having to make do with the Buckingham Palace swimming pool and a garden sandpit. Of all the royal homes, only Sandringham was anywhere near the sea, and visits there were traditionally in winter. A Stockholm newspaper, writing at the time about Prince Carl Gustav of Sweden, observed: 'Our little Prince spends his summer bathing and playing by the sea. But for Charles the outlook is gloomy; he is never allowed to bathe.'

But he was introduced to other delights that would one day grow into passions. When he was three years old his grandmother Queen Elizabeth, herself a green-fingered gardener of no mean skill, bought him a set of miniature gardening tools and showed him how to plant his first garden at The Royal Lodge, Windsor, where he was often to be found gravely watering the flowers. It was another significant strengthening of the bond with Queen Elizabeth, who relished the role of doting grandmother.

At about the same time he acquired his own detective, Sergeant Kelly, and his own footman, Richard Brown. 'Why haven't you got a Richard?' he would innocently ask other children he met. Both his mother and his nannies, fearful that the deference he was bound to be shown by all who came in contact with him might go to his head, insisted that he treat the staff with due respect. He was sent back to apologize to the Queen's detective on the occasion that he called him simply by his surname, omitting the courtesy of 'Mister'. To the same end, his mother hid from his eyes most of the tidal wave of newspaper photographs of himself.

The firm but gentle insistence on manners and consideration, and the fact that his young life was lived in a certain amount of solitude with its shortage of other children with which to rough-and-tumble, were already moulding his personality. The Queen has always maintained that, from the earliest age, all her four children had distinguishably different personalities. Charles was sweet-natured and thoughtful, both in his consideration for others and in his observation of the world around him. Some early pictures show him as a rather solemn child, but that is probably as a result of shyness, a trait which he has never fully overcome. There was always a hint of restraint, even withdrawal, unlike his outgoing sister, who always did the waving when they were in a car together. But it was Charles, with his concern for good manners, who led Anne by the hand up a station platform to thank the driver for the train journey they had just undertaken. His mask of restraint did occasionally slip; his mother once gave him a good spanking for sticking his tongue out at a crowd through a car window.

The most momentous event of Charles's young life occurred while his parents were far from home, undertaking a visit to Kenya, and he, as was the custom, was staying with his grandparents the King and Queen at Sandringham. On the morning of 6 February, 1952, Charles and his sister were kept in the nursery long beyond the usual time, with no sign of either grandparent. Charles became more and more insistent that he wanted to see Grandpa, whereupon a maid eventually weakened and told him that Grandpa had 'gone away'. Charles immediately demanded to see Granny. Queen Elizabeth took the child on her knee, explained that Grandpa had gone away, and broke down in tears. 'Don't cry, Granny,' said the child who had suddenly become Heir Apparent to the throne, hugging her tightly.

From the moment of the death of King George VI Charles was Heir Apparent, Duke of Cornwall, Duke of Rothesay, Earl of Carrick, Baron Renfew, Lord of the Isles, and Great Steward of Scotland. He was not, however, Prince of Wales, a title which is not automatic and has to be bestowed on the eldest son by the sovereign. Most importantly his mother, still at Treetops Hotel in the Aberdare National Park of Kenya, had become Queen at the age of twenty-five.

Apart from the absence of Grandpa, Charles's life changed little at first. He was kept well away from all the suffocating ceremonial of the State funeral; he continued to live at Clarence House, and his mother still bathed him. But he grew perceptibly closer to his bereaved grandmother, undoubtedly sensing her grief.

Soon after Easter that year, he noticed his first change; the family moved back into Buckingham Palace, and he was installed in a second-floor nursery painted in pale blue to resemble that at Clarence House as closely as possible. He now saw more of his father, who because of his wife's increasing royal commitments had been obliged, very much against his will, to give up his naval career; in his first months of enforced retirement, Philip would often sink into long black furies of depression and frustration. The Queen became preoccupied, not only with the immense weight of office suddenly thrust on her young shoulders, but also with preparations for her Coronation. Charles himself was soon aware of the activity: he would often stand at the window watching troops rehearsing below. On one occasion he was seen conducting a military band with a pencil from an open first-floor window; when the pencil was taken away he continued with the tassel of the window blind.

The burning question was whether or not Charles should attend the lengthy ceremony of the Coronation in Westminster Abbey, a spectacle that would thrill most of the population except those aged four or under. As a test of his patience, six months before the event he was taken to one of Sir Robert Meyer's children's concerts at the new Royal Festival Hall; but halfway through, boredom set in, followed by intense fidgeting and wandering attention, and he had to be taken home.

He was obviously too young to attend the full Coronation, despite now being the premier duke of the kingdom and head of the peerage, and therefore strictly speaking he should have been the first to swear the Oath of Homage 'to become your liege man of life and limb and earthly worship' to the newly-crowned sovereign. It was an unprecedented situation, for not since the creation of the Duchy of Cornwall in 1337 had a monarch been crowned with a successor so young. Elizabeth chose to run the risk of her son one day leading a revolt against her, and spared him the swearing. But it was decided that he should witness the highlight of the ceremony. He was led into the gallery above the tomb of Anne of Cleves just as the choir was singing Handel's majestic Coronation anthem *Zadok the Priest* and his mother, stripped of all finery save her earrings and wearing only a plain white robe, was about to be anointed with consecrated oil. Charles kept rubbing his head and passing his hand to his Granny for her to smell his new hair lotion, constantly firing questions at her and his Aunt Margaret. After a short while, Nanny Lightbody led him out by a side door and home to lunch.

Later that day he was taken out on to Buckingham Palace balcony to be confronted for the first time by a great adulatory, seething sea of uplifted faces, a sight that, although he now has no recollection of it, must have imprinted on his mind some vague image and clue to his eventual, inescapable fate.

Five is the age at which the law requires every British child to begin formal education: it need not be in school, but if not the child must receive some proper teaching at home. Towards the end of the Coronation year of 1953 Charles's fifth birthday approached, and his parents had to face the weighty decision of how he should be educated.

Prince Philip had had what amounted to a conventional British boarding school education, beginning at Cheam and ending at Gordonstoun, with a brief and unfortunate interlude at Kurt Hahn's original school at Salem in Germany, just as Hitler was coming to power in 1933 and Hahn was being arrested, chiefly for being Jewish. Philip, no academic, had thrived on his boarding school career and had enjoyed it immensely, as he had no home which he could properly call his own. He had been barely a year old when his father, Prince Andrew of Greece, had been sent with his family into exile after being rescued by a British emissary from a trumped-up charge of treason following the defeat of his cavalry regiment in Greece's border war with Turkey. For a while the family camped with assorted royal relatives around Europe, until Prince Andrew took to the gaming tables of Monte Carlo to die more or less broke, while Philip's mother retreated into a nuns' order of her own founding. Philip was eventually taken under the wing of his uncle Lord Louis Mountbatten who directed his education and subsequent naval career. It is little surprise that a boy of such rootless and dismantled background should take so happily to the public school system, ending up as head boy of Gordonstoun.

The Queen's education could hardly have been more different, being as it was almost entirely within the hermetic confines of Buckingham Palace at the hands of governesses and private tutors. Her father George VI and her grandfather George V were taught in precisely the same way, but it is a curious coincidence that in the case of all three, at the time when the pattern of their education was set none of them expected eventually to succeed to the throne.

On the matter of education, Prince Philip became seriously involved for the first time in his son's life and future. He, naturally, was all for sending the boy to school, and preferably the same schools as he himself attended. Fathers who take that view are frequently of the minority who profess to have enjoyed their schooldays, failing to consider that a hatred of school may be a desirable, even necessary, step in the formation of a rounded, imaginative adult. The Queen, although admitting that boys' schools were a subject on which she knew little or nothing, concurred that, in principle, Charles should be educated outside; she appreciated that an heir to the throne raised in the age of the Welfare State and universal secondary education could not be educated in the style of the Victorian aristocracy. She may also have felt a longing in her own private education for wider experience and contact with her own generation. The high-born Girl Guide troop brought into the Palace once a week was hardly the route to broadbased social intercourse.

What the Queen may have lacked in early contact with her common subjects she has always made up for with a great deal of common sense, and on the question of Charles she moved with a perceptive caution. She realised that for his first five years her son's experience had been every bit as sheltered as her own, and the growth of his social abilities outside his own family circle equally stunted. The tender plant raised in the royal hothouse might wither and shrivel if transplanted directly to the cold border outside. Charles's introduction to the world, she decided therefore, must be gradual.

Accordingly the Queen engaged Catherine Peebles, a shrewd, humorous Glasgow woman in her early forties who had been governess to Charles's cousins, Prince Michael of Kent and Princess Alexandra. Miss Peebles had no formal training, no degree or any other teaching qualification, but she exhibited that no-nonsense common sense and air of kindly firmness at which Scottish spinsters of a certain age are especially good, and which struck an immediate chord with the Queen. A schoolroom was set up in the Palace equipped with blackboard, table and globe of the world, and Miss Peebles commenced the awesome responsibility of educating the heir to the throne.

Miss Peebles found she had inherited a child with only a misty vision of the outside world. He could, however, tell the time, read just a little, write 'CHARLES' in a spidery hand, and could draw particularly well for his age. He had a good ear for tunes, and could count to a hundred. But although he was apparently conscientious he did not in fact concentrate well and displayed no great thirst for knowledge. He was, to be blunt, a plodder. He was correct, precise, mannerly and obedient, but nothing had yet seemed to fire his imagination.

In later years Miss Peebles recalled: 'He liked being amused, rather than amusing himself. He was very responsive to kindness, but if you shouted at him he would draw back into his shell and for a time you would be able to do nothing with him.' Instructed by the Queen that there should be no forcing, Miss Peebles had to work hard to draw her charge out of himself.

The school day began with a Bible story. Miss Peebles encouraged his painting and drawing, an area in which she saw a glimmer of imagination developing, found he could grasp history and geography well, but just like his mother had only the vaguest concept of mathematics. Teaching history to the future king was an awesome responsibility, but the resourceful 'Miss P' prepared a series of studies of 'Children in history' – some famous, some obscure – so that he could appreciate British history through the eyes of others of his own age.

In the afternoons they would embark on educational visits around London, to improving institutions like the British Museum, or for such novelties as a ride on the Underground – an eye-opening experience also visited upon his sheltered mother, but not until she was a teenager. Unfortunately the Press quickly caught on to these forays into the real world, so Charles and Miss P had to take refuge in secret walks in Richmond Park.

After a year Charles was reading well, writing less well, but Miss Peebles felt confident enough to introduce a little French into the curriculum. The one thing Charles was not getting was contact with other children, except for his weekly dancing lesson with Madame Vacani in the Palace, to which several other children came, and at which Charles for once appeared to lose his shyness and enter into the spirit of being taught how to move and stand elegantly.

Charles was approaching the age of seven when the Queen decided that she must grasp the nettle of the next stage of his development. There was no question in her mind that the move had to be made, but it was a move fraught with snares and uncertainties: Charles had to leave his shelter and enter the real world of other people, few of whom had a background anything like his own.

3

Into the World

THE ADULT CHARLES has said of his own upbringing: 'I've learned the way a monkey learns – by watching its parents.' It was inevitable that he would learn much of his royal role simply by watching. Indeed there is not really any other way; no university or polytechnic offers courses in kingship. His parents knew that perfectly well; what concerned them from the earliest years, and what was infinitely more difficult given the peculiarity of his position, was to develop him as a balanced, rounded and sociable person. To that end the Queen drew a deep breath, gathered her resolve, and in the autumn of 1956 she sent him to school.

Friends had recommended Hill House, a discreet pre-preparatory school for the children of diplomats and their like, opened five years before in a side street in the fashionable environs of Knightsbridge, near Harrods store, by Colonel Henry Townend, a bluff, affable character who was still running the school in 1988. A former Royal Artillery officer, he had taken the school's motto from Plutarch: 'A boy's mind is not a vessel to be filled, but a fire to be kindled.' Townend was invited to tea at the Palace, approved of, and told that no special treatment should be shown to Charles; every effort should be made to make him feel that he fitted in with the 120 other sons of gentlefolk at Hill House.

The Queen's choice, when announced, was not universally popular, especially among Labour MPs, who felt that by going to Hill House Charles was continuing to live in a sheltered world of privilege. They called instead for the heir to attend an ordinary inner-city State primary school. But the

Queen would have no truck with any such suggestion; it was, she felt, far too radical a step for an eight-year-old of Charles's background, and it would serve no useful purpose. Besides, she let it be known, he would stand out as such an oddity that the rest of the school life would be hopelessly disrupted. To represent the people, she implied, the heir to the throne did not have to be exactly like them.

Her principal fear, even about Hill House, was that the boy's life might be made a misery by Press attention, if posses of photographers hung around the school gate every time he came and went. At first Charles went, very discreetly, only in the afternoons, having spent the morning with Miss Peebles, until on the momentous day of 28 January, 1957, dressed in the regulation cinnamon-coloured blazer and cap, and attended by a vast gang of pressmen, he began his full-time schooling. He was indistinguishable from the other eight-year-olds, except that his was the only overcoat with a velvet collar. His mother was pleased with his first day, and relieved when it was over; the next morning, when she heard that a large crowd of Press and public were again on the pavement, she was reluctant to let him go. The situation continued for several days until she asked her Press secretary, Commander Richard Colville, to plead with the Fleet Street editors to call off their hounds. They did.

His first full day at school was a traumatic one; it coincided with the retirement of his nanny, Helen Lightbody, to whom he had grown exceptionally attached, and with the departure of Catherine Peebles to begin the education of his sister Anne. Traumatic or not, it did not prevent him many years later from visiting an almost identical set of circumstances on his son William who, on return from his first day at Wetherby school in Notting Hill, found that his nanny Barbara Barnes had rather suddenly left his parents' employment.

In later years, Charles recalled his years at Hill House as among the happiest of his young life, although he was academically undistinguished; his report at the end of his second term described him as 'determined but slow', with history and painting his best subjects, and arithmetic his worst. But his parents took the view that his lack of brilliance did not matter; sending him to school was more of a social than an academic exercise. Hill House introduced him to cricket and football but then, as now, he showed little enthusiasm for such team games: he much preferred swimming, at which he was adept by the age of seven, and wrestling, which Colonel Townend included in his curriculum to allow the boys to dissipate surplus energy.

At home in the holidays he had already learned to ride a pony. His father introduced him to sailing at Cowes, which he enjoyed after overcoming his initial sickness, but most of all he enjoyed going to Balmoral and painting. It was developing as his best form of expression, and its essential solitude seemed to suit his already introverted nature.

Encouraged by the success of Hill House, the measure of success being that nothing went disastrously wrong, that the Press retreated when asked, and that Charles had enjoyed himself, his parents felt able to proceed with the next stage of his development; inevitably, it would be a much bigger step than the first, fraught with many more problems.

Once again the cry went up for Charles to attend an inner London State day school; again it came principally from Labour MPs, and from Lord Altrincham – nowadays plain Mr John Grigg, having disclaimed his peerage for life because he objected to inherited seats in Parliament. A State school was briefly considered, and rejected. For one thing, the Queen and Prince Philip genuinely believed that the public school system provided a better education; for another, Charles would have been far too conspicuous amongst boys from council estates, he would have found it impossibly hard to mix with them, and the result would have been acute embarrassment on both sides. Another equally important consideration was that a city day school could never provide the required measure of security and privacy that a private establishment, out of town and in its own grounds, could.

Several schools were considered, and their headmasters sized up over tea at the Palace. But it was Prince Philip's old school, Cheam, which best seemed to fit the bill; Philip, who was very much in the driving seat when affairs of education were discussed, naturally favoured his own *alma mater*; although he had been something of an academic dunce he had enjoyed his time there and had shone at games. Cheam, originally sited in south London, laid claim to being England's oldest prep school; it had moved to a country location to escape the Great Plague of 1665, and was now near Headley, on the Hampshire-Berkshire border.

The early days that the first heir to the throne to go to school spent away from home were miserable. He had set off by train from Balmoral filled with gloom, apprehension and nerves, feelings hardly uncommon in a boy of nine leaving home for the first time. His forebodings proved justified; the other ninety-nine boys were stand-offish and treated him as a very considerable curiosity. His parents' fears about Press intrusion also proved well-founded despite Cheam's relatively secure grounds; stories about Charles, most of them fabrications, began to appear almost daily in the absence of hard fact, leading to a great deal of suspicion and ill-feeling inside the school as to which boys were earning their five-pound notes as tipsters. At the end of the first term the situation had become so bad that the Queen summoned the Fleet Street editors and told them she was considering taking Charles away from Cheam, and if she did it would be their fault entirely. Chastened, they called off the hounds.

Charles's early weeks at Cheam, he recalled afterwards, were dominated by a sinking feeling of awful isolation, but he soon learned one important lesson; after some of the initial stand-offishness of the other boys had worn off, those seemingly most anxious to make his friendship wanted it for what he was rather than who he was. The danger had been foreseen; his headmaster, Peter Beck, and his mathematics teacher, David Munir, were charged with keeping a discreet eye on him, and with their help he was guided towards several genuine friendships, including Charles Donald, who went on to Harrow, and Christopher Wilson, who went to Stowe.

Throughout his time at Cheam Prince Charles continued his progress as a lacklustre academic performer. His headmaster reported him as 'above average in intelligence, but only average in attainment'. He had an exceedingly wide general knowledge for his age, of both the historical and geographical, and could put it all in context, but he struggled to pedal uphill in the face of such disciplines as mathematics, Latin and Greek. He did shine at artistic and practical subjects; a coffee table he made in his woodwork class became one of his sister's most treasured possessions, and he earned praise for his drawing, painting and modelling.

He appeared to approach the obligatory team games with a dutiful enthusiasm, but his innate politeness got the better of him; it is not among the rules of rugby union, and certainly not in its spirit, that you apologize when bringing an opponent down with a flying tackle. Made captain of the first football eleven, he proved an outstanding disaster in losing every single match: at the end of his captaincy the score stood at: goals for, 4; goals against, 82. The football correspondent of the *Cheam School Chronicle* wrote of one match: 'Prince Charles seldom drove himself as hard as his ability and position demanded.' The belief, which in some public schools almost approaches a fetish, that team games are healthy, character-forming, and an aid to future social progress, is at best a proposition open to argument.

Charles found satisfaction and relief in an entirely different area: drama. He took enthusiastically to acting in school plays, as a conscious way of overcoming his shyness, even if it did mean delivering with a straight face such lines as Gloucester in *Richard III* declaring: 'Soon may I ascend the throne.' The *Cheam School Chronicle*'s drama critic was much kinder than its sports writer: 'Prince Charles played the traditional Gloucester with confidence and depth; he had a good voice and excellent elocution, and very well conveyed the ambition and bitterness of the twisted hunchback.'

Unlike his father, Charles endured Cheam rather than enjoyed it. His father had no firm home base from which to be wrenched, but Charles never seemed to let go the ties that bound him to the comfort and safety of home. He could not wait to get home to see his new baby brother, Prince Andrew, born in 1960, and even wanted to bathe him. It was partly character, partly his upbringing so far to which, despite the best efforts of his mother and father, he was hopelessly chained, and which acted like an iron ball on his subconscious desire to run free. There is an uncomfortably pathetic tone in the story of the young Prince being found by a teacher tidying the classroom long after he should have been in bed, and being told he would be in trouble with Matron. 'I can't help that, sir,' replied the Prince: 'I must do my duties.'

The English public schools, and the preparatory schools which feed them their partly-processed raw materials, are an easy target at which to hurl the slings and arrows of the envy of privilege. Some are excellent, others dreadful; all are expensive. The English who send their offspring into the system at an early age are performing the equivalent rite to the Spartans placing their new-born on a bare hillside to see if they survived the night. They succeeded in their task of supplying administrators to run the Empire and officers to staff the Army that defended it. Public schools are peculiarly English; other nations which enjoy both cultural and economic success survive very well by keeping their children at home and sending them to day schools. They have enjoyed a resurgence of late as a combined result of prosperity and middle-class dissatisfaction with the present State system which puts all abilities in the same school. Heads of State of other lands, even hereditary Heads of State, have survived successfully by going through their country's normal educational system.

But other countries are not England, and the public school system is to some extent a reflection of English society as a whole, which, despite the efforts of the post-war government at the time of Charles's birth, is still divided by money, breeding and birth, and its principal institutions are still largely in the hands of those with public school backgrounds. Given the circumstances, and given that Charles had at some stage to be prised out of his domestic cocoon, it is difficult to see what other practical choices were open to his parents. At least he suffers less than most from one of the commoner of public school vices, which is insufferable arrogance.

Charles was eventually made head boy of Cheam, a position he probably did not particularly deserve but one his masters felt he ought to have. To a sensitive pupil already overburdened with ideas of duty and right, that in itself could be regarded as a peculiar form of cruelty, and another hammer on the wedge prising the Queen's son apart from his more ordinary contemporaries. Charles was already more than sufficiently aware of his differentness; he has himself recalled the acute embarrassment he felt when, gathered with masters and other boys around a radio in the head's study, he heard his mother announce that she intended to create him Prince of Wales.

Cheam was a middle-of-the-road, conventional sort of establishment free from both great distinction and academic eccentricity. The same could certainly not be said of the next school to be imposed on the unhappy youth.

Gordonstoun sits exposed to biting northerly gales on the Morayshire coast of north-east Scotland, where the sinews of boyhood are stiffened as much by the climate as by any Platonic educational theory. It was the creation of Kurt Hahn, a German born into a Jewish family that had moved west from Warsaw in the mid-nineteenth century. Hahn's own school years had been spent at the Humanistic Gymnasium in Berlin at the turn of the century, which inspired in him a lifelong admiration for the moral philosophy of Plato.

During the First World War Hahn had worked in the Imperial German foreign ministry, which he left in disgrace after advising that a planned intensification of the U-boat war was a policy doomed to disaster. He rapidly became associated with those influential Germans pressing for peace by negotiation, particularly Germany's last Imperial Chancellor, Prince Max of Baden. In the ensuing peace, in a Germany largely rudderless and burdened with crippling reparations, he became private secretary to Prince Max and helped him found the Salem School, near Lake Constance in southern Germany. The purpose was to develop a generation of leaders for a new and restored Germany, and the philosophy was lifted straight from Plato's *Republic*: 'Our youth should dwell in the land of health, amid fair sights and sounds; and beauty, the effluence of fair works, will meet the sense like a breeze, and insensibly draw the soul even in childhood into harmony with the beauty of reason.' Unfortunately Plato had in mind a Greek city state, while Hahn was living in a nation bowed into sullen submission by defeat in war and the extraction of a high price by the victorious allies. Hahn always believed that German defeat in 1918, and the subsequent unsteady course of the Weimar Republic which permitted the rise of Nazism, could all be ascribed to a failure of leadership.

Needless to say, he rapidly fell foul of Germany's new Chancellor, Adolf Hitler. In 1932, after Hitler's telegram glorifying the murderers of Potempa who had trampled a young Communist to death in front of his mother, Hahn wrote to all his former pupils challenging them to choose between National Socialism and the ideals of Salem.

He was subsequently arrested, and was set free after five days thanks to a storm of protest from academics throughout Europe and from the British prime minister, Ramsay MacDonald; he fled in 1933 to the safety of England, and in the following year, having found a suitable house in Scotland, opened a new school on the Salem model at Gordonstoun. He brought with him his Platonic theories of education, which in essence meant exposing pupils to a range of personal challenges, dangers and discomforts, rather than have them with their noses in books all day. He borrowed some elements from the English public school system, which he admired, but he had little belief in the value of team games by which English schools set so much store; he thought they brought out the worst in boys, and he preferred that his pupils compete against themselves in such activities as running, discus throwing and mountaineering. His philosophy gave rise to the school motto *Plus est en vous* – 'There is more in you.' He also introduced a degree of democracy; pupils progressed up a bizarrely complex system of ranks and awards, largely on the decisions of their fellows rather than their masters. Two of his important guiding principles for the boys were service to the community, and trust; rather than mete out punishments for misdemeanour, he preferred boys to feel their own sense of guilt at not performing their due share of tasks and duties. Despite Hahn's background the new school was avowedly Christian, and Hahn himself became an Anglican at the age of fifty-nine. Gordonstoun opened its doors in 1934, and among its first intake of thirty boys was Prince Philip of Greece.

Philip had come in contact with Hahn the previous year as the result of a family argument about his education. Rootless after his parents' exile from Greece, he had been taken under the wing of Lord Louis Mountbatten and the other members of the English branch of his Battenberg family, who had ensured that he got the beginnings of an English public school education at Cheam. But the German side of the family, which greatly outnumbered the English, thought that they too should have a say, and that young Philip should experience the second half of his schooling in Germany. He was accordingly dispatched to Prince Max's school for leaders at Salem in 1933. It was a brief and unhappy episode; Hitler's National Socialism was beginning to permeate the school despite the best efforts of Hahn to keep it out; boys were under pressure to join the Hitler Youth and to give the Nazi salute, Philip happily being excused because he was a foreigner. But the dream was going sour, and as soon as Hahn escaped to England, Philip followed him.

Gordonstoun suited the extrovert, blunt, unacademic and self-reliant Philip perfectly, and it was perfectly natural that he should want to send his own son there. The introverted, artistic temperament of Charles had so far been something of a disappointment to him, for what father does not expect his son to be made in his own image? Gordonstoun, he thought, was the very place to make a man of Charles and get him away finally from the influence of all those confounded women.

Family opinion was divided. The Queen largely stayed out of the discussions, still protesting her ignorance of the arcane world of boys' schools. The Queen Mother favoured Eton on several grounds. First, it had a good academic reputation without demanding brilliance of its charges. Second, it was convenient, being on the doorstep of Windsor Castle and known facetiously in the district as 'Slough Grammar'. Third, Eton is the very pinnacle of the venerated old-boy network which the English public school system creates and nourishes; many personal friends of the Queen, and other eminent persons in British life, had their children at Eton, and there was therefore every chance that Charles would be accepted as an equal rather than a freak, and would be surrounded by plenty of his own kind with whom to make friends. It has been suggested since that Charles might not have had such a problem finding a wife if he had been introduced earlier through school friends to the circle of girls who were suitable.

Eton did not win the day. Philip, whose voice was the most influential in the discussions, and which had the support of Mountbatten, argued that if the boy went to Eton the future king could find that all the Cabinet members of his Conservative Government were old school chums, which would not be a good thing for the independence of the Crown.

Philip also brought up the problems of Press intrusion that Charles had suffered at Cheam, pointing out that while a reporter could get from Fleet Street to Eton in an easy hour, the hounds would think twice before undertaking the 600-mile journey from the front door of the *Daily Express* to Morayshire. With Philip in charge, there was never any real doubt that Gordonstoun would be the choice. He is not British, did not have an Eton or Harrow background, and therefore had no reason to see any advantage in a mainstream English public school. Indeed he had some reason for positive dislike of the system, as the aristocratic stratum of English society which was educated in it had taken a very long time to accept the Queen's husband. It could be said that Philip has never fitted in happily with the English aristocracy, being more at home with his German cousins. Charles himself was asked where he would prefer to go, but his request for Charterhouse as some of his Cheam friends were going there fell on the already deaf ears of his father.

By the time a very miserable Prince Charles arrived with his father at the gates of Gordonstoun one day in May 1962, some of the hard edge of Hahn's crusading zeal had been blunted. The founder had retired, and the school was in the charge of Robert Chew, who had joined as one of the original masters in 1934 and who was now tired, harassed, and approaching retirement. But it was still an unconventional place, leaning towards the founding principles of service to others and personal challenges rather than book learning. Many parents did, and still do, look to Gordonstoun to temper difficult or unruly offspring.

It had no academic reputation to speak of, and it required no entrance examination. To allay potential criticism that her son had been shunted off there as a closet dunderhead, the Queen insisted that Charles take a version of the common entrance examination for public schools; the boy produced a perfectly fair result.

After the uphill struggle to make genuine friends at Cheam, Charles had to start all over again in the essentially unfriendly atmosphere of Gordonstoun; it was, if anything, more difficult. His fellow pupils were not of the kind that would easily accept him and, as at Cheam, they were wary and stand-offish. There was only one other pupil there he already knew: Norton Knatchbull, Lord Mountbatten's grandson and now Lord Romsey. There were few others from his social stratum, and it is perhaps significant that of the boys from

Charles's year, the only one who gained any kind of fame apart from the heir to the throne himself is now the gossip columnist of the *Daily Express*.

The school was an austere place with few creature comforts, and Charles was plunged in at the deep end of cold showers and early-morning runs. Robert Chew, the headmaster, and Robert Whitby, Charles's housemaster, had been given strict instructions by the boy's parents that he was to be treated exactly as any other pupil, a well-intentioned directive which was nonetheless apt to backfire, as in the case of the cherry brandy incident.

On a school sailing trip to Stornoway, in the Western Isles of Scotland, Charles, drying out in a local hotel, was forced by the curious gaze of many pairs of eyes at the window to retreat into a back room, which happened to be the bar. Confused and harassed, he ordered the first drink which came into his head, a cherry brandy; alas for the hapless Charles one of the customers was an alert local journalist, who ensured that the story of the fourteen-year-old heir to the throne taking alcohol in a public bar circled the world. For that misdemeanour Chew took away all Charles's hard-won school privileges and reduced him back to the rank of a new boy, a decision Chew subsequently admitted to taking with misgiving and regret. Charles thought the punishment monstrously unfair, given the circumstances of the crime, but he had no avenue down which he could vent his frustration, and he had no choice but to bottle it up. He was completely boxed in, unable to indulge in the healthy, perhaps even necessary, pursuit of minor wickedness.

Team games had crept into Gordonstoun despite Hahn's mistrust of them. Charles played some rugby but did not enjoy it, having neither the motivation nor the required bullock's build. But he took enthusiastically to sailing on the school's own yacht *Pinta*, and at the same time felt the stirring of an innate desire to make music. That such a desire should be present at all is surprising in the son of artistic philistines, and must spring from the genes and influences of the Queen

Mother, who is notably more cultured, in the broadest sense, than her elder daughter or son-in-law. Whatever the present reign is remembered for, it will not be its artistic pace-setting.

Charles, having been forbidden the bagpipes, toyed with the trumpet, and made passable enough progress to appear in a school concert. His true enthusiasm, however, he saved for the cello; he had no great natural aptitude beyond a general artistic sensitivity, but he persevered at it with great seriousness and determination, if with no great encouragement from any quarter other than his wise and indulgent grandmother, and the inspiration of hearing the brilliant virtuoso Jacqueline du Pré. Many years later one of his contemporaries told the political weekly, the *New Statesman*: 'Gordonstoun all fitted in with Philip's idea of toughening him up – that's the rather unfortunate Germanic side of his character showing up. The boy was interested in music, and he absolutely squashed that.'

Charles did make friends, but slowly; the rest of the school could never entirely forget his separateness. He was the only boy there with his own detective, who shadowed his every movement, although the police Land Rover did provide useful personal transport after long night hours spent on a clifftop as a member of the school's coastguard lookout. At weekends Charles would as often as not be away from the school, invited to lunch or shooting parties at the home of Sir Iain Tennant, the Lord Lieutenant of Morayshire, or making a desperate escape to Balmoral to be in the comforting and familiar company of his grandmother.

Visitors noticed that, unlike other boys who would take their parents, relatives and friends on a tour of the school and introduce them to fellow-pupils, Charles would take his callers on long walks and tours of the Morayshire countryside. But he did have other lifelines to sanity, one of which was his art class and his burgeoning love of the physical pleasures of pottery. He formed a close friendship with his art master Robert Waddell, a kindly and amusing man in whose small bachelor flat in the school grounds Charles would spend many hours of refuge listening to Waddell talk about art.

This fired in him an interest which he has retained ever since. In the mainstream of school he remained shy, awkward and unhappy, bottling up all emotion.

Then he had a lucky break. A new English master, Eric Anderson, who subsequently went on to be Head Master of Eton, arrived at the school bringing with him a passion for drama, which had lain dormant at Gordonstoun for some years. Charles had begun to come very slightly out of his shell, and had begun to win some popularity by doing exceedingly life-like impressions of the master's voices, and of the myriad mad characters on the then current and wildly popular BBC radio *Goon Show*, a brilliantly surrealistic creation. When Anderson announced that he intended to mount a school production of Shakespeare's *Henry V*, Charles shyly volunteered for the relatively minor part of Exeter. On stage all his shyness fell away; he was by common consent brilliant, and everyone wondered why he had not been awarded the part of the king. It emerged that Anderson had feared that he might be accused of toadying if he gave the best part to the most important pupil.

At the next production, the appropriately Scottish *Macbeth*, there was no mealy-mouthing over who was the undisputed star of the company, and Charles was deservedly given the leading role. His parents came to watch, causing additional stage fright in the rest of the company, but Charles was, by all accounts, magnificent. The school magazine drama critic wrote: 'Prince Charles was at his very best in the quiet poetic soliloquies, the poetry of which he so beautifully brought out, and in the bits which expressed Macbeth's terrible agony of remorse and fear. In the second part of the play he equally well expressed the degenerate hardening of Macbeth's character, the assumption of cynicism in an attempt to blunt the underlying and too painful moral sensitivity.'

His performance clearly displayed a mature understanding of the character of Macbeth and of the moral questions posed in the work; there may have been some connection with the fact that shortly before the production Charles was confirmed in the Anglican church, a necessary requirement for a future monarch under the Act of Settlement of 1701 which specified that Britain should have an exclusively Protestant throne. Confirmation was preceded by a series of religious discussions with the Dean of Windsor, at which Charles showed a commendable grasp of the essence of the Anglican faith and the significance of the act of confirmation. It was one area in which his father had little or no influence; having switched easily from Greek Orthodox to Anglican, Philip had only the vaguest interest in organized Christianity, and only a minimal belief in it.

Ever since then the inward-looking streak in Charles's nature has made him, in the broadest sense, a religious person, that is to say one aware of a dimension beyond man's everyday existence. He has maintained his Anglican faith stoutly, but he has sought religious experience elsewhere, from pondering the nature of the self with Laurens van der Post, to desiring to celebrate Roman Catholic Mass with Pope John Paul II in Rome during the Wales's Italian tour of 1985.

At Gordonstoun, despite its considerable distance from Fleet Street (no problem to a newshound on *Daily Express* expenses), Charles continued to have occasional trouble with the Press, despite still being an essentially private figure whose sole official duty during his school years was to attend the state funeral of Sir Winston Churchill. One of his school exercise books went missing, eventually to be published in a German magazine, with the unlikely explanation that Charles himself had been forced to sell it because his parents were too mean with his pocket money. And on a New Year skiing holiday with his relative Prince Ludwig of Hesse in Bavaria, the photographers drove him off the slopes and back into the *Schloss*, a taste of much more of the same to come in future years.

Despite the tribulations, Charles in 1964 managed to sit seven O level examinations and to pass five of them, in English language, English literature, Latin, French and history; his old foe mathematics had got the better of him again, as had physics. But he was unhappy, unsettled and bored. Gordonstoun did not appear to be bringing out the best in him; he wanted to leave.

A compromise was reached, in which Charles had little say. The Queen, who on her post-Coronation tour of Australia in 1953 had promised to send out her eldest son to visit her Antipodean subjects one day, realized that this might be the perfect time to fulfil her undertaking. The Australian Prime Minister Sir Robert Menzies, on a visit to London, was summoned to Balmoral for discussions, and it was decided that provided he returned to Gordonstoun to sit his A levels, Charles might profitably spend a term at Geelong Church of England Grammar School near Melbourne, regarded as the closest comparison that young and relatively egalitarian country could offer to Eton; it numbered among its former pupils old boys of such subsequent eminence as Rupert Murdoch. Geelong had an outstation at Timbertop, in high, remote outback country 200 miles to the north, where boys spent one school year learning the art of physical and mental self-reliance. In January 1966, at the age of seventeen, Charles set out for Australia with his detective and his equerry, David Checketts, filled with his customary gloom and foreboding that he was on his way to an earnest, hairy-chested establishment that was probably no more than Gordonstoun with good weather.

In the event, Timbertop was in many ways the making of him. Away from the close, fetid atmosphere of the British upper class, where everyone was extremely conscious of precisely who and what he was, he was placed instead among boys who did not care half so much whether or not he was the future king of England – and of Australia, unless Republicanism there gains a greater hold. They were a good deal more free of inhibitions and prejudice, and cared more about whether the man within was a decent sort than about his position. Timbertop, although supposed to instil the same sort of values of discipline and self-reliance as Gordonstoun, was in fact a good deal more informal about it. The boys lived together under the eye of two or three masters, but with few rules and regulations, little timetable, and only a token amount of academic work. Charles was supposed to be studying for his A levels, but the books remained closed for most of the time in favour of the outback life: felling trees, shearing sheep, panning for gold, exploring the empty country. He began to learn, almost for the first time, natural face-to-face social relations with his own generation; he shared a room with a sheep farmer's son, and he knew he had been accepted when his classmates cheerfully addressed him as a pommy bastard, which in Australia comes close to being a compliment.

He was almost entirely untroubled by Press intrusion; Australian newspapers kept to the bargain set up by Checketts that, having been given a free run of Timbertop for one day with Charles, they would then leave him alone.

While at Timbertop, Charles had his first experience of real live crowds, when he joined a regular school expedition to visit the Australian mission stations in Papua New Guinea. As his aircraft touched down at Port Moresby he could see through the window that a crowd of hundreds had gathered, patently with the sole object of seeing him. He was panic-stricken, and refused to leave the plane until Checketts more or less propelled him physically towards the waiting sea of faces. He found making small talk with them infinitely easier than he had imagined, and to this day he has rarely hesitated to wade into a crowd. He ended up by staying for two terms at Timbertop; before he left he got Checketts to read a brief statement to the Australian Press which positively glowed with appreciation for the friendly treatment he had received at their hands, describing his sojourn as 'the most wonderful period of my life'.

He returned from six months in the outback with a new self-confidence which Gordonstoun had been unable to give him, and when he reappeared on the Morayshire coast that school never again got the better of him. He sat, and passed, A levels in history and French, achieving respectable grades in both despite his lack of study among the gum trees. Although still far from being a hail-fellow-well-met sort of character, he was more at ease in personal relationships. His artistic temperament enjoyed a brief flowering; he returned to the cello, sang Bach, Britten and Mozart in school concerts, becoming a reasonable sight-reader of music, and he played and sang the Pirate King in Gilbert and Sullivan's operetta *The Pirates of Penzance*.

He reached his eighteenth birthday, an event marked by the firing of gun salutes at the Tower of London and Edinburgh Castle; and he became legally able to assume the throne without the need for a regent, and legally able to act as Councillor of State in the absence of his mother abroad and to declare war and make peace. Much more important to him, he was made Guardian of Gordonstoun, the school's name for its head boy and a position held by his father thirty years before. Unlike at Cheam, the promotion was unquestionably deserved this time, thanks to the maturity and poise acquired at Timbertop. For once, his father was proud of him.

The boy who left Gordonstoun was a somewhat happier one than the boy who had arrived. He found the process of trying to absorb its ethos unpleasant and at the time unrewarding. And yet in his life since, in his interest in young people, his social awareness and his concern for the community, he constantly espouses much of what Kurt Hahn believed in. He said himself many years after the experience was behind him: 'I did not enjoy school as much as I might have, but that was because I am happier at home than anywhere else. But Gordonstoun developed my willpower and self-control, helped me to discipline myself, and I think that discipline, not in the sense of making you bathe in cold water but in the Latin sense – giving shape and form and tidiness to your life – is the most important thing your education can do.'

It is not a view of education that is universally held; many would argue that the most important thing education can do is to teach you to question, to think and to ponder, to move easily amongst your fellow men, treating all with equality, tolerance and respect, and that a little indiscipline is necessary for a full enjoyment of life. It is Charles's misfortune that he still does not move through life easily, being by nature shy, introverted and solitary. But it is his achievement not to have allowed his education, with its emphasis on willpower and self-control, to have destroyed his essentially questioning mind and searching soul.

And one of his own, small, private triumphs was, at the second attempt, to pass his O level in mathematics.

4

A Peace Disturbed

LORD BUTLER of Saffron Walden, Master of Trinity College, Cambridge, submitted himself to interview by the *Daily Mail* in 1967 on the delivery of a distinguished new undergraduate into his care, and he cheerfully opined that the boy's parents were, from his own donnish standpoint, a couple of philistines. 'Quite frankly, you know, the Queen and the Duke are not university people; they're horsy people, common sense people. The Queen is one of the most intelligent women in England and brilliant in summing up people, but I don't think she's awfully interested in books. You never see any lying about her room when you go there, just newspapers and things like that. Whereas Prince Charles has a tremendous affinity for books – they really mean something to him.'

Whether to send their bookish son to university was a decision which exercised the Queen and her husband well before Charles was due to leave Gordonstoun and well before his crucial A level examinations had ever been sat, let alone graded. It was a decision they did not feel able to take alone; quite apart from the fact that the Queen rarely acts without consultation, even in family matters. Prince Philip was less than wholeheartedly in favour of university; he has always nursed a certain suspicion of the worth of academic study, particularly in the non-specific disciplines. In 1965, therefore, the Queen arranged a dinner party at which to discuss the matter; she invited her new socialist Prime Minister Harold Wilson, the Archbishop of Canterbury Dr Michael Ramsey, the Dean of Windsor Dr Robin Woods, the Chairman of the

University Vice-Chancellors' Committee Sir Charles Wilson, her private secretary Sir Michael Adeane, and the family's *eminence grise* and would-be puppetmaster, Mountbatten.

Various options were discussed, including a spell at one of the English redbrick universities, and whether Charles should sit for a degree or merely dabble in a few courses that might add to his breadth of knowledge in general and his understanding of the British Constitution in particular. This latter was difficult; academically the boy was still something of an unknown quantity, being regarded by his schoolmasters as a bit of a plodder but at least having the virtue of application.

Previous Princes of Wales, all academic dunderheads whatever their other qualities, had spent a term or two at Oxford or Cambridge; in their youth Edward VII, Edward VIII and George VI had all had brief tastes of college life, but had used the occasion as a social opportunity rather than for any serious process of learning. That is not necessarily by definition a waste of undergraduate life, especially for an heir to the throne whose entry to his unchosen profession does not depend on the passing of examinations, but neither the Queen or Prince Philip nor any other of the advisers around the dinner table had any great desire to see Charles repeat the lifestyle of the future Edward VIII, who used his brief span at Oxford merely to sharpen the edge of a gay blade.

Charles himself had made it clear that he greatly liked the idea of university, and wanted to go. The Queen was more for the idea than against it, aware of her son's need for contact with his contemporaries, a need which boarding schools had not entirely satisfied. She and her son both also knew that a spell in college would probably be the last chance for the foreseeable future that Charles would have for any kind of study and contemplation, and for a reasonable degree of privacy. The question of whether he should merely stick a toe in the academic water, or whether he should jump in for the total immersion of reading for a degree, would have to wait for a while. The immediate question was where he should go.

Mountbatten was, as usual, in no doubt whatsoever; he

should go to Trinity College, Cambridge, as his grandfather King George VI had done, and he should follow that with a naval officer's training at the Royal Naval College, Dartmouth, as his father had done. Considering his own distinguished career at sea, Mountbatten could not countenance the thought of the heir to the throne missing out entirely on the sharp taste of salt. Trinity was attractive to all concerned, not least to Charles himself, who has always tended to the traditional rather than the experimental. It appealed because its quiet position in the city of Cambridge offered a reasonable degree of peace and security. But it appealed most of all because of the new Master it had acquired just before the decisive Buckingham Palace dinner party.

Richard Austen Butler had himself been educated at the rival Pembroke College, Cambridge, but his great-uncle Henry Montagu Butler had been Master of Trinity in the earliest years of the century. What mattered, however, was that 'Rab' Butler had had an exceptionally long and distinguished political career, always at the pragmatic centre and never on the wilder shores of either extreme. He had sat as Conservative Member of Parliament for the old country market town of Saffron Walden, not far from Cambridge, since 1929, and there was little of public affairs he did not know inside-out.

During the wartime coalition government he had been Minister of Education and architect of the watershed 1944 Act which set the mould for post-war secondary education in Britain. In a succession of post-war Conservative governments he had been in turn Chancellor of the Exchequer, Home Secretary, Lord Privy Seal, Foreign Secretary, and Deputy Prime Minister, the last under Harold Macmillan. He was an old-style liberal Conservative with a profound social conscience, of the kind Thatcherism has largely swept away, and of the kind the Queen might well have voted for if indeed she had a vote to cast. His middle-of-the-road stance was close to that of the moderate socialist opposition leader Hugh Gaitskell, giving rise to the term 'Butskellism' as a label for centrist politics. In 1965, having twice narrowly failed to win the leadership of the Conservative party, he retired from politics to his second love of scholarship, ennobled to the House of Lords with the title of his old constituency.

Butler was an old personal friend of the royal family, and continued to be so until his death; in 1976 he sold his country house at Gatcombe Park in Gloucestershire to the Queen in order that she might give it as a home to Princess Anne for her family. He was a happily married family man to whom no personal scandal had ever attached, and he was regarded as the ideal choice to oversee the academic and moral welfare of the Prince of Wales.

Charles went up to Cambridge armed with two A levels from Gordonstoun, in history and French, causing the annual conference of the National Union of Students to debate a motion of protest that the normal requirement for entry to that university was three. Naturally there was never any serious question that his admission would be refused, but his acceptance was bolstered by the report of Trinity's senior tutor, Dr Denis Marrian, who conducted a standard entrance interview and pronounced the Prince 'capable enough and interested enough to take an honours degree'.

Charles was uncertain of what subjects to read, knowing that there was some, largely unspoken, pressure on him to train for the job and to immerse himself in constitutional history, Trinity having a particularly strong history department. But Lord Butler, anxious to further the best interests of his charge, waved any such concerns aside; he told Charles that he should at least begin by reading a subject which genuinely interested him, to give his academic career a sporting chance of success and to avoid quashing his eager spirit with boredom. Study of the Constitution could wait. Charles, fired by his visit to Papua New Guinea during his spell at Geelong, favoured archaeology and anthropology, an option popular among Cambridge arts undergraduates in search of the generalist rather than the specialist and with no particular inclination or aptitude towards the narrower humanities.

That is not to suggest that it is a particularly soft option; no Cambridge degree course is.

Dr Marrian explained to him that he could take 'ark and anth' in his first year as a start towards a degree; he could then switch to another subject for the second part of his degree course, or he could abandon thoughts of a degree and merely paddle in assorted pools of passing interest. Encouraged by Butler, Charles determined from the first that he must try to complete the degree course, both from a sense of his own pride and from his inborn dutiful desire not to let anyone down. It was not going to be easy, and Butler knew it even more than Charles; although the boy was intelligent and inquisitive his background, both at home and at school, had not been ablaze with the fire of academic study. In addition, he was in danger of constant interruption from the demands of his life outside; Butler, in an effort to give the student some peace and allow him to concentrate on his studies, fought a constant but generally hopeless battle to keep public engagements for Charles at bay.

The new undergraduate arrived at Cambridge to huge crowds and a positive storm of media interest, which briefly unnerved him; fortunately the interest of the crowds, if not the newspapers, was short-lived, and he was able to enjoy relative privacy during his time at Trinity, strolling or cycling around the city unmolested like any other undergraduate; Cambridge is somewhat immune to the dazzle of celebrities, and considers itself superior to most of them.

From the first suggestion that he might go up to Trinity Charles had insisted that he live in rooms in the College along with his fellow-students; he wished to confront his shyness, reserve and tendency to solitude rather than to emulate his predecessor Princes of Wales who had spent their undergraduate days in splendid isolation in large private houses on the edge of town. Nor did he have any desire to be seen enjoying obvious privileges; experiences at both Cheam and Gordonstoun had taught him that his position already made it difficult enough for him to mix as an equal with his contemporaries. Even so, small details of his Cambridge life conspired to set him apart from the beginning.

He was given room number 6 on the first floor of E staircase in New Court at Trinity, a quiet corner overlooking the River Cam and the Backs, that sequestered ribbon of calm running through the city where the ancient college walls back on to the river banks. It was like any other undergraduate's rooms, except that as soon as it had been allocated a squad of tradesmen arrived from Sandringham to fit it out with new carpets and curtains; a brand new communal bathroom was installed on the stair, and the Prince's quarters were equipped with two luxuries not bestowed upon ordinary undergraduates – a telephone and a small kitchen, the rest of the student population having to make do with public callboxes and a gas ring. There were, inevitably, mutterings about favouritism and expense although, for the telephone at least, there were perfectly good security reasons.

In his early days at Trinity Prince Charles encountered the same difficulty that had faced him on the occasions he started at a new school: that of making friends. Many shied away from embarrassment or because, in the climate of that time, princes were not politically desirable or fashionable people for students to be associating with. Lord Butler saw from the beginning that his noble charge faced the dangers, firstly of isolation, and secondly of confusion. The atmosphere of university is, after all, much more free and less structured than that of school, and the experience was for Charles entirely new; until then, when he was not living according to the well-defined rules and confines of boarding school, he was immersed in a family environment stiff with order, timing and convention, where the ability to do as one pleased on the spur of the moment was markedly less than for ordinary mortals.

Accordingly the Master of Trinity, every evening before dinner, set aside three-quarters of an hour for Charles to come to his lodgings and see him if he wished, where the Prince could discuss any topic or worry in the informality of Butler's sitting room. He even gave Charles a key to the side door of the Master's Lodge with the instructions that he could come and go whenever he wanted. Charles enjoyed the privilege and used it to the full; it provided him with the same kind of refuge that the art master's apartment had done at Gordonstoun.

Once the new undergraduate had found his feet and gained some confidence, the regular evening meetings developed into privileged private tutorials that any serious student of twentieth century political history would have given his eye teeth for. Butler, although kindly, solicitous and wise towards his young acolyte, nevertheless had no intention of acting merely as a passive guardian of Charles's welfare; he described in great detail the British political scene and its personalities, giving freely of his opinions as to who among his former Commons colleagues were able and trustworthy, and who were mere bags of wind. Having always been near the political centre, and anyway having retired from active politics, Butler had no particular axe to grind, except perhaps against those members of the Tory party who had denied him the leadership. Charles, by nature a listener, soaked it all up. Butler later wrote: 'I found him talented – which is a different word from clever, and a different word from bright. He grew. When he arrived he was boyish, rather immature, and perhaps too susceptible to the influence of his family.' Mollie Butler, the Master's wife, found him charming, sensitive, and with an insatiable desire to know everything; but her woman's intuition detected underneath the seemingly open and pliable exterior a core of steel, which could be interpreted either – she does not say which – as a soaring determination to achieve goals born of a disciplined mind, or a curmudgeonly stubbornness born of high rank and a narrow field of vision.

A combination of reticence, natural introspection and remoteness of position have conspired to ensure that Prince Charles has never been an easy mixer or maker of friends. At Cambridge he relied initially on those few he already knew, including his cousin Prince Richard of Gloucester (now Duke of Gloucester) who was at Magdalene College reading architecture, and Robert Woods, son of the Dean of Windsor. The circle did widen in time, but never as much as it might have done; three-quarters of Trinity's 650 undergraduates were of grammar school background, but Charles seemed to make little effort to adventure into their company, nor they into his. He preferred instead to associate with young people of a background closer to his own, joining the University Polo Club and rapidly gaining his half-blue. One of the advantages of a university education is the opportunity it provides to mix with contemporaries of all social backgrounds and points of view, but in Charles's case it was an opportunity that might profitably have been made more of. There were exceptions like Hywel Jones, the son of a Nonconformist minister from the radical-red valleys of South Wales, who had read Marx by the age of fourteen and who occupied a room on Charles's stair. Jones so impressed the heir to the throne with fluent Welsh socialist argument that Charles asked Butler if he might join the University Labour Club; he was very quickly disabused by the Master of the notion that he could nail his colours to any such obvious political mast, whether right or left. It was an early practical lesson on the place of the Crown in the British Constitution.

Prince Charles spent his first year largely in dedicated study, except for a hugely enjoyable visit to the Neolithic cave paintings of the Dordogne in the company of his archaeology tutor Dr Glyn Daniel, and was rewarded in the first part of his tripos examination with an upper second pass, definitely an above-average result. Charles was pleased, and Butler was delighted, urging the Prince to stick with 'ark and anth', and holding out the strong possibility that if he did so the first modern heir to the throne to complete a university course could come out with a first-class honours degree. But for once Charles was stubbornly determined not to heed the Master's advice; an interest in his antecedents and a growing awareness of his responsibilities of his eventual office had convinced him that for the second part of his course he must tackle history. No matter that his history tutor, Dr Anil Seal, far from being an expert on the British Constitution, was a modern historian with a particular interest in India; there was always Butler and his private informal tutorials on matters closer to home.

With a satisfactory first year behind him, Charles began to spread his undergraduate wings a little, figuratively and literally. He took flying lessons, and made his first solo flight. He sang in the Madrigal Society, and played his cello at a public concert. With Butler's prodding he joined the Dryden Society, Trinity's amateur dramatics club, on the grounds that it would give him confidence on public occasions and particularly in television interviews.

From his acclaimed performance as Macbeth at Gordonstoun, the Dryden Society took him to the opposite extreme of the dramatic canon, playing a padre in *The Erpingham Camp* by the savagely witty and rampantly homosexual Joe Orton, a role which required him to be pelted with pork pies and to have a custard pie thrown in his face. Needless to say, the performance attracted as much attention from the theatre critics as a major West End premiere. Three months later the royal thespian had graduated to a part in the annual satirical revue staged by the university's celebrated Footlights Club, nursery to many a now-famous professional comic actor. It was not, perhaps, the most biting of satire, but then undergraduate humour is highly variable in its degrees of cleverness and invention. Charles was still deeply attached to his beloved *Goon Show*, which although wildly inventive in its crazed surrealism and a landmark in comedy, was very much the creation of an earlier decade, its principal writer Spike Milligan and its performers drawing largely on the madness of their military service for inspiration. But Britain was now in the Sixties, the so called 'swinging Sixties' when humour and a great deal else besides underwent quite dramatic changes.

All periods and eras are to some extent arbitrary definitions and artificial dates on the calender of time, but the Sixties in Britain was an unusually identifiable epoch, deeply imprinted on the minds of most people of Charles's generation. In a way, by being at university at all and by almost living the life of a normal undergraduate, he was a product of it. And yet in so many other ways, poor fellow, he missed it.

Above all, the Sixties was the decade of the young, for it was they more than any other group who found themselves with money in their pockets, and with a new spirit of self-confidence. The burgeoning rock music industry gave them their own culture and heroes who grew in stature the more their elders despised them. Perceptions of the established order of society were loosened by films like *Room at the Top*, based on a John Braine novel, which promulgated the working-class hero, and *Darling* starring Julie Christie, which portrayed a world of glamour and easy sex which was essentially classless and therefore within reach of all. Upstart financiers like Jim Slater and the direct-sell washing machine king, John Bloom, gave the impression that anyone could make a million. Goonish humour gave way to political satire, to *Private Eye* and *That Was The Week That Was*, in which the ruling class was held up to ridicule. The ruling class had only itself to blame after the revelations of their behaviour and morals in the Profumo scandal of 1963. Why, the rest of the country asked, should the ruling class have all the fun?

The political climate changed, at least on the surface. The tired old Conservative government fell and gave way by the tiniest of majorities to the Labour administration of Harold Wilson, bursting with promises that Britain would be regenerated in the white heat of the technological revolution. The level of political consciousness was raised in the population at large, first by Bertrand Russell leading thousands of middle-class people, who would never have dreamt of demonstrating about anything before, in protest against nuclear weapons. As the decade progressed, the articulate young found another political cause which helped to unite them, America's involvement in Vietnam.

In fact it was all hopelessly ephemeral and insubstantial, an illusion or even a delusion, this notion that Britain was great again and that the old order of society had finally been dismantled. As the decade drew to its close the dream began to go sour, with the rise of the drug culture and the realization of the nonsense of seeking Nirvana through Indian maharishis, some of whom proved to be much better businessmen than Jim Slater. Margaret Thatcher, whose premiership has been a crusade for a return to the virtues of thrift and sacrifice, said in an interview in the *Daily Mail* in 1982: 'We are reaping today what was sown in the Sixties; fashionable theories and permissive claptrap set the scene for a society in which the old virtues of discipline and restraint were denigrated.' Only two years before, *The Times* had taken a more constructive view of the period: 'The Sixties was the decade when England truly emerged from its post-war depression and became a country of joyful and envied achievement.' Jean Shrimpton, the fashion model who encapsulated the era, said in an interview at about the same time: 'There was energy then, and if you had an idea, however silly, you could get it on the road. People were willing to listen – too much so, but it was better than not listening at all. It was a terribly naïve period; it was like falling in love. You didn't see anything very clearly.'

For those who were young then, it was more basic than that; it was, quite simply, enormous fun, and the young of the Sixties who are now middle-aged remember it with great affection, and can probably cope with the infinitely more serious Eighties that much better as a result.

Among its less desirable facets, the Sixties was the high summer of dubious property speculation which threw up forests of ghastly, inhuman, featureless office blocks in the inner cities, of the kind that Prince Charles now rails against, branding their developers as worse than the Luftwaffe for wanton destruction of the environment. He has become vociferous in his condemnation of hideous excrescences like Paternoster Square in the City of London, an utterly insensitive development of blank grey office towers thrown up in the very shadow of St Paul's Cathedral to the greater glory of the fast buck.

But that apart, Charles's present-day outlook owes little to the philosophy of the Sixties; it was a slightly later era that left more of a positive mark on him. But looking at him as he approaches his middle years, one cannot help but feel a tinge of regret that he was not in some way more able to share that interlude of abandon, silliness, unfettered self-exploration, and sheer fun before the realities of a hard world came crowding in again.

Not that his life at Cambridge was in any way monastic, and he himself has said that he looks back on his under-graduate days with great affection and nostalgia. By his own standards he was free, although even then his public life was never far away. He would eat out with friends in the cafés of Cambridge, or more grandly at the Pink Geranium restaurant in the village of Melbourn outside the city.

And he discovered girls. The ever-attentive Butlers introduced Charles to Lucia Santa Cruz, the daughter of the Chilean Ambassador to London, who was working as a research assistant on Butler's memoirs, *The Art of the Possible*. She was three years older than Charles, and vastly more experienced in the ways of the world; she too was given a key to the side entrance of the Master's Lodge, and although the romance came and went in a very few months, Charles never again lacked for a female companion. Lucia returned to South America and married, and Charles became godfather to her first child.

Although he did not fall to being a disciple of the Sixties, there were aspects of his Cambridge life which helped to colour his latterday thinking. Charles and a small group of his friends frequently enjoyed, as students do, discussions far into the night on the meaning of life. Among the regular participants were Professor Donald McKinnon, of the chair of Divinity, and the Rev. Harry Williams, an ordained priest and a Fellow of Trinity. Williams made a particular impression on Charles, because his life seemed to be an odyssey of self-exploration; he wrote several books, including *Objections to Christian Belief* and *The God I Want*, all of which seemed to be a painful wrestling with his own soul in an effort to find an elusive religious truth. Although never anything more than a mainstream – indeed devout – Anglican, Charles was impressed by Williams's questioning attitude and his apparent unwillingness to accept received religious doctrines at face value.

Soon afterwards the uneasy Christian gave up his Trinity post and disappeared into an obscure religious community in Yorkshire, but Charles kept in touch with him, and indeed asked him to participate in his wedding at St Paul's in 1981.

There were other brief flashes of the Charles-to-come. The Cambridge undergraduate newspaper *Varsity*, to celebrate its 21st birthday, asked Trinity's best-known student to contribute a piece on his impressions of Cambridge life. 'For me, life at Trinity means every modulation of light and weather, like the orange-pink glow from the stone of the Wren Library in the last rays from a wintry sun,' mused the aesthete who many years later would talk to an audience of Canadians about life being a mirror in a lake.

But not all his impressions were quite so poetic. He went on to write of the everlasting sounds of the Great Court fountain, 'and of photographers' boots on the cobbles'. At that stage he still regarded the antics of the Press with a wry amusement, and only in later years did he come to look on newspapermen with a certain impotent desperation. His *Varsity* contribution was also the source of a much-quoted passage, and the inspiration for his best-known stage role, when he wrote of the early-morning noise beneath his window of the city coming to life: 'This is something I find hard to accustom myself to, particularly the grinding note of an Urban District Council dust lorry's engine rising and falling in spasmodic energy at seven o'clock in the morning, accompanied by the monotonous jovial dustman's refrain of "O come all ye faithful" and the headsplitting clang of the dustbins.'

He got his own back on the dustman by portraying him in the Footlights revue, but the dustman did not mind; a record company had signed him up. Charles was equally satisfied; after his article appeared Cambridge City Council put the Trinity dustbin collection back by two hours.

Throughout the undergraduate life of the Heir Apparent, Lord Butler did his best to fend off extraneous distractions, and was particularly keen that Charles should be shielded as much as possible from the call of public duties, in order that he might concentrate on his work and, equally important, enjoy himself while he had the chance. It was no easy task, and it was one of the few areas in which Butler failed in his intentions. While still at school Charles had attended the state funeral of Sir Winston Churchill, one of the greatest assemblies of crowned heads and political leaders ever seen. Within weeks of arriving at Cambridge he had attended his first State Opening of Parliament to hear his mother repeat, as though they were her own, the words written by her government on what legislation they intended to enact in the coming year. And he had flown to Australia to represent the Queen at the funeral of a former Australian Prime Minister, Harold Holt. In addition Charles was frequently rostered for more minor royal appearances in Britain, tasks which Butler referred to disparagingly as 'balcony jobs' and urged the Prince to turn down. But not even Butler could slow down the gradual development of Charles as a public figure; his dramatic, spectacular, formal debut as Prince of Wales was looming, and it was about to create by far the most serious diversion in his entire academic career.

The investiture of Charles as Prince of Wales within the grand ruined walls of Caernarfon Castle in 1969 was one of the few major acts of positive public relations ever undertaken by Buckingham Palace, and as such it was a tremendous success. It also said something about how the public's view of the royal family had changed during the Sixties, and how the Queen had moved skilfully to remain in tune with her subjects.

In the early years of her reign Elizabeth II relied, quite naturally, on the old guard of advisers and courtiers inherited from the earlier age of her father. She was uncertain, bowed down with responsibility and feeling her way. She was remote; her subjects knew little of her and her family, except through the pathetically obsequious outpourings of former nannies and the like in cheap women's magazines. The nation had great sympathy and respect for the job she had undertaken and for the circumstances in which it was forced upon her, but she was distant, stiff and unreachable, and a poor public performer whose pronouncements were dreary and starched. Some of her admirers, the elderly Winston Churchill in particular, nonetheless viewed her almost as a goddess. Others thought that her remoteness was opening a dangerous gulf between Crown and people.

Lord Altrincham, a journalist and proprietor of a worthy and serious periodical, *National and English Review*, voiced those latter concerns in an issue in 1957: 'The personality conveyed by the utterances which are put into her mouth is that of a priggish schoolgirl, captain of the hockey team, a prefect and a recent candidate for confirmation. Like her mother she appears unable to string even a few sentences together without a written text. When she has lost the bloom of youth, the Queen's reputation will depend, far more than it does now, upon her personality. It will not then be enough for her to go through the motions; she will have to say things which people can remember and do things on her own initiative which will make people sit up and take notice. As yet there is little sign that such a personality is emerging.'

The author made it quite clear that the blame lay, not with the Queen herself, but with the second-rate circle of advisers who surrounded her, 'a tight little enclave of English ladies and gentlemen'. Altrincham was decidedly pro-monarchist, but such details went over the heads of the public, who heaped hate, scorn and obloquy on his head. The town from which he took his title disowned him, the *Observer* newspaper, supposedly of liberal outlook, for which he worked, sacked him, and a member of the League of Empire Loyalists walked up and hit him in the middle of a television interview. Other commentators, including the much-respected Malcolm

Muggeridge, who voiced similar concerns about the excessively buttoned-up style of the monarchy, were treated with equally intemperate disgust.

For the next dozen years the Queen took a series of small, careful but significant steps to bridge that gap, helped by the gradual replacement of the old courtiers and her own improving confidence. She abandoned the presentation of debutantes at court, a curious ritual in which young women with well-heeled or nearly-famous fathers essentially advertised themselves on the upper-class marriage market. She agreed to deliver her Christmas broadcast on live television as well as radio, an exceedingly nerve-racking experience for her. She instituted Thursday lunches at the Palace, and invited quite ordinary subjects from industry, the arts and many other fields of endeavour. She went to the theatre, even to see quite daring shows such as the satire *Beyond the Fringe*.

She was helped to acclimatize the monarchy to the mood of the Sixties by her sister, who married Antony Armstrong-Jones, not only a commoner but also a practitioner of the then exceedingly fashionable trade of photography. The fact that Tony and Margaret, who formed the apex of a London smart set much as the future Edward VII had once done, were able to move around the 'in' spots of London without being unduly mobbed or stared at was itself an indication that the public was beginning to take a more relaxed, more mature view of the royal family. The stiff view of the Queen as goddess in her temple had softened, and the obsessive interest in every minor detail of royal private life had not yet begun.

The Queen was further helped to attune herself to the Sixties by the fact that she got on exceptionally well with the first Labour Prime Minister of her reign, Harold Wilson, to the dismay of the Conservative old guard who regarded him as a dangerous charlatan, and who even contemplated, with the tacit support of none other than Mountbatten, the engineering of a coup to secure his overthrow. The Queen's esteem for Wilson was recognized in her personal gift to him on his retirement in 1976 of the Order of the Garter, the highest order of chivalry in the land.

For all that the Queen, assisted by the antennae of her husband who had much more opportunity to mix and to speak freely with her subjects, sensed that the gap between monarch and people was not yet fully closed, and that if her son was to be effective in his task of continuing the preservation of the institution, the Crown would have to ensure that he had the people's support. She had announced at the time that he first went to Cambridge that he would be invested as Prince of Wales in two years' time, and the matter had preyed on her son's mind ever since.

It was a wonderful opportunity to relaunch the monarch at a time when its popularity was in something of a lull. The principal weapon in the public relations battle was the sanctioning by the Queen of a BBC/ITV television film about her family life, containing such apparently mundane but previously unseen and even undreamt-of scenes as the entire family cooking sausages on a barbecue at Balmoral.

Screened deliberately just before the investiture the film, *Royal Family*, was a tremendous success; it showed the Queen and her brood, if not altogether accessible, at least human and in many ways quite ordinary. The film opened a door on the private lives of royalty that now bangs so violently in the wind of Fleet Street prurience that it may damage its hinges. Charles himself was given his own exposure; he conducted radio and television interviews in which he chatted easily and freely about schooldays and university life, and even performed some of his Goon voices from the Footlights revue. He was seen to be an amiable, honest and really rather articulate young man.

But a far more serious and potentially much more dangerous battle was that to win over the Welsh whose Prince he claimed to be. Welsh nationalism was a rising and occasionally violent political force; Gwynfor Evans had just been elected to the Commons as the first Welsh Nationalist MP, and everywhere in the Principality there was pressure and demonstration against English dominion and in favour of a resurgence of the native language and culture. Many Welshmen saw the planned investiture as a sordid English trick to buy them off, little better than Edward I's original subjugation of their land. By the time the ceremony took place numerous threats against Charles's life had been issued and fifteen terrorist bombs had gone off, the last of them on the morning of the investiture causing an innocent child to lose a leg. The newly invested Prince of Wales dwelt unhappily on that last incident for a long time afterwards.

It had been decided from the beginning that the Prince of Wales should be properly schooled in the language and culture of his Principality, and that he should spend one term away from Cambridge at the University College of Wales, Aberystwyth. Butler was displeased to lose his star undergraduate for so long; George Thomas, Secretary of State for Wales in the Wilson government, who was appointed Charles's mentor in all matters Welsh, thought that sending him there for a brief spell was patronising to the Welsh people, although when it was made clear to him that the Queen's mind was made up he lent his wholehearted and enthusiastic support. But in the rising tide of Welsh militancy even the Queen began to fear for her son's safety, and the investiture and its preliminaries became dominated by a nightmare of security precautions.

It is to Charles's eternal credit that, faced with such opposition, he entered the anti-royalist den of Aberystwyth as Daniel entering among the lions, confronted his detractors, and disarmed them with his openness and his desire to understand their objections. When they shouted at him, he went up and talked to them; sometimes they listened, and sometimes he turned away disappointed because they merely ranted. His Welsh language tutor was a strangely inspired choice; Edward Millward was President of Plaid Cymru, the Nationalist political movement, and no friend of the London government. Without giving an inch from his own position, he schooled

Charles very thoroughly in what the aspirations of his movement were.

He also proved to be an excellent teacher of his native tongue, just as Charles proved a surprisingly able pupil. Only six weeks into his course the Prince stood up before a crown of 5,000 at the Welsh League of Youth Eisteddfod in Aberystwyth and delivered a seven-minute speech in word-perfect Welsh which he had composed himself. It was a masterstroke, and no mean achievement. The crowd, initially hostile, was instantly won over, and roared and cheered its approval. Even Gwynfor Evans, the Nationalist MP, was obliged to offer his congratulations, and to describe the performance as 'amazing'.

Interviewed at the end of his Aberystwyth term, Charles said:'If I've learnt anything in the last eight weeks, it has been about Wales in particular, and its problems, and what these people feel about Wales. They're depressed about what might happen if they don't try and preserve the language and culture, which is unique and special to Wales. And if something is unique and special, I think it's well worth preserving.'

The investiture was a somewhat contrived ceremony that owed much to Lloyd George's creation for the previous Prince of Wales in 1911, updated for the Sixties with its Habitat-style plywood chairs, perspex canopy over a Welsh slate throne, Lord Snowdon as Constable of Caernarfon Castle in a high camp uniform he designed himself, and a thoroughly ugly crown of Welsh gold for the Prince. It was a triumph, watched by a world-wide television audience of at least 500 million who heard Charles speak again in fluent Welsh, and saw the Queen present her twenty-year-old son to the Welsh people. The people who had been so suspicious now accepted him gladly, for he had taken the trouble and the courtesy of getting to know them.

George Thomas, with whom Charles developed a lasting friendship and who subsequently had his mellifluous Welsh tongue put to good use as Speaker of the House of Commons, finally retiring ennobled as Lord Tonypandy, had done his work well, satisfying both his own political party who wished to defuse the explosive issue of Welsh Nationalism – and were quite happy to use Charles towards that end – and his own countrymen, who were made to feel that the English Crown embraced them while recognising their separate identity. After the Caernarfon ceremony Charles made an equally triumphant four-day tour of his domain; Llewelyn ap Gruffydd, the last of the true Welsh princes defeated by Edward I in 1282, could hardly have had a better reception had he risen again in that week.

But the twenty-first English Prince of Wales could not afford to bask in his success for long; Trinity, and the neglected study for a history degree, beckoned with some urgency. In this final year he returned to the stage in another revue, this time titled *Quiet Flows the Don*. And Lord Butler had one last flash of annoyance when the Prince was hauled off for the duration of his Easter vacation to tour Australia and New Zealand with his parents, in celebration of the 200th anniversary of Captain Cook's voyage of discovery. His final examinations, six papers of three hours each, taken barely a month after his return, contained such essay questions as 'How and to what extent did George III control his ministers before 1784?' and 'Was Winston Churchill an unsuccessful peacetime prime minister?'

The eventual outcome was a lower second class Bachelor of Arts honours degree, a creditable performance for one who spent his three-year course with so many interruptions and with so much else on his mind. Butler was convinced that, but for the diversion of the investiture and the term spent away at Aberystwyth, Charles could easily have achieved an upper second, and had he stuck to 'ark and anth' throughout, he could even have achieved a first.

The quality of the result was not, perhaps, the most important thing, except to prove to the doubters that Charles was no gormless bonehead at the tail end of the tired Hanoverian genes; he had become the first modern heir to the throne to graduate. The real value was in the enjoyment and satisfaction that the experience gave him, and the home truths he learnt in the Master's Lodge. It could be argued that the experience would have been richer without the interruptions and with a wider circle of friends; but he nonetheless left a much maturer man, having acquired the ability, which he has exhibited frequently since, to think independently of his family.

'I think I can say,' said Lord Butler as his charge departed for the next stage of his education, 'that we have done a good job at Trinity.'

5

'No Better Training
for Kingship'

THE NEWS that His Royal Highness the Prince of Wales, Bachelor of Arts, historian, television megastar, comic actor and sometime cellist was to follow his university education with a military career was not greeted with universal acclaim. Was it not inappropriate and outdated that the Heir Apparent, particularly one seen during his investiture exposure to be sensitive, intellectual and an altogether amiable chap, should be pushed into a job which was essentially about killing people?

Despite the recent Soviet invasion of Czechoslovakia and the consequent raising of the temperature in the arsenal of Europe, militarism was severely out of fashion, particularly among the young generation which was largely united across the Western world in condemnation of American involvement in Vietnam. The British Army watched with dismay as its recruiting figures dropped at the rate of 15 per cent a year.

Prince Charles felt the need to justify himself in public, and took the opportunity in a speech when receiving the freedom of the City of London soon after his Cambridge graduation. 'It is pointless and ill-informed to say that I am entering a profession trained in killing ... I am entering the RAF and then the Navy because I believe I can contribute something to this country by so doing. To me it is a worthwhile occupation, and one which I am convinced will stand me in good stead for the rest of my life.'

At this remove it sounds a po-faced reply lacking the ring of total conviction, and it is unlikely to have won over any of the doubters. But with the voices of his father and Mountbatten loud among the counsels that debated the course of his life, Charles never really had any other option. Mountbatten was fond of recalling how his father Prince Louis of Battenberg, who rose to be First Sea Lord, had reassured the future King George V that there was no more fitting training for kingship than to have served in the Navy, and how he himself had repeated the maxim to the panic-stricken George VI as he was dragged unwillingly to the throne on his brother's abdication.

The notion of schooling monarchs-in-waiting and other members of the royal family in a military career owes more to tradition than to necessity. It was all very well for kings to be generals in the days when the role of a monarch was to hold together an unruly country by force of arms, and it is a very long time since Henry V cried 'God for Harry, England and St George' on the field of Agincourt. There has not been much call for British kings to lead their armies in person since William of Orange secured the throne for the Protestant faith in his defeat of his Catholic predecessor James II at the Battle of the Boyne in 1690. In the last battle fought on British soil, when the Jacobite cause was finally extinguished at Culloden in 1746, King George II was quite happy to leave the fighting to a professional general, 'Butcher' Cumberland. The military career of the future Edward VII was exceedingly brief and distinguished only by his initiation into the pleasures of the boudoir. That of Elizabeth II was almost equally brief, and imposed by the special circumstances of wartime, although her short spell as a motor mechanic in the Auxiliary Territorial Service did turn her into a particularly competent driver and the only British monarch trained in the maintenance of a diesel truck engine.

There have, of course, been those who positively wanted a military career. The present Duke of York, for example, saw the Navy as an attractive full-time job, and did not baulk for a moment when his unit was involved in front-line fighting and great danger in the Falklands campaign in 1982.

Others who have wanted a military career have found

themselves unsuited to it. Prince Edward, presumably from a burning desire to match and preferably outshine the military exploits of his two elder brothers, attempted the most gruelling, masochistically difficult officer training course of all, in the Royal Marines. He was either ill-advised, or too strong-headed to heed advice, but he was in the end unable to adjust to the prime necessity of any Marine Commando unit, which is total mutual dependence. When he left he expressed a desire to follow a career in arts management, which he subsequently embarked upon.

The argument has occasionally been advanced that the monarch-in-waiting requires at least some military experience because he or she will in time become titular head of the armed forces and will be obliged to conduct a great many military rituals through the inevitable clutch of colonel-in-chief appointments. But the present Queen is living proof that this is largely a nonsense; besides, both her mother and her daughter are colonels-in-chief of a variety of regiments, and their combined active military experience is precisely nil.

There are, however, strong attractions in a military, especially a naval, career for an heir to the throne: it is ideal for keeping him away from the political arena, the public eye and the Press, and it forces him into contact with his fellow men. The error is made by those who imagine that the Services have a monopoly of the teaching of discipline, responsibility and human relationships.

In many ways Charles seemed a far from ideal candidate for Service life. That side of his character which had been shown to the public revealed him as a bookish, sensitive character. Dermot Morrah, in a blandly uncritical biography published in 1968, declared: 'No British Prince since the Stuarts has cared more sincerely for the things of the mind and the spirit.' *The Times*, reviewing the book, said he would have made an excellent schoolmaster.

The schoolmaster *manqué* had in fact been a late developer. Born with a shy and vulnerable nature, he had been channelled into a hairy-chested Hooray-Henry educational stream, chiefly at the instigation of his father who thought so highly of it. Whatever its other merits, the broadening of the mind into egalitarian attitudes is perhaps not at the top of the list of attributes of the public school system. Cambridge had begun to loosen the shackles on Charles's thinking, conditioned as it was by the overpowering constraints of his background, but most of his public pronouncements still remained firmly anchored in the safe, conventional, traditional bedrock of his family upbringing.

It was a long time afterwards that he admitted his school-days had not been a period of unalloyed joy. In an interview at the time he remained unquestioningly loyal to the system he had endured: 'I suppose I could have gone to the local comprehensive or the local grammar, but I'm not sure that it would have done much good. I think a public school gives you a great deal of self-discipline and experience and respon-sibility, and it is this responsibility that is so worthwhile.'

He was an undergraduate when much of the student popu-lation of Western Europe was in ferment, seized with a revo-lutionary fervour against the established educational order which culminated in virtually open war between the students of the Sorbonne in Paris and the fearsome French riot police. In the tranquillity of his room overlooking the Cambridge Backs, Charles was untouched by it all. Jack de Manio, the radio presenter whose trademark was misreading the studio clock at a time of day when the nation was trying to get itself to work, asked the Prince about student demonstrations in his pre-investiture radio interview. This time Charles tempered his Establishment outlook with a desire to understand the opposite view, an indication that Cambridge had begun to loosen up his preconceptions.

'We all hear about students today,' de Manio said, 'and you are still a student, and thank heavens not all students demonstrate. But in your view, why do they do it and how can one solve the problem?'

Prince Charles replied thoughtfully. 'I can't help feeling that because students and many people feel so helpless and so anonymous in life and society that demonstrating is one useful way of making known your own particular opinions about world affairs, and domestic affairs and things like that. It may also be because perhaps it's enjoyable, a lot of other people do it. I have a feeling that a lot of people are very serious about it – a lot are not so serious about it, and it develops into sheer mob hysteria, which is very frightening I would think. As to solving it this is, I should have thought, a very, very difficult problem. At Cambridge at the moment they've set up several working parties between dons and students, and I think this is a great help.'

His views on marriage at that time were, however, rather more rigidly conventional; it was clearly a subject to which he had not given more than a passing thought. 'You've got to remember that when you marry, in my position, you are going to marry somebody who perhaps one day is going to become Queen. You've got to choose somebody very carefully. The one advantage about marrying a princess, for instance, or somebody from a royal family, is that they know what happens.' Brides from outside royal families, he was to discover some years later, are capable of learning.

There were, however, some rather more accurate glimpses of the Charles to come. During his public exposure at the time of the investiture, he addressed a Welsh audience, still numbed by the appalling tragedy of Aberfan when a vast tip of colliery spoil slid and entombed a school full of children, on what was to become one of the major concerns of his later life. 'My object is to be alarmist and to say that there is a very small line between extinction and survival – and this applies to the country as well – and that legislation should be enacted now and not vaguely in the future. In South Wales nearly an acre [one third of a hectare] disappears under mine wastage every three years. I could go on until I am blue in the face and you are, I hope, aware of many of the problems. An enormous percentage of the population of Britain and Wales seems to be totally unaware except when it is too late. The most distressing aspect of the whole question is the dormant state of public opinion in this country. If it could be awakened somehow, the whole task of making our environment habitable would be immensely easier.'

His own awakening environmental concern sprang from a number of sources; the trigger of Aberfan, his own sensitive perception, the broadening of an undergraduate mind. But it also came from his father. Undiplomatic he may sometimes be, but unintelligent he is certainly not; Philip championed the cause of conservation long before his son helped to make it fashionable, and has for years hammered away like some Biblical prophet without honour in his own country at the ominous portent of diminishing resources.

Unfortunately, his style over the years has given him a bad Press and, as he himself admitted in self-deprecation but not entirely without truth on a recent visit to Norway, nobody listens to a word he says.

Interviewed by Grampian Television in Aberdeen at the time of the investiture, Philip, in the course of justifying the public ritual at Caernarfon against a certain amount of criticism, made a wider point: 'I think it [the Monarchy] functions because occasionally you've got to stick your neck out. You can't just be wholly negative about this. I think if you feel strongly enough about it, and you feel you're doing the right thing and that it is in the interests of people – sensible and intelligent people – you should go ahead and do it in spite of the fact that you may be criticized for it. The idea that you don't do anything, on the off-chance you might be criticized, you'd end up like a living cabbage, and it's pointless. You've got to stick up for something you believe in.' In spite of considerable differences of outlook and style between himself and his father, it was a philosophy which Charles was already nurturing, but which was not yet ready for its full flower. He was still inexperienced and in many ways hopelessly naïve.

To guide him through the day-to-day snares and thickets of a suddenly expanding public life he had the practised hand of Squadron-Leader David Checketts. Checketts knew the ropes, and his master, well; he had been attached as equerry to Prince Philip's office, and had accompanied Charles as helpmate and guardian during his two terms at Geelong school, where the two developed a friendship that went well beyond the needs of the job in hand.

He had been transferred full-time to Charles's service when the latter went up to Cambridge, and now had the far-from-unpleasant task of organizing the Prince on a succession of domestic and foreign appearances that were deemed necessary to be crammed in between his official public unveiling at Caernarfon and the impending demands of a Service career. It was an undoubted help in the projection of Charles that Checketts was a part-time director of Neilson McCarthy, a public relations consultancy; certainly in those early years of increasingly high profile, Charles rarely seemed to put a foot wrong.

As already recorded, he travelled with his parents to Australia and New Zealand in 1970 shortly before his Cambridge finals, and immediately stole the headlines away from the Queen, his televised performance at Caernarfon still fresh in the Antipodean consciousness. After trying the national obsession of surfing at St Kilda Beach near Melbourne, he complained that the experience had been like swimming in undiluted sewage. The Mayor of St Kilda was furious: 'When that young crank came here he didn't have the brains to tell us he was going to St Kilda, or we would have cleaned the place up.' Another local worthy fulminated: 'Who does he think he is – the next King of England?' From New Zealand he went on alone to visit Expo 70 in Tokyo; there he met the president of the Sony electronics corporation, who he heard was considering building a plant somewhere in Western Europe. 'Why,' asked the Prince of Wales, 'don't you take a look at Wales?' Two years later Charles took great satisfaction in opening a Sony television factory at Bridgend, Glamorgan.

That year he also travelled with his father to the Council of Europe conservation conference in Strasbourg, attended

President de Gaulle's funeral in Paris, and undertook a two-week tour of Canada, after which he met up with Princess Anne in Washington and paid a courtesy call on President Nixon before the latter's Watergate disgrace. Nixon set aside ten minutes for a chat in the Oval Office, which lasted for nearly an hour and a half, the President being so impressed with his young visitor's grasp of world affairs. (In view of subsequent revelations, the chat is presumably enshrined somewhere on tape.) But the outstanding feature of the visit was Nixon's apparent determination to pair off Charles with his then-unmarried daughter, Tricia; they were sat together at every official meal, and were even left alone together for long periods. Charles was embarrassed to the point of annoyance; he did not like Tricia. The American Press, however, was aglow with praise for the dashing young man, and equally strong in its dislike of Anne, who looked sullen and bored. 'The Prince is full of pep, the Princess acts pooped,' said one Washington headline.

Charles was again embarrassed, but for different reasons, during his first major foreign tour in his own right later that year, to Fiji, Tahiti, Bermuda and Barbados. At the latter, the president of the local university union greeted him with a black power salute. 'Do you always shake hands like that?' asked the heir to the throne, not having the faintest idea what the gesture meant.

Overall, the Charles that the world at large saw was an enthusiastic, slightly immature, very amiable individual, essentially rather conservative and traditional, not least in his dress which, with turn-ups on all his trousers, was at least a decade out of date. The fact that he had not been altogether pulped and reconstituted through a public relations machine was in itself appealing and endearing. The author Andrew Duncan, trying to write an intelligently critical appraisal of the monarchy but unable to find much of a bad word about Charles, said of him in 1970: 'He has the gentlemanly tranquillity, almost softness, of an intellectual but without the academic qualifications.' The tranquil gentleman, however, had a deep love of the physical, which chiefly manifested itself on the polo field, another item in the mixed ragbag of inheritance from Mountbatten and his father.

The British Raj in India discovered polo as a legacy from the Moghul emperors, who in turn had borrowed it from the ancient Persians. The first polo match played in England was between the 10th Hussars and the 9th Lancers on Hounslow Heath in 1871 when a spectator observed: 'It was admitted by all who were looking on that the game was more remarkable for the strength of the language used by the players than for anything else.' British royalty eagerly took to the game in 1881 when the future George V called at Buenos Aires on a world cruise and was given a demonstration by members of an already well-established local league. It has been popular with the House of Windsor ever since. Mountbatten, a fanatical participant in anything competitive, wrote the game's definitive textbook and transmitted his enthusiasm to his nephew Philip, who became a founder member of the Household Brigade (now Guards) Polo Club at Smith's Lawn, Windsor, in 1957, and did his best to keep up the early reputation for strong language on the field of play.

Charles's first introduction to the game appears to have been at the age of four, when he and Anne watched their father referee a chukka or two of bicycle polo in the grounds of Windsor Castle. By the age of fourteen, having tried out some of his father's more docile ponies, he took to the game with enthusiasm, and was presented with two ponies of his own, named La Quininia and La Sombra. Mountbatten, sensing his natural aptitude, leapt in with enthusiasm as a coach, although for Charles it was as much as anything an escape from the show-jumping ring, for which he did not share his sister's enthusiasm despite his own competence on horseback.

Charles reminisced with affection about La Sombra: 'She was exactly like the Maltese Cat in Kipling's story. She knew so much more about the game than I did. When you went to try a backhand she would turn so fast that I spent half my time around her neck to begin with. She taught me an awful lot. She was a marvel.' He was soon included in scratch sides, and was noted for never shirking taking on an opponent; he managed to fit in some polo during his school sojourn in Australia, which did wonders for his game, and shortly before going up to Cambridge he was playing in his first tournament at Smith's Lawn, his side beating Ronald Ferguson's team in the final. Constant practice, and the wherewithal to buy more and better ponies, improved his game considerably, and by the time he was ready to enter the Services his handicap had gone from minus two to plus two; polo, being a perverse sort of game unlike the infinitely more sensible golf, has a handicap system which goes up as the player improves. The knowledgeably obsessed within the game judged him to be distinctly better than average given that, unlike some of them, he had many other things to do besides practise.

His skill and his enthusiasm both increased during his Services career and after it, to the extent that he was playing in an international match for England against Spain three days before his wedding, with Major Ferguson glibly assuring the world that he was far safer among a field of such experienced players than he was driving his car down the M4 motorway; in fact during the game two other players suffered a head-on collision and lay stunned on the ground for a full six minutes.

Polo is patently rough, tough and dangerous at high speed; then, as now, it went a long way to satisfying the Prince's need for danger, challenge and physical sensation. Playing once at Palm Beach, Florida, he collapsed in the heat and gasped to his equerry, Oliver Everett, that he was certain he was going to die; thanks to a brief rest and the administration of salt tablets, he did not. He has himself said of polo: 'I love the game. I love the ponies. I love the exercise. It's the one team game I can play. It's also a very convenient game for me; you can't just nip out of Windsor Castle and enjoy a soccer game.'

It was therefore no flabby wimpish aesthete who presented

himself at the Royal Air Force College, Cranwell, in March 1971 to enrol as a flight-lieutenant for officer training. He arrived in due style; having already discovered the mental and physical stimulation and exhilaration of piloting an aircraft, and having managed somehow to squeeze in more than 80 hours' experience in the air while at Cambridge, he naturally flew himself in at the controls of a twin-engined Beagle Basset. The RAF were particularly pleased to have him; as the junior service they had always felt deprived of their rightful quota of royal recruits, and the presence of Prince Charles on the strength was worth ten thousand recruiting posters. His father has said that, left to his own devices, he would probably have chosen the Air Force rather than the Navy for his own career, but the Mountbatten influence was too strong. If Charles had been an entirely free agent he too would in all probability have stuck with his beloved aeroplanes; he remains a better pilot than he ever was a sailor.

The normal graduate course at Cranwell lasts for twelve months, but for Charles it was telescoped into five. His report at the end spoke glowingly of his natural aptitude for flying, that he would make an excellent fighter pilot at supersonic speeds, that he excelled at aerobatics in jets, and that he had all-round ability. Because training young men to fly highly expensive machines at supersonic speeds is a serious business, it must be assumed that the report was a fair assessment of his skills and not merely a hyperbole by some well-meaning brasshat anxious to show the RAF and its new recruit in the best possible light, and with one eye on the recruiting figures.

Had it been a misguided attempt at flattery, Charles would have taken it badly, and indeed there were moments during his brief Air Force career when he showed grave displeasure with the way he was being treated; any hint of mollycoddling or favouritism caused him to become quite bad-tempered. His trouble was, and to some extent remains, that since his earliest years he has suffered greatly from what he regards as unearned reverence, from being voted one of the best-dressed men in Europe at the age of five to Service chiefs speaking like prerecorded messages about how brilliant he was at everything he put his hand to. He was particularly annoyed to discover that the two aircraft allocated for his training at Cranwell had been modified to make them easier and safer to handle; that, he felt, was cheating, and a trick that would deny him his due respect.

The feeling that he was being shielded from danger was in the end counter-productive to those who ordained it; Charles insisted on flying supersonic in a Phantom jet scrambled from RAF Leuchars on the east coat of Scotland and taking it over Balmoral before heading out into the North Sea. And he insisted on making a parachute jump, which is not in the normal curriculum for Cranwell officer cadets; both his mother and the Ministry of Defence expressed reservations, which they felt were somewhat justified when the jump turned out less than perfectly. Heart in mouth, Charles launched himself from the aircraft high above Studland Bay near Poole in Dorset on a summer evening with a large crowd watching from the cliffs; within seconds he had swung upside down in the harness and caught his feet in the parachute rigging. His entry into the water was deeply undignified, and he gave himself quite a fright, although his own account played down the danger: 'It was very odd. Either I've got hollow legs or something. It doesn't often happen.The first thing I thought was: "They didn't tell me about this." Fortunately my feet weren't twisted around the lines, and they came out very quickly. The Royal Marines were roaring about in little boats underneath and I was out of the water within seconds . . . a rather hairy experience.'

He survived, and at the passing-out parade the following month his father, who as Marshal of the Royal Air Force took the salute, so glowed with pleasure and pride that he even joked with his old enemies, the Press photographers.

Prince Charles found more strictures hemming him in when he moved on in September 1971 to his sea training at the Royal Naval College, Dartmouth. The senior officers planning his career had decided that he must not be

ABOVE Godparents at Charles's christening. Seated on either side of his mother are his great-grandmothers the Dowager Marchioness of Milford Haven (Duke of Edinburgh's grandmother) and Queen Mary. Standing (l to r): Lady Brabourne (Mountbatten's daughter), Prince Philip (proxy for Prince George of Greece), King George VI, the Hon. David Bowes-Lyon (brother of Queen Elizabeth), the Earl of Athlone (proxy for King Haakon of Norway), and Princess Margaret. *(Royal Archives)*

BELOW One of his mother's most treasured photographs, and one of the last of King George VI; the young Prince with his grandparents and baby sister Anne on his third birthday in November 1951. The King died three months later. *(Press Association)*

ABOVE First day at
Gordonstoun, 1962; Prince
Charles with his father and
Captain Iain Tennant of the
school's Board of Governors.

LEFT The twenty-first English
Prince of Wales since 1301 is
presented to the Welsh people
at the Queen's Gate of
Caernarfon Castle at his
Investiture in 1969.
(Syndication International)

ABOVE Explaining the responsibilities of captaining HMS *Bronington* to Prince Andrew, with support from Officer of the Watch Lieutenant James Ringrose. *(BIPNA)*

BELOW The outgoing captain of *Bronington* with retirement gifts from his crew on leaving the Navy at Rosyth, Scotland, in 1976. *(Syndication International)*

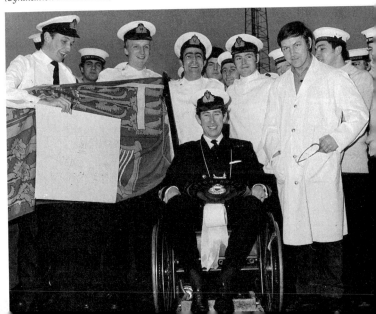

ABOVE Action man at the controls of his Wessex helicopter.

LEFT 'Okay, Corporal, catch this one!' Undergoing severe unpleasantness at the Royal Marine Commando training centre, Lympstone, Devon, in 1974. *(MOD)*

ABOVE LEFT Badminton, 1976. *(Newspix)*

ABOVE RIGHT At Balmoral. *(BBC)*

BELOW LEFT Charles with his godson, Charles Tryon, and parents Charles and Dale 'Kanga' Tryon. *(David Graves)*

BELOW RIGHT A formal portrait taken in the Grand Hall of Windsor Castle. *(Peter Grugeon)*

ABOVE Shooting pool in 1981 at the Pear Tree coffee bar, Derby, a county council 'drop-in centre' for unemployed young people. *(Ron Bell)*

BELOW 'I would like a hat like that.' Stand-up comedy at the Stoke Mandeville Paraplegic Olympics, Buckinghamshire, in 1984. *(Mike Maloney)*

LEFT 'Like this, do you mean?' A brave attempt at break dancing in front of appreciative unemployed youngsters at Middleton-on-Sea, Sussex, in 1985.

BELOW At the 1979 annual conference of the traditionally moderate steelmen's union, the Iron and Steel Trades Confederation, watched by its general secretary Bill Sirs (left). *(Ron Bell)*

ABOVE At Smith's Lawn, Windsor, with Honorary Grandfather Mountbatten, a fanatic for polo and all other competitive sports. (*Mike Lloyd*)

BELOW 'They that go down to the sea in ships . . .' Prince Charles reads the lesson from Psalm 107 at Mountbatten's funeral service in Westminster Abbey on 5 September, 1979. The entire royal family sits in mourning before the catafalque. (*PA*)

allowed to fly Buccaneer strike aircraft or Sea King anti-submarine helicopters, because they were too dangerous; he must not serve in the Polaris nuclear submarine fleet, because it was too political; he must not serve on the aircraft carrier *Ark Royal*, the largest in the fleet, because he would be swamped and lost in its enormous crew; and he must be kept away from the Navy's two current theatres of action, patrolling the fisheries in the so-called 'cod war' with Iceland, and attempting to impose a blockade of the East African port of Beira against the rebellious white Rhodesian colonists who had unilaterally declared themselves independent of the mother country. Some of those restrictions did not trouble him unduly; others did. All he really wanted to do was to get his hands on a flying machine again.

The running, however, had to wait for the walking. Being at Dartmouth was like being back at school, with all the basics of seamanship to be learned from scratch, and an enormous weight of family tradition bearing down on him, sitting on his shoulder like some dolorous vulture waiting for him to fail. There was, primarily, the example of his father, who in 1938 had won the King's Dirk, a prize for being the best cadet in his year. And, as ever, the spectre of Mountbatten, another outstanding old boy, hung over his endeavours.

The influence on him of both men remained strong. Mountbatten he greatly admired, wished to emulate, and desired greatly not to disappoint. Towards his father the feeling appears to have been slightly different, with a definite edge of competition, as though he were saying to the man who had the natural father's desire to see his son grow up in his own image of bluff and extrovert masculinity: 'I'll show you that, despite my more introverted and studious nature, I'm just as good as you are.'

The goad was sufficient to drive Prince Charles to achievement; at the end of his basic training he came top of his year in navigation and seamanship. His father was detained in Berlin on the day of the passing-out parade, so a delighted

Mountbatten took it upon himself to fly down for the ceremony, no doubt basking in a warm sun of reflected glory. During Charles's naval career the two men grew considerably closer, the relationship strengthened by the common interest in ships, and more often than not shore leave for Charles meant a visit to the Mountbatten home at Broadlands, within easy driving distance of Portsmouth. There the younger man found companionship, mutual admiration, and a sympathetic ear for his troubles, much more so than he would have done at home, where he tended to encounter the natural tendency of all fathers, figuratively speaking, to have the whip out. The nature of Charles's upbringing and his natural *gravitas* also tended to drive him towards an older generation rather than his own for close friendship.

Mountbatten's attitude to his young acolyte was not entirely uncritical, for he had the measure of Charles's character, faults included. He detected in him the germ of a blinkered, stubborn streak, which some might call determination and others pig-headedness, and which, the honorary grandfather thought, could all too easily develop into an unwelcome trait of selfishness and thoughtlessness. Mountbatten knew that the previous Prince of Wales, later Edward VIII, had displayed it, that too often he cared only for himself, and that it had ultimately been his undoing. It is a trait which perhaps befalls easily those whose daily details of life are largely taken care of by others, and who cannot walk down a street without weeks of advance planning by an army of staff.

During Charles's time in the Navy the two men found themselves together in the Caribbean. Charles suddenly changed his mind about how he wanted to spend his Easter weekend, which meant that the United States Coastguard had to summon up a shadowing escort. The action earned Charles a stern note from Mountbatten: 'Of course you were legally right; the US Coastguards could recall a crew from Easter weekend leave if you really wanted them. An officer was on duty and had no claim for the extra days with his fiancée. But how unkind and thoughtless – so typical of how your Uncle

David [Edward VIII] started. When I pointed this out you flared up – so I knew you had seen the point. I spent the night worrying whether you would continue on your Uncle David's sad course, or take a pull.' Chastened, Charles abandoned his plan, and the coastguard spent Easter with his beloved.

After his basic training Sub-Lieutenant The Prince of Wales spent the next nine months at sea on board the guided missile destroyer HMS *Norfolk*, 5,600 tons (5,690 tonnes), a medium-sized vessel with 33 officers on board which meant that Charles's duties were not unduly onerous. He tasted a wide variety of tasks, from cooking bread and butter pudding in the galley to handling an unaccustomed commodity – money – in making up the crew's wages. Unlike at Cambridge, where he could enjoy the luxury of keeping his own company if he wished, the tight confines of a destroyer forced him into the company of the other officers and men, at least most of the time; he was afforded the rare privilege of his own cabin, a tiny hutch 7 feet (2 metres) square but a refuge nonetheless into which he could, and often did, withdraw into solitude. His former shipmates recall that he was always eager to know about themselves and their families, and was always perfectly willing to talk about himself, but that his own family affairs were a subject strictly off limits. Although ship-board life is an artificial environment compared with normal life ashore, and although it is drummed into a trainee officer to be friendly towards the enlisted men but never familiar, Charles probably came closer while in the Navy to knowing ordinary people than at any previous time. His allies were a genuinely inquiring mind and a sense of humour; senior officers who pointed out his errors tended to be threatened gently with the Tower. His fellow-officers enjoyed his company sufficiently to take him ashore at the French naval base of Toulon and show him the more exotic sights of that city's red light district.

Norfolk was followed by a spell on HMS *Minerva*, a much smaller Leander class frigate with a complement of only 17 officers and consequently greater responsibility. Its first commission took Prince Charles to the West Indies, where he was encouraged to mix diplomatic with naval duty, calling on local dignitaries at every port of call and receiving their hospitality, a bonus which the rest of the crew sometimes enjoyed as well. At one stage *Minerva* called at Hamilton, Bermuda, and Charles strolled on the lawn of Government House with Sir Richard Sharples, the Governor. A week later Sir Richard was assassinated by terrorists on the same spot, and with *Minerva* due to call again for repairs, Charles was temporarily transferred to the survey ship *Fox*. That apart, the voyage resembled more of a luxury cruise at times; he called at the Bahamas to represent the Queen at the independence celebrations, tried deep-sea diving in the shark-infested Caribbean waters, and danced until 5 a.m., with his ship due to sail at 6.00, in the nightclubs of Caracas, Venezuela.

During periods ashore he found time to organize a dinner party for his parents' silver wedding anniversary, and after their thanksgiving service in St Paul's Cathedral went walkabout among the concrete tower blocks of the City of London's Barbican high-rise housing development, about which he was suitably rude in public. He attended his sister's wedding in Westminster Abbey, and as a gesture of conciliation he paid a private visit to the Duke of Windsor at his home in Paris, eight days before his death. Charles could never bring himself to share the feeling of bitterness against the Windsors that his grandmother had harboured ever since abdication had forced her husband on to the throne.

Charles's next ship, the frigate *Jupiter*, took him on another sunshine voyage as its communications officer to Australia, New Zealand, Samoa, Hawaii, Fiji and California, across the South Pacific where the Royal Navy once patrolled in earnest in defence of tiny far-flung fragments of Empire. He was mobbed by girls when he tried surfing in Queensland (he at least found the water cleaner than in Melbourne), and mobbed by fellow-officers who on one occasion threw protocol to the winds and attempted to debag the heir to the throne. Charles was clearly forewarned; they got his trousers off, only to find another pair underneath. They got those off, only to find yet another pair, whereupon they gave up, and he sighed with relief. It was not the climate for extra trousers.

His spell on *Jupiter* over, Charles was at last allowed to tackle what he had been waiting for since his first day at Dartmouth. To equip him for helicopter flying he was subjected to another fiercely telescoped training course of 105 hours' instruction in 45 days, including 26 hours of solo flight in a Wessex V codenamed Whisky Alpha, and a brief spell at the exceptionally tough Royal Marines training school to understand the lives of the men the helicopter crews supported. Again it annoyed him that everywhere he flew he was shadowed by another Wessex carrying full emergency equipment. He hated such special treatment, but his superiors in this instance had the greater wisdom; during training he had to make three real emergency landings, once for computer failure, once for engine failure, and once when a metal fragment of the helicopter's engine housing lodged itself among the moving parts.

But he thrived on the dangers, as though they were necessary for him to prove that he was as good as anyone else; the feeling of disadvantage born of privilege is a thread running through most of his adult life, and still surfaces regularly in his constant anxiety about achieving something useful and concrete. He said of his favourite occupation: 'I adore flying, and I personally can't think of a better combination than naval flying – being at sea and being able to fly. I find it very exciting, very rewarding, very stimulating and sometimes bloody terrifying.' And on the subject of terror, he remarked on another occasion at about the same time: 'If you're living dangerously it tends to make you appreciate your life that much more, and to really want to live it to its fullest.' The latter observation was made while on helicopter training in Canada, when he donned an inflatable diving suit and disappeared under the Arctic ice for half an hour.

While ashore on one occasion he insisted on taking the submariners' escape drill, a frightening and potentially dangerous routine which involves rising fully clothed from a simulated wreck at the bottom of a 100-foot (30-metre) deep tank of water at the naval base of Gosport. He performed it three times, from successive depths of 30, 60 and 100 feet (10, 20 and 30 metres); two seamen subsequently died attempting the same routine. He had no need of the attempt; it was not an obligatory part of his training. But once again the daredevil in him impelled him to show that he could overcome the disadvantage of his favoured birth.

He also took the opportunity of brief Arctic isolation to grow a beard, and was still sporting it when he made a flying visit to London to be installed by the Queen as Grand Master of the Most Noble Order of the Bath at Westminster Abbey. By the morning of the ceremony the beard had been reduced to a moustache, suggesting an outburst of maternal disapproval, and by the time he had returned to duty even the upper lip had been shaved clean; the Navy allows a full set of whiskers, or none at all.

He was almost sorry when given command of his own ship in 1976, for it meant the end of regular helicopter flying. HMS *Bronington*, at 360 tons (365 tonnes), was one of the smallest and most elderly ships in the entire fleet, an unglamorous wooden minehunter of hideous instability whose previous captain reported that she had a tendency to roll even on wet grass, and whose equally unglamorous duty was to plough up and down the cold, turbulent waters of the North Sea looking for mines. Her pennant number was 1115, and she was known as 'Old quarter past eleven'. Charles commanded her for ten months, during which time he was seasick more often than in the entire rest of his seagoing career. He relinquished her, and his naval career, at Rosyth in Scotland, pushed by ship-mates along the quayside in a wheelchair with a lavatory seat around his neck in an arcane naval farewell. As his old ship approached retirement in 1988, a group of naval enthusiasts in Portsmouth was urging its preservation alongside HMS *Victory* and HMS *Warrior*, the first ironclad battleship.

His career he judged to have been a success, not least because he had shown himself the equal, if not the superior, of his father. Philip had gained his helicopter licence at the age of 35, Charles at 25; Philip had been given his first command, of HMS *Magpie*, at the age of 29, Charles at 27. It was almost as if he were saying: 'I have satisfied you. Now I feel entitled to be my own man.' The Navy had also given him a hitherto unknown personal freedom and privacy; for the first time in his life, he was not accompanied everywhere by a detective.

During spare moments away from the sea he had returned to bookishness, delving in the Royal Archives for evidence that the ancestor who most intrigued him, George III, was not mad at all but suffered from a purely physical condition. He wrote an extended foreword to John Brooke's new biography of the monarch, and subsequently made a television film on him with Alistair Cooke, in which he said: 'I am determined to clear his name. It's very unfortunate if one is misunderstood in history. I personally would hate to be misunderstood.' The theme kept returning in a number of articles and reviews he wrote, including one for the magazine *Books and Bookmen*: 'The vulgar view of King George III is quite simply that he was mad and, to make matters worse, that he also succeeded in losing the American colonies. The fact that he had wide and civilized interests, was a good patron of the arts and sciences and devoted a vast quantity of time to affairs of State has been conveniently neglected.' In less serious vein, he was happy to turn in a witty review for *Punch* of the first novel by his old friend and former *Goon Show* performer, Harry Secombe, and to provide the foreword for a collected volume of *Goon Show* scripts.

He might well have made a modest living, and enjoyed himself, as a historian and freelance writer, except that he would have suffered dreadfully from the agony of wondering whether his work was being published because of who he was rather than for its intrinsic merit. The Duchy of Cornwall revenues ensured that making a living, modest or grand, was not his difficulty; indeed throughout his naval career he donated his pay and allowances to the King George's Fund for Sailors.

But he was about to face the dilemma that had confronted many of his predecessors in their long wait for the throne; what was he going to do with his time?

6

Princes without Position

THERE WAS a suggestion from the British Government, some while ago, that as the Queen advanced in years the Prince and Princess of Wales, for the sake of finding them a proper job to do, might move into Buckingham Palace and take over the more public and ceremonial duties of the monarchy. But the Queen would have none of it, and wrote to the Home Secretary, 'Her Majesty thinks it would be most undesirable to constitute the Heir to the Crown a general representative of herself, and particularly to bring him forward too frequently before the people. This would necessarily place the Prince of Wales in a position of competing, as it were, for popularity with the Queen. Nothing should be more carefully avoided.'

The Queen was Victoria, the Home Secretary Sir George Grey, the year 1864, and the Prince of Wales he who, after an interminable wait of forty-two years from his majority of eighteen, finally ascended the throne for a brief reign as King Edward VII. The suitable occupation of princes-in-waiting has long troubled the minds of the well-meaning, usually to no effect whatsoever, and the troubled minds have generally belonged to politicians rather than monarchs. Those who nowadays would place Prince Charles in some ill-defined well-defined role have been merely thumbing through ancient volumes of Hansard to ape their parliamentary predecessors of an earlier age.

Edward, Prince of Wales, suffered mightily from his father and from his mother, who suffered from Mr Gladstone. Despite the most strenuous efforts to mould him into the paragon of a constitutional monarch, Edward spent his life in devoted pursuit of the path of voluptuousness rather than that of righteousness; yet he reigned admired, respected and loved, as a favourite uncle is, and he died mourned by millions whose bedsheets he had not even rumpled. The good intentions of those who would have shaped him in the end counted for nothing; the man's own innate character carried him through.

Victoria in 1837 inherited a throne whose foundations she regarded as needing serious underpinning with piles of stability and propriety after the foibles and fornications of its two previous incumbents, her uncles George IV and William IV, the latter of whom had neglected to leave any legitimate heirs. Further blatant immorality, she feared, would seriously affect the stability of the whole monarchical edifice. The Queen and her beloved consort provided the perfect paradigm of the Christian family, monogamous to the point of monotony, although Victoria left sufficient asides in her journals to indicate that she relished greatly the pleasures of the marriage bed; urged by her doctors after the birth of her ninth child in seventeen years to abandon procreation for the good of her health, she protested at the prospect of no more fun. Outside her boudoir, however, she and Albert were granite pillars of rectitude, and they determined to ensure that their eldest son would be equipped to continue the monarchy at a similar level of the highest moral elevation.

Prince Albert, although a man of great energy, art and intellect, was also imbued, when the occasion demanded, with an awesome Germanic seriousness. For the young Albert Edward's education he drew up the most rigorous and comprehensive programme of study with the assistance and guidance of a severe German educationalist, Baron Christian von Stockmar, who attributed the waywardness of Victoria's uncles to the failure of their father, George III, to impose a proper education on them; he told Victoria that that singular omission had 'contributed more than any other circumstances to weaken the respect and influence of royalty in this country'.

His parents never had a moment's thought of sending the young Prince of Wales to school. Being both of predominantly Germanic upbringing, they viewed the native British aristocracy with a degree of disdain and suspicion, a class of pliable moral fibre much given to frivolity; to send Edward – Bertie to his family – to school would merely expose him to their infections. His education, therefore, must be conducted in the sterile, unpolluted atmosphere of the best private tutors. It was in fact conducted with excessive, almost brutal, regimentation; there was barely a moment in young Bertie's life when his nose was not to the grindstone of some mind-improving activity. His father wished no opportunity for his mind to wander to unworthy thoughts, and besides, a rigid timetable was essential if he were to absorb all that was necessary for the perfect monarch of the future. Albert insisted he be taught absolutely everything, even down to a course in bricklaying at Osborne House.

But Bertie was distinctly unpromising academic material. Like his latterday successor he was dim at mathematics, and was taught the subject only insofar as it applied to gunnery; also like Charles he had some talent for drawing and painting. But the strain of his education was enormous, and when his safety-valve blew to the sound of violent temper fits his father would devise complex punishments, none of which did the slightest good. His tutor wrote to his parents: 'Many of his peculiarities arise from want of contact with boys of his own age, and from his being continually in the society of older persons ... He has no standard by which to measure his own powers.'

Yet he was an extremely affectionate child, affable and easy-going by nature, and he showed great devotion to his parents in spite of their severity. He suffered from constant unfavourable comparison with his elder sister Victoria, but his mother, in his early years at least, looked upon him kindly, and had every intention of taking him into her full confidence when the time was right. When the Prince was nine she noted in her diary: 'We talked of Vicky and Bertie, Albert saying the latter ought to be accustomed to work with and for us, to have great confidence shown him, that he should early be initiated into the affairs of State. How true this is! So wise and right.' How wise indeed, but future events turned Victoria against ever acting upon it.

At the age of fifteen he was briefly released from his tutorial treadmill and sent, in the care of his Saxe-Coburg relatives, on a study tour of Germany where, at a dinner, he innocently kissed a pretty young girl. Innocent it was, for he subsequently had to be filled in by friends on the most basic facts of life. Yet it was seen back home as an act of gross moral turpitude. The Chancellor of the Exchequer wrote to a colleague in disgust of 'this squalid little debauch. The Prince of Wales has not been educated up to his position. This sort of unworthy little indulgence is the compensation.'

Prince Albert's devised punishment was to announce that his son would be 'kept away from the world for some months'. He was sent to live with two of his tutors for a spell of intensive mental and social polishing, which included such nameless torture as reading immense mountains of Sir Walter Scott, much admired by his Scotophile parents, and other solidly improving works. The youth was bored to distraction, and his mother's opinion of him began a distinctly downhill slide. The year after the German peck she wrote: 'I feel very sad about him. He is so idle and weak. God grant that he may take things more to heart and be more serious for the future and get more power. The heart is good, warm and affectionate.' At the same time his father noted distressing attempts at self-assertion: 'Unfortunately he takes no interest in anything but clothes. Even when out shooting he is more occupied with his trousers than with the game.'

His parents thought him dull, but one of his German uncles was at least able to spot a virtue: 'Bertie has remarkable social talent. He is lively, quick and sharp when his mind is set on anything, which is seldom. But usually his intellect is of no more use than a pistol packed on the bottom of a trunk if one were attacked in the robber-infested Apennines.'

He was sent briefly to both Christ Church College, Oxford and Trinity College, Cambridge, although with no intention at either that he should stay long enough to read for a degree. At both, his isolation from his contemporaries was compounded by his parents' insistence that he did not live in college, but in his own private rooms some distance away. Not that he could be kept entirely from all human intercourse; whilst at Trinity his tutor wrote despairingly to his father that Bertie had 'a love of excitement, which carries him almost unconsciously into the company of the idle and the frivolous'. He further compensated for his deprivations by employing a first-class chef at his lodgings, and began to exhibit the early signs of expanding girth.

Some fresh air was at last admitted to his fetid life of study when, at the age of nineteen, his mother despatched him on an official visit to North America, where he learned the art of opening municipal buildings and laying foundation stones, including that of the Federal Parliament building in Ottawa. The tour was an enormous success, with fulsome welcomes, huge crowds and public holidays in every town. To some extent he basked in the reflected glory of his mother, but in addition his easy manner, when it was allowed to flower, made him immediately popular, and Monsieur Blondin even offered to wheel him in a barrow along his tightrope stretched across Niagara Falls. Bertie made to accept eagerly, but was restrained by his retinue. America showed him freedom, and there he found his true metier: when he returned home his mother noted in her journal that he had become 'extremely talkative'.

In the eyes of Victoria and Albert, Bertie was a young man wide open to the temptations of the flesh. If he was to retain some semblance of their hoped-for paragon, an early marriage was essential to help guide him down the planned paths of righteousness. At that moment, however, the extensive European royal caste was somewhat short of eligible princesses, and the choice was a narrow one. Princess Alexandra of Denmark would not have been their first choice, given a wide field: she was but sixteen, there was moral laxity in her family, and the Danish throne was politically suspect for its alliance with the doubtful Prussians. Still, she was pretty, if a little scatterbrained, and the wheels of an arranged marriage began slowly and discreetly to grind into motion. To his parents' relief, Bertie seemed pleased and intrigued at the prospect, but for the moment he had other priorities on his mind.

For years he had pestered his father to be allowed to join the Army and in 1861, during Bertie's summer vacation from Trinity, Prince Albert relented; the Prince of Wales should go to Ireland for a ten-week infantry training course – of the most rigorously intensive kind that could be devised, naturally – at the Curragh camp outside Dublin. His fellow-officers, solicitous for his welfare and anxious that his training be fully rounded, smuggled into his quarters one Nellie Clifden, an actress, and for many a night she unwound his mind from the day's laborious science of gunnery.

When the present sovereign's second bachelor son chose to enter a liaison with an actress whose *forte* was for parts other than costume drama, the Queen limited her reaction to an admonition that the popular Press was making an unseemly meal of it, and that the dignity of the throne might be better served by a switch of his allegiance. When news of Nellie Clifden snaked back to Buckingham Palace through the serpent tongues of London club gossip the effect was, by comparison, volcanic. Victoria and Albert were utterly mortified; it at once justified their desire for an early marriage, yet at the same time appeared to jeopardize the plans they were so carefully laying in Copenhagen. On Bertie's return, Albert travelled up to his rooms at Cambridge to have it out with his son, who was both honest and contrite, and ended up being forgiven by his father.

But on the journey, the Prince Consort caught a chill; three weeks later he was dead of typhoid at the age of only forty-two, and for very many years afterwards Victoria blamed the premature loss of her beloved Albert, quite unreasonably, on the day he had to travel in damp weather to admonish their wayward son. 'Oh, that boy,' she wrote in her grief. 'Much as I pity, I never can or shall look at him without a shudder.'

Walter Bagehot, the journalist and amateur constitutional historian whose treatise *The English Constitution* has never been bettered as a definition of the appeal and the role of monarchy, took a more understanding view: 'Princes of Wales over the ages have been offered whatever is most attractive, whatever is most seductive. It is not rational to expect the best virtue where temptation is applied in the most trying form at the frailest time of human life.'

The Queen, desolate at her loss, withdrew from London into years of seclusion. Bertie meanwhile, having met Princess Alexandra and having fortuitously found her attractive and appealing, entered quite happily into his mother's desired safe haven of marriage, although for the rest of his life it proved to be little more than a home port. The ceremony took place at St George's Chapel in Windsor Castle, in the days before royal weddings were regarded as public spectacles to be played before the crowds in central London. Taking up residence in Marlborough House near St James's Palace, the couple instantly and naturally assumed the role of leaders of London society, filling the social vacuum created by Victoria's self-imposed seclusion, and severely taxing Bertie's £50,000 a year income from the Duchy of Cornwall. 'The Prince of Wales, in the flower of his lusty youth, and with the most beautiful Princess in Europe by his side, inaugurated with startling suddenness and inimitable gusto a social sovereignty which endured until he died,' wrote his biographer Philip Magnus.

Bertie, freed from the dreadful confines of his youth, determined to live life to the full, and could not bear to be idle or alone for a moment. If not entertaining, or playing whist for high stakes, he would chase fire engines, tipped off by the captain of the London Fire Brigade, and would wade in to assist in rescues, unannounced and largely unrecognized. His present-day successor makes night-time forays to see London life with more circumspection, but in Bertie's day there was no tabloid Press to chase him, and even if there had been it would not yet have acquired the technology of printing photographs.

Victoria, from the safe distance of Osborne House on the Isle of Wight, viewed her son with some disdain. 'Oh, how different poor foolish Bertie is to adored Papa, whose gentle, loving, wise, motherly care of me, when he was not twenty-one, exceeded everything.' There was now no question of her taking the Prince of Wales into her confidence in matters of State, as had once been her avowed intention: 'After '61 I could hardly bear the thought of anyone helping me, of standing where my dearest had always stood.'

Bertie's blithe abandon, and more importantly his mother's withdrawal into apparently endless sepulchral mourning, soon became a political issue, with the monarchy at a low ebb of popularity and republican clubs established in at least fifty British towns. Prime Minister Gladstone wrote to a Cabinet colleague in 1870: 'For our time as a government, and my time as a politician, Royalty will do well enough in this country, because it has a large fund to draw upon, which was greatly augmented by good husbandry in the early and middle part of this reign, and which is not yet exhausted. But the fund of credit is diminishing, and I do not see from whence it is to be replenished as matters now go. To speak in rude and general terms, the Queen is invisible and the Prince of Wales is not respected.'

Seeing no immediate hope of luring the Queen from her seclusion back into the public eye, Gladstone concentrated his attention on formulating a plan to divert the energies of the Prince of Wales into channels more elevating than London café society. A proper job for Bertie had been talked about for years, to no effect; Gladstone thought he had found the perfect answer in Ireland, just as some latterday royal advisers thought they had found the perfect answer for Prince

Charles as Governor-General of Australia. Bertie would spend the winter months of each year in Dublin acting effectively as Viceroy of Ireland, the existing Viceroy having been conveniently shuffled off to some other high office. Dublin Castle seemed the ideal base: it was a long way from the fleshpots of London; Bertie would be seen to be occupying a genuine office, in which there was much ceremonial but not too much intellectually taxing labour; and he would be learning the art of monarchy at first hand. Mr Gladstone was much taken with this plan.

But the Queen would have none of it. She told her Prime Minister that he was interfering intolerably in her domestic affairs; she pointed out forcibly that the Irish were hardly the most loyal of her subjects, and that the heir to the throne would inevitably become entangled in the thorny thicket of Irish politics; and beside, she added almost gratuitously, it would be bad for his health. Bertie himself showed no enthusiasm; he told Gladstone he would rather spend his time being attached in rotation to all the Government ministries in Whitehall to learn something of their workings.

Bertie never did get himself a proper job, at least in the formal, restrictive sense that Gladstone had in mind. But the Prime Minister, as it transpired, was worrying unduly over the decline in monarchical esteem. Bertie fell victim to typhoid, the very ailment that had killed his father, and for a time it was greatly feared that he too might be carried off in the full bloom of life; but when he recovered there was such an outpouring of national rejoicing that 13,000 people crowded into a service of thanksgiving for his recovery in St Paul's Cathedral, and the Queen, Prince and Princess were treated to thunderous applause from the multitude as they rode through the streets of London.

Thereafter he continued his long wait for the throne largely untroubled by pressure for his moral and spiritual improvement. He was, as Charles is in a very different way, a man of his time. The straitlaced morality of the era was a hypocrisy, at least among that class with the money and mobility to break the code, and the gymnastics of the boudoir were quite as energetic and inventive as anything propounded in the rather synthetic 'free love' days of the 1960s, as indicated by Mrs Patrick Campbell's celebrated dictum: 'It doesn't matter what you do in the bedroom, as long as you don't do it in the street and frighten the horses.'

Bertie probably engendered more envy and admiration than opprobrium for his exploits, and was liked for his essential kindliness; he was known for looking after the interests of his mistresses long after the flush of ardour had passed, even inviting a bevy of discarded paramours to his Coronation, seating them in a gallery of Westminster Abbey which was instantly christened 'The King's loose box'. He had an ally too in the Press, which unlike the prurient tabloids of today drew a discreet veil over his indiscretions; except for *The Times*, which noted obliquely at the time of his accession that 'he must often have prayed "Lead us not into temptation" with a feeling akin to hopelessness.'

It should not be forgotten that in his long wait for the throne he conducted a distinguished and active public life. He allied himself to no particular domestic interests, as Charles has done, and he did not accept the suggestion of moving into Buckingham Palace to set up alternative court while his mother hid in widow's weeds at Windsor. But he travelled widely and often in Europe, not only for his own delectation but also as Victoria's ambassador among the other royal courts of Europe, to most of whom he was related, at a time when all but Switzerland and France were still ruled by hereditary and usually interrelated monarchs.

He travelled further afield too in the cause of Empire, including to India to prepare the sub-continent for his mother's declaration as its Empress. He was, by nature, a diplomat. He had humanity, wit, and above all, great style, which somewhat forgave him his trespasses in the eyes of his subjects. Despite the trepidations of his mother and of her Prime Minister, he never really put the stability of the throne in any doubt. When he finally came to it in his sixtieth year in 1901 he was a trusted, avuncular figure with a twinkle in his eye; he suited well the era named after him, the short, bright coda at the end of the majestic Victorian symphony, the last gay fling before British society was melted down in the flames of the Great War, to be reforged with different perceptions and values. And in throwing off the shackles of propriety with which his parents attempted to bind him in his early years, he demonstrated that there is no training for a future king except that he earn respect by being himself.

His successor King George V did just that, earning the respect of the nation by his very ordinariness, and by an unwavering adherence to a clear and simple perception of where his duty lay. He was by no stretch of the imagination clever or innovative; he was in his domestic attitudes and in the treatment of his children the last Victorian, a relic of the nineteenth century surviving well into the twentieth. But he had one great virtue, as defined by his official biographer Harold Nicolson: 'The influence which King George exercised during the twenty-five years of his reign was due, not to any exceptional gifts of imagination or intellect, but to the consistency of his principles and beliefs.

'It was this consistency which enabled him, throughout an angry phase of transition and disbelief, to symbolise stability and to command universal confidence.'

Prince George, being the second son of Edward VII, was not raised to inherit the throne, but his elder brother Prince Albert Victor, known to his family as Eddy, was a rather backward child who died in manhood while his father was still Prince of Wales. Their father, who had suffered so much at the hands of his parents' quest for perfection, determined that he would not visit the same frightful rigours on his own children, and their early education was conducted at Sandringham in the gentler hands of the Reverend John Neale Dalton, father of Clement Atlee's post-war Chancellor of the Exchequer, Hugh Dalton.

Gentler it may have been, but the boys were still insulated from their contemporaries. Observing that the two brothers were inseparable, their tutor wrote to Queen Victoria: 'Prince Albert Victor requires the stimulus of Prince George's company to induce him to work at all. The mutual influence of their characters on one another (totally different as they are in many ways) is very beneficial.'

The future King Edward VII, as an antidote to his own hermetic education, had intended to send his eldest son to public school and university, but the boy was patently not up to it, and in view of his tutor's observation he was sent in the company of Prince George to join the Navy, a natural career for the second son as has again been shown in much more recent times.

Prince George learned much of seamanship, but little of statesmanship, on the training ships *Britannia* and *Bacchante*. Yet the experience had the effect which his father desired, which was for him to mix with his own generation. George found it a hard school, as he wrote many years later: 'It never did me any good to be a Prince, I can tell you, and many was the time I wished I hadn't been. It was a pretty tough place, and so far from making any allowances for our disadvantages, the other boys made a point of taking it out on us on the grounds that they'd never be able to do it later on.' What he did learn was iron discipline and unquestioning loyalty, which was to stand him in good stead in his quarter-century of kingship. He even ran his family as though they were the scallywag crew of some naval brigantine, to the extent of allowing his pet parrot Charlotte to peck his breakfast crumbs, and the cardinal sin in his house was unpunctuality. He is recorded as having relented only once, when his second son's fiancée Elizabeth Bowes-Lyon, full of trepidation and apology, arrived two minutes late for dinner. Charmed almost to distraction by the delightful young woman, the King protested that he must have sat down two minutes early.

He believed that the qualities which made a good monarch were much the same as those which made a good sailor, and he enumerated them to an intake of naval cadets at Dartmouth: 'Truthfulness, without which no man can gain the confidence of those below him; obedience, without which no man can gain the confidence of those above him; and zest, without which no seaman is worth his salt.'

After the death from influenza of Prince Eddy at the age of twenty-eight in 1892, Edward Prince of Wales developed a particularly close and loving relationship with his second son George, declaring that they were more like brothers than father and son. Father took son completely into his confidence, and on his accession to the throne in 1901 King Edward freely shared with the new Prince of Wales all State papers and secrets. And yet, despite this closeness, George seemed to revert to strict old Hanoverian ways, at least in the matter of his children. In that attitude he was certainly abetted by his wife Princess May of Teck, who had been manoeuvred by Queen Victoria towards an arranged marriage with Prince Eddy, and into whose affections Prince George stepped smartly on his elder brother's death.

George and May (who took the name of Queen Mary on her husband's accession in 1910) were stiff, temperamentally unsuited to parenthood, and although undoubtedly loving and caring, found the greatest difficulty in showing it. The Queen's biographer James Pope-Hennessy said of her: 'Her withdrawn, reserved manner, her cool, even temperament, made it unlikely that she would ever inspire a violent emotion.' She and her husband, he declared, had 'restricted human responses'. Certainly she recoiled in distaste from the physical aspects of pregnancy and childbirth, and she left no clue, as Victoria did, of any underlying sexuality beneath her Bible-black skirts. Nevertheless she achieved six children.

David, her eldest, writing in later life as Duke of Windsor of his own birth, records on the very first page of his autobiography that his father made a note in his diary of 'a sweet little boy' being born. 'Somehow I imagine this was the last time my father was ever inspired to apply to me that precise appellation.' The infant David was put in the care of a strangely sadistic and possessive nanny who, when she presented her charge for evening inspection by his parents, would twist and pinch his arm so that he would cry and be given straight back to her. Nanny finally disintegrated in a nervous breakdown, possibly because she had not been awarded a single day off in three years.

If the family atmosphere surrounding the young David and his brother Bertie was one lacking in demonstrative affection, it was also one of almost total philistinism. Their father distrusted all matters of the intellect, as though afraid they might upset the rigidity and direction of his purpose. His diaries are full of details of the number of birds he shot, but they are almost entirely devoid of any wider opinion or observation on his life and times. Even their cramped home at York House, Sandringham, had a distinctly suburban air, described by Harold Nicolson: 'Its rooms, with their fumed oak surrounds, their white overmantels framing oval mirrors, their Doulton tiles and stained glass fanlights, are indistinguishable from those of any Surbiton or Upper Norwood home.' Prince George would have no truck with the adventurous or the excellent; his son's summing-up of an essentially good and simple man was: 'He believed in God, the invincibilty of the Royal Navy, and the essential rightness of whatever was British.'

He also believed that his children should be educated exactly as he had been, which meant private tutors followed by the Navy; he dismissed out-of-hand suggestions that times had changed and that the boys would benefit from a spell at preparatory school. So David and Bertie spent an insulated childhood at Sandringham, finding much solace in each other's company and in occasional football games with the village boys, and went early to naval cadetships, thus ensuring that they grew up quite as ill-educated as their father. The naval regime was harsher even than the public schools of the period, and Bertie in particular took it badly, occasionally coming bottom of his class in matters of knot-tying, rope splicing and compass-boxing.

David was sixteen years old and still at Royal Naval College, Dartmouth when King Edward VII died, his father became king, and he automatically became Duke of Cornwall. He was created Prince of Wales and a Knight of the Garter in time for his father's Coronation in 1911 at which, taking precedence over all other peers of the realm, he swore homage to his father.

The twentieth English Prince of Wales since 1301 wrote of his Installation in later years: 'This ceremony had been allowed to lapse for centuries. But surprisingly enough the Welsh radical, Mr David Lloyd George, who only a few years before had shocked my family with his famous Limehouse speech attacking inherited privilege, decided that its revival would appeal to the national pride of his people.' David hated the ceremony, from the preposterous dress down to the gobbets of platitudinous Welsh which Lloyd George had taught him and which he dutifully repeated: '*Mor o gan yw Cymru i gyd*': 'All Wales is a land of song.' But he hated it most because, in the midst of the ceremony with all its bowing and scraping of Welsh wizards and bards, he claimed to have made a painful discovery about himself. 'I recoiled from anything that tended to set me up as a person requiring homage . . . if my association with the village boys at Sandringham and the cadets of the Naval Colleges had done anything for me, it was to make me desperately anxious to be treated exactly like any other boy of my age.' His father's cure for such self-doubt was to pack him off to sea again at once as a midshipman.

For all his rigidity, King George had wit enough to appreciate that the skills of the quarter-deck were, by themselves, perhaps not enough to broaden his son's preparation for kingship; wary though he was of intellectuals he was persuaded that David would benefit from a short spell at Oxford reading languages, history and political economy, always provided of course that there were trustworthy people to keep a close eye on the boy.

Having a close eye kept on him was a matter of constant resentment to David: his father appeared to have a remarkably efficient spy network which reported back in detail his every movement and action, wherever in the world he might be, and when he returned to Sandringham he would invariably receive the dread summons to present himself in the library, where the King would take issue with his dress, or his behaviour, or the company he was keeping. King George, like other members of his family before and since, was an authority, a pedant even, on matters of dress and in particular the correct details of uniforms; one man in his presence wearing the wrong tie could ruin his whole day. His boiled-shirt sartorial conservatism was greatly upset when his son wholeheartedly embraced the Oxford fashions of the day: two-tone brogue shoes, trousers with turn-ups, and the vogue for three-quarter length breeches that came to be known as plus-fours. Later, when touring India, David was irritated by the efficiency of his father's intelligence system which ensured a constant stream of messages from Sandringham nitpicking at minor solecisms of dress or etiquette before the maharajahs.

He made little of Oxford's academic atmosphere. With his limited formal education he was excused the entrance examinations; once there he showed little interest in study, and much in hunting with the South Oxfordshire hounds. But unlike his grandather shut away in private lodgings, David was allowed to live in Magdalen College as an ordinary undergraduate and to mix freely with his contemporaries.

His charm blosssomed; he was bright and intelligent if not intellectual, well able to conquer his natural shyness with a powerful air of self-assurance, and above all a good listener. Sir Herbert Warren, President of Magdalen, wrote in *The Times* of David's spell in his care: 'Bookish he will never be; not a Beauclerk, still less a British Solomon. Kings, perhaps fortunately, seldom are this last. That is not to be desired, but the Prince of Wales will not want for power of ready and forcible presentation, either in speech or in writing. And all the time he was learning more every day of men, gauging character, watching its play, getting to know what Englishmen are like, both individually and still more in the mass.' That charm and ease was to make him a hugely popular, even idolized, figure wherever he went in a fast-changing and uncertain world which then, as now, craved heroes who strode above the toils and snares of common existence.

When the skies of Europe finally fell in on the last age of innocence in 1914, the Prince of Wales, like millions more of his generation, could not wait to get to the action in France. He fought hard and long against all attempts to post him at a safe and non-combatant distance from the front line; when, after constant pestering of his superiors, he was appointed ADC to Lord Claud Hamilton at 1 Army Corps General Staff near Bethune, he took every opportunity to visit the front line, constantly walking or cycling over very dangerous ground to gather his reports from the trenches. His courage and his manner endeared him to the extent that his brother officer Oliver Lyttelton called him 'the most charming and delightful human being that I have ever known'.

In 1915, while at home on leave, he fell in love for the first time, with Lady Coke, daughter of the Earl of Leicester, a near neighbour at Sandringham; not surprisingly, in view of later events, the lady was married, and twelve years older than himself. The affair lasted for three years, and generated a fulsome correspondence between Norfolk and the Western Front; it ended when he switched his attentions briefly to Lady Rosemary Leveson-Gower, daughter of the Duke of Sutherland, the only known time in his life that he paid serious court to an unmarried woman. But by then he had already met another older, married woman. Mrs Freda Dudley Ward was petite, intelligent and greatly gifted with charm, flat-bosomed in the Twenties fashion that replaced Edwardian bustiness. She so riveted his attention for the next sixteen years that he largely excluded other women from his life, except for purely physical encounters, at a time when he might profitably have been casting around for an eligible wife with whom to have children. She was utterly discreet, as Lillie Langtry and Mrs Keppel had been about their association with his grandfather, but in the end, by absorbing him at a critical period of his life, she performed for him the same disservice that Mrs Fitzherbert had done for George IV in keeping him off the marriage market.

She was succeeded in David's affections by Lady Furness, the former Thelma Vanderbilt, who appealed because she was married, older, intelligent and American. He liked Americans and their refreshing candour; it fitted perfectly with his desire to flee the stifling family nest of tradition and be modern in harmony with the jazz age.

Thelma Furness introduced him in turn to another American, Wallis Simpson, already divorced once and soon to be heading for a repetition; through his obsession with her David finally found the depth of spiritual companionship that had long eluded him, although they had known each other four years before, as Wallis later wrote, 'we crossed that line that marks the indefinable boundary between friendship and love'.

For all that has been written since about the Windsors, the true reasons for his addiction to married women can only be surmised, beyond their normal attraction to single men: their sexual experience; the sweet sharp stimulus of forbidden fruit; and the divine luxury of enjoyment without responsibility. All the Prince of Wales's serious paramours had the further common factor of considerable wit, intelligence and drawing-room conversation to match his own. And all drew the displeasure, suspicion and odium of his father. Seeing David and Wallis dance at his Silver Jubilee ball in 1935, King George fulminated to Lady Airlie with a rare perception: 'I pray to God that my eldest son will never marry and have children, and that nothing will come between Bertie and Lilibet and the throne.' And he remarked with equal vision to his Prime Minister, Stanley Baldwin: 'After I am dead the boy will ruin himself in twelve months.' His prayers were answered; Bertie acceded as George VI, and Lilibet as Elizabeth II.

Such has been the subsequent interest in the man that the received version of his life story has become set in the aspic of a great romance; it is too readily forgotten that, before his brief unhappy reign, he was a spectacularly effective Prince of Wales.

He was twenty-five years old when he returned from the Great War, and the perennial question arose of how he should be employed. His father wanted to keep him at home to learn kingship but David Lloyd George, by now Prime Minister, wanted to send him on a tour of the Empire to convey the mother country's thanks for their contribution to the war effort. Whilst awaiting a decision, the 23rd Duke of Cornwall took himself on a tour of Duchy properties, expressing sentiments and concerns remarkably similar to those voiced by his successor more than sixty years later. Visiting the Duchy housing properties at Kennington in south London, he was distressed to find a great deal of dereliction and poor living conditions among his tenants. That the Labour-controlled Lambeth Borough Council had put up curtains in the windows of empty flats to make them look occupied did not fool him for a moment. 'We hope to alter the present state of affairs,' he declared as he toured the estate; and he did, ensuring that a large amount of Duchy money was invested in much-needed improvements.

Later in 1919, Lloyd George having won his point, David set sail for Canada and the United States on the first of several major Empire tours. It was, of course, an immense success. He initiated the custom, in whatever town he paused, of mounting a rostrum and allowing everyone who wished to come and shake his hand. The novelist Compton Mackenzie, swept away by his own enthusiasm as much as the Prince's, wrote: 'King George had all the talents but none of the genius of royalty. If his son may have lacked some of the talents he had the genius of it beyond any except a dozen princes in the history of man.'

What David had a genius for was the patina of public relations. *The Times* correspondent covering his Canadian tour wrote: 'Some of his speeches he reads; sometimes he speaks from notes which he hardly looks at; sometimes he just talks as a friend to friends. When he is on his feet he loses all self-consciousness. You hear without effort every word he says. He has a happy knack of saying the right things in the right way, and his clear boyish voice has a quality of sympathy and sincerity which makes the speaker one with his audience.' Good speaker though he was, almost all his texts were written for him by his private secretary, Sir Alan Lascelles, or by other aides. Back at Sandringham, the King received his regular reports and sat in the library muttering that his son was acting with insufficient dignity.

He never could please his father, a fact which caused him to muse at some length in his own memoirs: 'How does a monarch prepare his eldest son for his duties? I had a general idea of what was expected of me. But beyond all that there was no carefully conceived plan for equipping me for eventual assumption of kingship. In that respect, I dare say, my father was no different from most other fathers; he left my mature development pretty much to chance. Perhaps one of the only positive pieces of advice that I was ever given was that supplied by an old courtier who observed: "Only two rules really count. Never miss an opportunity to relieve yourself; never miss a chance to sit down and rest your feet." '
And on his performance in Canada: 'About this time my father had a serious talk with me. "You have a much freer life than I ever knew," he said. "The war has made it possible for you to mix with all manner of people in a way I was never able to do. But don't think that this means you can now act like other people. You must always remember your position and who you are." ' The Duke of Windsor went on to concede that he never really did know who he was.

Subsequent tours of Australia, New Zealand and India were conducted with equally wild success, although one of his travelling entourage, Lord Louis Mountbatten, was sufficiently close to him to see behind the smiling front which appeared to have transcended the healthy atmosphere of self-confidence into the rarer air of self-esteem. Mountbatten wrote long afterwards: 'I soon realized that under that delightful smile which charmed people everywhere, and despite all the fun that we managed to have, he was a lonely and sad person, always liable to deep depressions.'

His moodiness was no doubt fuelled by thousands of miles' separation from Mrs Dudley Ward, occasionally eased by abandoning some long-awaited public function at the last minute in favour of female company. Or it may have been a deeper unwillingness to accept the burdens and responsibilities of his position; his public smile rarely faltered, but off-stage he was often given to a childish petulance if the tide was not flowing exactly his way.

Yet on the public stage at home, he was a tireless and admired performer for many years. Seeing the deprivation and distress of the Depression, his sadness and concern appeared perfectly genuine. He contributed generously from his own pocket to the Miners' Relief Fund, and he was a regular supporter of the National Council of Social Service, drumming up money and volunteers for schemes to relieve the Depression's worst effects among the unemployed. His war service also formed in him a deep bond with ex-servicemen; he took a close interest in the formation of the British Legion, and became its first Patron.

He was distant from his father, who never shared the confidence of State papers with him or with his brother who succeeded him, and he spent much of his life in fear of him; time and again he received the awful summons to the Sandringham library, usually for a dressing down and rarely for praise. He was determined to be his own man in his own age; the Great War had changed British society out of all recognition, although the aristocratic old guard, watching him plunge into the 1920s dancing craze in his trendsetting clothes, still regarded him as a bit of a cad.

During the last days of his life he was visited at his home in the Bois de Boulogne by Prince Charles, a gesture of reconciliation by the present Prince of Wales to the former. Charles knew well enough that his family held the Duke of Windsor in less than the highest regard, and he knew in particular of the coldness towards the Windsors felt by his grandmother Queen Elizabeth, who is always supposed to have laid the ultimate blame for her husband's early death at the feet of

Wallis Simpson. But the Abdication happened long before Charles was born, and he is not one to bear old grudges. What drove him more than anything else to the house in Paris was his insatiable curiosity and his desire to meet such a famous historical figure while he still could.

On the Duke of Windsor's death in 1972 the Prime Minister of the day, Edward Heath, had the grace to lay his virtues before the House of Commons: 'There must be men and women on Tyneside, and in Liverpool and South Wales, who are remembering today the slight, rather shy figure, who came briefly into their lives, and sometimes into their homes, in those grim years . . . I have no doubt that the Duke by his conduct as Prince of Wales and as King has paved the way to a form of monarchy which today is more in tune with the times than would have been thought possible fifty years ago.'

He was the living embodiment, not of an improper or incomplete preparation for kingship, but of the fact that monarchy is more than gladhanding. His upbringing cannot be entirely blamed, for it differed little from that of his brother who reigned with success and gained admiration as George VI. Perhaps the essential difference is that King George VI met and married a quite exceptional woman.

7

The Emerging Conscience

CHARLES had been on shore leave from the Navy in 1972 when one day he happened to listen to BBC Radio 4's early-morning news programme *Today*, still his principal daily source of world affairs along with *The Times*. There he heard an interview which riveted him. George Pratt, a senior London probation officer, was describing the imminent launch of a new scheme for dealing with young offenders, whereby they would be made to perform some kind of community service rather than be put in detention to mix with other members of the criminal classes. Pratt hoped that the performance of good works might ignite some small spark of pride in youths who otherwise felt they had little of value to live for.

The interview was a revelation to Charles, who had not previously contemplated the possibility that young people might turn to crime simply because their lives were entirely devoid of anything positive.

The circumstances of such people could not possibly have been more different from Charles's own; he was weighed down with purpose, however vague it might be. Yet a chord was struck across the chasm. Charles himself had been imbued with the ideal of community service as preached by Kurt Hahn and practised by his disciples at Gordonstoun; the ethos was enshrined in the school motto *Plus est en vous* – 'There is more in you' – embodying Hahn's philosophy that character was built from personal challenge (preferably of some physical kind) and service to others. Charles, although unhappy during much of his rigorous and often lonely existence at

Gordonstoun, nevertheless felt on reflection that the experience had done him a power of good, and that it could well do good to others. George Pratt was summoned to a meeting with the Prince, a summons he did not feel able to ignore.

By the time they met David Checketts, on Charles's instructions, had been busy contacting a wide range of other bodies with an interest in youth, and the meeting became a wide-ranging round-table discussion between Charles, the probation service, the police, social services and various youth welfare organizations. Of the Prince's sincere desire to help in some positive way there was no doubt; his increasing realization that the country over which he would one day reign was in danger of becoming a divided one of haves and have-nots was troubling his innate social conscience. It was also stirring his feelings about his own privileged position which, if not exactly a feeling of guilt, was a conviction that his was an existence that needed to be justified.

By all accounts, the professionals at the meeting were not impressed by Charles's notion that the philosophies of Gordonstoun could be applied to the deprived inner cities. Hahn's theories of character-building and self-discipline through danger, adventure and physical exertion, they felt, were all very well when applied to those already motivated towards some kind of success or achievement. But down on the streets, in the black ghettoes and in the areas of high and chronic unemployment, where a feeling of hopelessness tended to quench ambition, they would be seen as elitist, irrelevant, and simply another facet of authority which the under-privileged young had ample reason to mistrust.

Still, in the discussion across the table, each side learned something important about the other. Charles, in many ways still innocent of life beyond his own world, had his first serious introduction to the problems of inner cities, which were to flare into violence some years later. And the welfare professionals, among the first of a great many such groups which Charles tends to pick, sometimes almost at random, to inform and advise him, learned much about the Prince of

Wales. They found that, despite his initial ignorance, he was a good listener without preconceived ideas, and that what he heard did not simply float out of the other ear. They also found a steely determination, a stubbornness even; having decided that he should enter the field of helping the disadvantaged young, he was not now going to be put off the notion, although he was willing enough to take advice on how best it should be tackled.

And they found, most of all, that his concern was perfectly genuine. No one had suggested it would make for a good public relations image, no charity had come begging his patronage. Like many of his stances and causes since, it was born out of a naïvety and good faith that is almost touching; Charles has never succumbed to the taint of cynicism.

Further meetings were called, with ever-greater numbers of participants, but the consensus remained that Charles should not become involved in mainstream youth work; it could become political, being an area that to a large extent belonged in the hands of local authorities, and it certainly had its quota of failures. The Prince remained determined, and a scheme of sorts was hammered out, with Pratt put in charge of its execution.

There was agreement that a great many youths throughout the country, possibly teetering on the edge of bad ways, would be greatly encouraged if only they could be helped to achieve some very modest ambition that was of benefit to the community, even if it was only finding enough money for a new football team strip. Charles's view was that if financial help was to be viable and acceptable, it needed to be offered quickly, without any hint of form-filling or other bureaucratic procedures, and there should be no interviews of the applicants or any other examination of their credentials; they would have to be taken at their word, and there should be no strings attached to any grant.

Furthermore, he believed, just handing out cash on its own was not enough; any scheme, however small, that he agreed to support should have guidance and help from an interested adult. And finally, he would prefer that the beneficiaries were not told the source of the money.

Police and probation officers were sent to find some worthy causes. A policeman in Cornwall, plagued by a local group of young hooligans, was able to tell them that if they formed themselves into a lifesaving team, the police would pay all their fares and expenses. They were too astonished to refuse, but it was a long time before they discovered who their real benefactor was. In London, a group of school drop-outs who were already in trouble with the law had expressed a wish to go camping, and Charles sent them £37.50 for their rail fares together with a tent and some cooking utensils begged from the Army.

Money was raised from City of London livery companies and from private donations, although in the very early stages Charles had been quite willing to make grants out of his own Navy pay and allowances. For over three years George Pratt and his contacts sought out small but deserving causes throughout the country, rarely making grants of more than a few pounds at a time. Every application was sent by diplomatic bag to whichever ship Charles was serving on, and he read them all, scribbling his comments in the margin. Not many were refused, but then not many knew that the offer was there.

What gratified Charles most of all, and eventually persuaded him that the scheme should be put on a formal and permanent footing, was the large number of letters of thanks, and enthusiastic reports of how the money had been used, from recipients who had discovered the identity of their benefactor. It was a novelty to him, and a particularly warming one, to feel he had done some modest good on a one-to-one basis to people who were far removed from his own privileged circle. The recipients in their turn were pleasantly astonished that the grandest young man in the land could descend from his Olympian heights to attend to their own minor backyard frustrations which no one else seemed to care much about. He was still reticent about having his own name emblazoned across his good works, but he was persuaded that visiting in person some of the schemes he supported would be an enormous additional boost to the participants, and that if he were going to go out and about he might as well come clean.

The Prince's Trust was formally set up in 1976, not long before Charles left the Navy; it was lodged with the Charity Commissioners as a registered charity, which helps to keep its proceeds out of the clutches of the taxman, and the Queen gave her consent for its emblem to be a capital C surmounted by a crown. Its original goal, although worthy, had been vague: Charles himself described it as 'to encourage disadvantaged young people who had not been motivated by more conventional methods. My original hope was to help them recognize their own potential by encouraging them to use their talents and energies to pursue self-help projects, some of which might enable them to help others.'

Now its policy was more clearly defined: to provide small grants to young people between the ages of fourteen and twenty-five who, a) produce their own proposals aimed at setting up self-help activities which contribute to their welfare or personal development, and which may sometimes enable them to help other people; b) make the application themselves, either individually or as a spontaneous group, but not as an existing organization; c) are socially, economically or environmentally disadvantaged or physically handicapped; and d) would not anticipate further funding from the Trust after the initial grant.

From small beginnings, the scope and scale of the Trust has grown out of all recognition. Its first annual accounts after its formal establishment showed a total of £7,471 awarded in grants; by the following year the sum had grown to £30,000, and by the time of its tenth anniversary in 1986 it was paying out £206,689 in a year, while still holding to its original principle that no single grant should exceed £300. Its early grants were mostly in aid of leisure or sporting activities, but young people soon made it clear that, much as they appreciated their leisure, what they really wanted was the chance of a job. The Trust therefore branched out in 1982 into the Youth Business Initiative to give start-up grants to young entrepreneurs on condition that they accept the guidance of a bank manager, accountant or other experienced mentor for their first twelve months.

In its first three years up to 1986, YBI helped launch 1,435 young people into their own businesses, and in 1986 alone it handed out grants of £90,000. It claimed in the same year that of all the awards made, over eighty per cent of the businesses were still trading after their first crucial year, and many were employing additional staff. Of those which failed, their founders nonetheless felt more often than not that the experience they had gained, and the evidence of their own self-motivation, helped them to find work elsewhere. An astonishing range of businesses has been launched, from a traditional West Indian bakery selling its cakes to Harrods, to stained glass window renovation.

The Trust still goes about its business without much publicity, except when rock bands like Dire Straits stage fundraising concerts at Wembley Stadium, and Charles is seen making a few brave jerks out of time with the beat while his wife sways in perfect and familiar harmony. With over 1,000 grants a year now being made, it is a long time since Charles vetted every application or took an active part in the Trust's day-to-day running; that is now largely accomplished by regional committees, many of whose members are young people who in the past have themselves been recipients of Trust cash. But he remains an assiduous visitor to Trust-funded projects, and has always urged the committees who hand out the money to take risks, and not to be afraid of backing the most unlikely or unpromising applicants.

That very policy has led it into a certain amount of trouble. Anthony Beaumont-Dark, a backbench Conservative MP for the Selly Oak district of Birmingham, claimed in 1987 that the Trust was in fact 'an inefficient shambles' which gave money away without any proper check on how it was used, and which regularly failed to provide the promised back-up support and advice to many of the young entrepreneurs that it launched into business. 'I think the Trust is a disgrace,' he said. 'It is badly controlled and it is obvious that they have not been monitoring the businesses. I don't doubt Prince Charles's good intentions, but I believe it would be better to help fewer people more thoroughly rather than spread it around so much.'

John Pervin, the Trust's managing director, retorted at the time that the scheme should not be judged by how many businesses succeeded, but by how many lives had been changed. 'We never want to give the impression that the Prince's Trust is a soft option; it's soft in the heart but hard in the head,' said Pervin. He did admit, however, that there might be room for a better monitoring of the Trust's money. Surprisingly, the Trust keeps no detailed record of what happens to the businesses it helps to set up.

Most of the Trust's work has been refreshingly far removed in its execution from the bracing approach of Kurt Hahn's two best-known memorials, Gordonstoun and the Outward Bound schools; Charles remains firmly convinced of the value of such an approach, but he has had the good sense to understand that it is not always appropriate. Nevertheless it did creep in in 1982, when the Trust ran the first of a number of residential training projects for the young unemployed; eighty teenagers from inner city areas were taken to Scotland and, under Army supervision, built a mountain path to a viewpoint above Loch Lomond. Since then similar gangs have been at work restoring the earthworks of Iron Age forts at Badbury Rings and Maiden Castle in Dorset. The Trust's schemes have been no more or less successful in finding their participants real and permanent jobs than have similiar projects run by the Government's Manpower Services Commission, but at least the Trust is not accused of creating artificial work simply to make the unemployment figures look better, nor does it make undue claims for its schemes.

One youth leader who took a party of Trust teenagers on two weeks' hard physical labour on the ramparts of Maiden

Castle reported back to Charles: 'They experienced two weeks which they will never forget. More importantly their ideas, plans and opinions have changed – some quite radically, others less so; but to be sure, they have changed. And not just from the effects of hard work and the beautiful countryside. Having access to people who have cared for them, despite their appearances and past behaviour, has had a marvellous effect on them. A little love and care has done wonders.

'The group are variously planning to revisit Dorset, go to Europe, canoe up the Nile and a hundred other things. My fear is that, once motivated to such heights, this energy and self-belief will come to nought. If this is to be the case, then ought we to elevate them in the first place? I ask this question because of the success you have achieved; I know that the Trust wished to develop its residential training programme in a major way, and I can see now the absolute necessity for, and fairness of, such an idea.' Hahn would have loved that young man.

If the Trust has been discreetly adventurous in its encouragement of youth, Charles's public pronouncements on related subjects have tended much more towards the Outward Bound mainstream, which he still patently sees as the answer to many social ills. Making his maiden speech in the House of Lords in 1974 he chose, as is convention, a non-party political topic; he called for more government money to be invested in the planning of the nation's leisure, and for the appointment of a Minister of Leisure. It is reasonable to infer that the appointment of a government minister implies that his area of responsibility becomes more organized, and it is certainly not a universally-held belief that leisure time would benefit from an injection of government bureaucracy. Although widely quoted on the day simply because of the identity of the speaker, Charles's words went the way of most other maiden speeches to the Upper House, into the catacombs of the infinite storehouse of oblivion.

He raised the subject again in the House of Lords two years later, and revealed for the first time that he had been raising money to help young people, but again it went largely unremarked. Then, in 1977, he went on television and radio to launch the Queen's Silver Jubilee Appeal which, his mother had decided, should raise money chiefly for the benefit of the underprivileged young. Charles had written his own script which was passed through various Appeals committees for approval; it was full of praise and encouragement for the young being able to do character-building things on, under and above Scottish mountains in Scottish weather and suchlike activities, which some committee members felt did not perhaps strike the right note of universal appeal. With some trepidation they suggested Charles might tone it down a trifle, and to his credit he did. The final version still retained a ruggedly masculine, public schoolish flavour, but any further criticism is quite unwarranted. The Jubilee Appeal raised a remarkable £16 million, of which half a million was sent to Charles personally at Buckingham Palace – not the authorized address. The response was doubtless in large measure a reflection of the esteem and affection in which the Queen herself was held, but the Prince's own personal machismo was clearly cutting quite a dash as well.

During Jubilee Year Charles paid a routine visit to Lewisham in south London to see the Moonshot Club, a centre for young unemployed blacks, exactly the sort of place that the Jubilee Appeal wanted to give money to. The visit, however, turned out to be anything but routine.

Lewisham is an area with a large immigrant population, and tension between blacks and the police was already running high. Twenty-four black youths had recently been arrested on charges of mugging (nineteen were subsequently convicted), and when Charles stepped from his car, he immediately noticed a group of anti-police demonstrators standing nearby. Having learnt to confront, and often thereby to defuse, opposition while surrounded by Welsh Nationalist students at Aberystwyth, he determined to go and talk to them, against the advice of his staff. He made straight for one wearing a 'Stuff the Jubilee' lapel badge, who turned out to be Kim

Gordon, secretary of the Committee to Free the Lewisham 24 and an activist in the black section of the Trotskyite Socialist Workers' Party, not an organization noted for its support of constitutional monarchy.

Charles asked what the demonstration was about, and Gordon enumerated a long list of local blacks' grievances against the police. Whereupon Charles summoned Commander Douglas Randall, head of the Metropolitan Police P Division which had made the arrests, and suggested that the two sides get together to discuss their grievances. By the next day, he was in serious trouble. The black activists dismissed him as simply naïve, while the police took exception to his interference in an area of extreme delicacy, especially when the case of the Lewisham 24 was still untried and therefore *sub judice*. Few could be found anywhere who thought his intervention helpful.

Nevertheless within a very short time the two sides did get together, at a conference of police and youth leaders chaired by Prince Charles himself at Buckingham Palace. There was much plain speaking on both sides, and some positive good appeared to come from it. Relations between police and young blacks did improve for a while, but unfortunately the constructive attitude built up was insufficient to contain the eruption four years later of a rash of serious rioting in Brixton, Bristol, Liverpool and other British cities with large black ghettoes. When these riots broke out just as the nation was supposed to be celebrating his forthcoming marriage, Charles was shocked to the core; he was still unaware of quite how much pent-up frustration, anger and despair there was in the run-down inner cities, but it was an ignorance he shared with the majority of the white middle-class population.

One of those particularly displeased by Charles's intervention at the Moonshot Club was his own private secretary David Checketts, who for twelve years since their joint adventure to Geelong School in Australia had been his meticulous guide and mentor, steering him with great skill through the snares and pitfalls of an emerging adulthood of public life and bringing him thus far more or less unscathed. Checketts had taken a safely traditional view of the Heir Apparent's role, that he should stay out of politics and trouble, and by and large he had managed to keep his charge on that straight and narrow course. He thought the royal intervention at the Moonshot Club a major breach of propriety, and said so.

In fact, it was an indication of a number of changes taking place in Charles; he was now 28 years old and, freed from the restrictions and responsibilities of the Navy, was displaying an increasing independence of mind and a desire to do as he pleased. Those around him were beginning to see again flashes of the steely core that Lady Butler had noticed at Trinity; he was, for sure, a good and earnest listener to others' views, but he was increasingly deciding for himself whose view he should listen to. Checketts had perhaps been there too long and too close; maybe he was becoming a touch too proprietorial. From the Jubilee onwards the relationship between the two men began to deteriorate, sometimes plunging into open rows. Charles liked less and less being advised on what he should be doing; he was, in his own relative way, rebelling against the suffocating strictures of the system which had created him. Checketts, for his part, grew increasingly critical of his master, not least because, in the years between Navy and marriage, Charles often seemed to him bent solely on his own enjoyment. Two years after the Moonshot incident Checketts packed his bags and left, to be rewarded subsequently with a knighthood for his spell of very considerable service.

Visiting the Moonshot Club and other projects thought worthy of Jubilee Trust money did much to stir Charles's interest in the plight of the inner city young, but it also acted as a warning to him of the minefield he could so easily stray into, and for the time being he moved on to safer ground.

He took over from Mountbatten as World President of United World Colleges, an organization whose aims greatly appealed to him as they added an international dimension to the Hahn ethic. And he lent his active support to Operation Drake, another scheme which fitted perfectly his own notions, born of experience, that what the listless and deprived young needed to wind them up was physical challenge and adventure. Drake was the creation of the explorer Colonel John Blashford-Snell, and involved taking 400 young people aged between seventeen and twenty-four on various stages of a round-the-world voyage on the 150-ton (152-tonne) sailing brigantine *Eye of the Wind* and putting them to work on a variety of research and community projects on the way.

The murder of Mountbatten by Irish Republican terrorists in the summer of 1979 temporarily stopped Charles dead in his tracks; it was a devastating and cruel loss which knifed him to his very core, and he spent many hours alone walking the moors of Balmoral searching within himself for reasons, logic and justification for such a bloody act. He found none. But he was sustained by a strong religious faith which has always been with him, by sharing the grief with his contemporary Norton Knatchbull, Mountbatten's grandson, and by the patient encouragement of old and trusted friends like Laurens van der Post. Only he himself can ever fully know how the experience affected him, but he appeared to come out of it convinced that he should shoulder Mountbatten's principles and work on behalf of the young, and determined more than ever that he should be his own man pursuing beliefs, opinions and interests that were his own.

Sometimes the path he had chosen for himself seemed ill-defined, and sometimes he seemed to be following it without a map. The loss of the guide in whom he had placed so much faith appeared often to make him easy prey for any proponent of the unconventional who happened to catch his ear, although soon after Mountbatten's death he had acquired a new private secretary who tried, with no obvious success at all, to keep him reined in to a safe and conventional role of good works and uncontroversial statements.

The Honourable Edward Adeane was an old-style courtier *par excellence* with a background to match. His great-

grandfather Lord Stamfordham had been the last private secretary to Queen Victoria, and a major influence on the moulding of the future King George V. His father Sir Michael (later
Lord) Adeane had been the present Queen's private secretary
until 1972. Edward himself, educated at Eton and Cambridge,
was an eminent barrister, eleven years older than Charles in
age and light-years apart in attitudes. Front-line visits to West
Indian clubs in Lewisham were not at all to his taste; Brooks's
Club in St James's, with its all-male clientele of kindred gentlemanly spirits and absence of riff-raff, was his natural *milieu*.
He was impeccably dapper in dress, elitist in outlook, and
punctilious in manner. Empathy with the underprivileged
was not a trait that obviously shone in him, but he was
regarded as the man to keep Charles pointing in the right
direction. He lasted a little over five years which, given the
conflict of personalities, is in itself surprising.

The eruption of race riots, of looting and burning, and the
image of British policemen fending off petrol bombs behind
riot shields during the summer of 1981 shocked Charles deeply, but confirmed his long-held belief that inner-city deprivation was one of the major social ills in the kingdom
that he would eventually inherit, and one which appeared
insufficiently high on the list of priorities of Mrs Thatcher's
Government. True, in the wake of rioting in Toxteth, a desperately run-down area of Liverpool in the shadow of the
city's two cathedrals, the Prime Minister had despatched one
or her more able and energetic ministers, Michael Heseltine,
to show the Government's concern. Heseltine set in motion a
development corporation to attract new industry to the city,
the clearing of a stretch of filthy and decaying riverside to
make way for a garden festival, and the restoration into a
tourist attraction of the finest block of Victorian dockside
warehouses in the country. But essentially Thatcherite Conservatism is the doctrine of self-help which does not believe
in throwing large amounts of money at inner cities to revive
them. In that, if in little else, Prince and Prime Minister
agree.

Charles's reaction to the riots was to redouble his enthusiasm for a repeat of Operation Drake, but on a much larger scale. The scheme came to fruition in 1984 as Operation Raleigh, in which 4,000 young people, many from deprived backgrounds, took part in a voyage of discovery and good works.

Again, community service was a major plank in the project, and it is a theme at which Charles still hammers away. In 1987 the Economic and Social Research Council, a government agency which promotes sociological and related academic work, produced a report on the attitudes and lifestyles of young people living in Liverpool, Swindon, Kirkcaldy and Sheffield; in it Professor Frank Coffield of Durham University said that more than 12 million youngsters aged between sixteen and nineteen in Britain and Western Europe were facing a 'crisis of exclusion' from the economic, social and political lives of their communities. Charles, invited to provide a foreword, floated again the idea of a compulsory period of national community service for all youngsters, which would make positive use of unused energy that could otherwise turn into anti-social behaviour. The idea of civilian conscription, he said, should not be 'swept under the carpet each time it is raised because there is a chorus of criticism from a vociferous minority.

'Talking about what is good for young people is notoriously dangerous. Ever since I became involved in the problems faced by young people I have tried very hard to put myself in their position, or at least to operate from the basis of what I felt when I was young. In all the things I have tried to do for young people I have been guided by a firm belief in the value of being challenged, at some point in your life, as an individual who is part of a team. I have seen in so many cases (not just my own) the effect of such challenge on the development of the individual and the subsequent increase in self-confidence.

'I believe that we need to consider the whole question of some form of national community service more seriously. Basically, all of us at some stage or other – especially when we are young – need to be encouraged to do things that we initially don't like the idea of but which, on doing them, we find to be not nearly so bad as we originally feared.' But, he cautioned, organization and leadership were needed to bring out the potential of youth, and he cited the Prince's Trust and his Youth Business Initiative as examples.

Had Charles's public pronouncements of social concern been limited to extolling adventure and challenge as a route to character-building and keeping young tearaways off the streets, he would have been an entirely unremarkable mouth-piece for conventional Gordonstoun wisdom, and his attitudes would have appeared not greatly different from those of his father, who after all set up the Duke of Edinburgh's Award Scheme on the basis of a similar philosophy. But Prince Philip does not wear a bleeding-heart social conscience on his sleeve; his attitudes spring from certainties – the certainty of what his own position is, his unquestioning acceptance of it, and the equal certainty that his power to change the world in any way by public act or pronouncement is at best minimal. He has in his time put many a bomb under a complacent backside, beginning in 1951 when, as President of the British Association for the Advancement of Science, he told science and industry to work more closely together for the benefit of both, thereby breaking the long-standing tradition of royal platitudes.

He is best remembered for telling British industry to 'get its finger out' – people still think he was attacking lazy workers when he was in fact getting at their managers – but his crusade, if he has had one, has been simply to chivvy along the complacent; he has never regarded it as his public business to reshape society, whatever he might think in private.

Prince Charles is far less certain about himself, and therefore about the world he lives in. He will not automatically accept the *status quo*, and in his search for certainties and truths he will pay great heed to those who propound a view that is not conventional or established. Thus was he drawn into the great debate on architecture.

Early in 1984 he was attending a dinner at the Royal Academy when he chanced to meet Jules Lubbock, a lecturer in architecture at Essex University and architecture critic of the left-wing weekly magazine *New Statesman*. Lubbock engaged the Prince in conversation on the subject of one of the young academic's favourite hobbyhorses – community architecture. Charles listened fascinated, although the concept was not entirely new to him; he had already been made aware of it by his cousin the Duke of Gloucester, a trained architect who had been forced to give up his practice when he inherited the dukedom on the sudden death of his elder brother, but whose firm, Hunt Thompson, was making a name for itself designing 'people friendly' housing.

The idea of community architecture was born in the late 1960s as a reaction against the official local authority policies of wholesale slum clearance, comprehensive redevelopment plans, the destruction of whole neighbourhoods by urban motorways, and the rehousing of thousands in soulless tower blocks on vast, bleak estates. Housing had become a numbers game, and the people who had to live in the planners' megalomaniacal creations had been largely forgotten. The community architects' reaction was to build small, to preserve and refurbish where possible, and to put the needs and desires of the tenants first. But what most appealed to Charles was its element of self-help, of involving the tenants in the planning and occasionally even the building. Some early community architecture schemes had operated in a similar way to neighbourhood law centres in inner cities, with the professionals giving advice and guidance to the customer rather than imposing their own schemes.

Charles's opportunity to sound off on his latest enthusiasm came several months later when Michael Manser, President of the Royal Institute of British Architects, unaware that the Prince of Wales was in the process of forming some particularly strong views on the architectural profession, invited him to address the RIBA's lavish 150th anniversary dinner at Hampton Court Palace. Charles consulted Lubbock and other like-minded architects, but the speech was essentially his own; the assembled architects, expecting to be coddled with royal praise for their 150 glorious years, could not have been more surprised by what they heard.

The speech is best remembered for its description of a proposed extension to the National Gallery in Trafalgar Square as being like 'a monstrous carbuncle on the face of a much-loved and elegant friend', but it was in fact a much more wide-ranging and uncompromising attack on the attitudes of architects. 'A large number of us have developed a feeling that architects tend to design houses for the approval of fellow-architects and critics – not the tenants. The prime requisite for a good architect should be to be concerned about the way people live, about the environment they inhabit and the kind of community that is created by that environment.' Community architecture, he said, had shown that architects did not have a monopoly of knowledge on taste, style and planning.

The architects were greatly put out. Peter Ahrends, who had designed the monstrous carbuncle, dismissed Prince Charles's remarks as offensive, reactionary and ill-considered. Manser, his host for the evening, was little better pleased but at least more constructive; he suggested the Prince hold a dinner at Kensington Palace to discuss architecture, in the clear hope that Charles might pay some heed to the established view. The dinner took place in December 1984 and was not a great success, but Charles struck up an immediate friendship with one of the guests, a northern architect named Rod Hackney.

Hackney had become the leading practitioner and apostle of community architecture after mobilizing his own neighbourhood at Black Road, Macclesfield, into refurbishing its dwellings when he discovered that the local council had scheduled the area for comprehensive redevelopment – a polite way of saying they intended to bulldoze it flat and move the tenants against their will into new council housing. Since then he had, as as result, become involved in a number of self-help refurbishment schemes throughout the country. Charles immediately asked to see some of his work, and Hackney took him to Macclesfield and to his birthplace of Liverpool, where he had helped to rescue some housing in a particularly depressed area of the city.

Charles was greatly impressed by what he saw. It nurtured his belief that inner cities could be saved, that bad housing was a major contributor to anti-social behaviour and unrest. The idea of people helping themselves on a small scale appealed to his own philosophical outlook already moulded by van der Post, and by his reading of the work of E.F. Schumacher, author of *Small is Beautiful*, whose principal concern was applying appropriately small and simple development schemes to Third World countries but whose ideas had a much wider appeal at a time when the 'God of Bigness' seemed to rule in all things.

Hackney, however, made one mistake: he revealed to the Press that he was advising Charles, and that the Prince had been making hitherto unpublicized and undercover visits to see for himself the deprivation of inner cities. Worse, he disclosed Charles's private fear that he would inherit a Britain sharply divided into haves and have-nots. Charles suddenly felt betrayed; troubled by his own insecurity, he felt that such disclosures could all too easily turn him into a laughing-stock and diminish the effect of his message. More seriously, Hackney's disclosures brought Charles perilously close to the political arena, with the attendant danger that the Government would attempt to silence one or both of them. Relations with Hackney cooled markedly, although he continued to be one of the Prince's circle of advisers if no longer the leading light. In the end, neither partner came to any harm; Charles continued to berate the architectural establishment with ever-increasing sharpness, and in 1986 the rank outsider Hackney was elected President of the RIBA. That alone showed that Charles had a great deal more support than some of the profession's most conservative figures were prepared to admit.

Charles returned to the fray early in 1985 with a speech to the Institute of Directors, which was a direct appeal to industry to do more to help the inner cities, and to central and local Government to stop dragging their feet. He enthused about the community architecture projects he had visited and said he had been 'electrified' by the atmosphere he had found there.

'There is a direct link here with many areas of the Third World, where there has been no shortage of massive development schemes. The majority seem to be designed and executed from the top by people who frequently have little concept of life in the rural areas and perhaps who know little about the aspirations of local communities. There often appears to be an entrenched belief that those who run government committees and development boards know what is good for those who try to wrest their living from the land, whereas in fact it is the small-scale community-based schemes which tend to have the greater long-term success. The secret, then, lies in the simple business of allowing the "ordinary bloke" to express his views and preferences and to realize the very considerable potential which exists in so many people.'

He went on: 'There is much resistance that stems from the intertia and conservatism of the financial institutions and developers, while the main obstacles are to be found in the paternalism of central and local Government, general bureaucratic inertia and the lack of effective management.' He called on industry to make derelict land available at peppercorn rents for small workshops and housing projects, and on local authorities to cut the red tape that prevented, for example, the setting-up of small workshops in areas defined as residential. And he concluded: 'The potential long-term problems of social unrest, if companies continue to avoid the fundamental issues of inner-city areas, will be to their detriment.'

He was deeply disappointed that his appeal for business to invest in the inner cities appeared to fall on deaf ears; hard-headed business, unconvinced that there was any return on such investment, failed to share his idealism. He was, however, delighted when later in the year he was invited to become president of an organization called Business in the Community, which had been in existence for four years and which numbered the chairmen of a great many of Britain's major public companies and nationalized industries among its members under a young and energetic chief executive, Stephen O'Brien. BiC was not so much in the business of handing out money to regenerate inner cities, more in persuading major companies to lend advice and occasionally trained personnel to help small business schemes to get off the ground. After its annual general meeting in 1987, Charles led a group of its industrialist members into the heart of Spitalfields, a decaying area on the edge of the City of London, and was shocked by what he saw of the working conditions in the rag-trade sweatshops operated by the Bengali community which has taken over much of the district. 'Something must be done,' said the Prince, echoing the impotent words of Edward VIII visiting unemployed Welsh miners in 1936. Unfortunately, the Bengali landlords who owned the ratholes and employed their fellow-Asians in such bad conditions all seemed to be visiting their families in Bangladesh the day Charles called.

The apparent unwillingness of the business world to embrace wholeheartedly the gospel of community architecture determined Charles to do more about it himself. One day in October 1985, sitting on the royal train in a siding in Somerset, he and Hackney conceived the idea of a new charity to raise money for inner-city community architecture projects, to be called Inner City Aid. Its launch the following year was, however, badly bungled, for on the same day Charles launched Youth Business Trust, yet another of his burgeoning crop of charities, aimed at helping young entrepreneurs. It was gradually realized that the two were in direct competition for funds, and Inner City Aid was effectively put on ice and stopped from further fundraising, causing the resignation of its director Charles Knevitt, architecture correspondent of

The Times. The Youth Business Trust, with the more strident voice of Lord Boardman, chairman of the National Westminster Bank, at its head, was allowed to continue, and after a year had raised £2.5 million to Inner City Aid's £33,000. The conflict was a clear indication that Charles, although passionately committed to concepts, is less good on detail; his staff, who could so easily have avoided such a class of interests, are not always kept fully informed and not always listened to, as his two previous private secretaries discovered. His interests are also too disparate and uncoordinated; the money raised in his name sometimes gives the impression of being divided into too many penny packets. Representatives of all his charities meet four times a year, supposedly to coordinate strategy, but even that is not always enough to keep them all pulling in the same direction. And the boss has his fingers in too many pies to give each one close attention.

In public, he continues to hammer away at his theme, which in essence is that a renaissance in architecture, and consequently in the quality of city life, will be brought about only when the experts climb down from their ivory towers and start listening to the view of the ordinary man in the street. In a much-reported speech at the end of 1987, when he bitterly attacked the tower blocks of the City of London which obscure the view of St Paul's Cathedral, and remarked that the bombs of the Luftwaffe had at least left behind nothing more offensive than rubble, he said: 'We, poor mortals, are forced to live in the shadow of their [architects'] achievements. Everywhere I go, it is one of the things people complain about most. Large numbers of us are fed up with being talked down to and dictated to by the existing planning establishment.'

That speech followed closely a campaign against high-rise building in the City that had been waged for some time in the columns of the *New Statesman*, an indication that Jules Lubbock still had the Prince's ear. Charles's normal method of speech writing is to invite ideas from a number of people, cut and paste them into shape, and add a gloss of his own. But after some time in the architectural bear-pit, he no longer needs to rely entirely on the opinions of others; he has built up his own substantial knowledge of the subject, although admittedly a great deal of it has been drawn from experts far removed from the profession's establishment. It goes hand-in-hand with his various schemes for encouraging self-help in the city: the individual against bureaucracy.

He continued his theme in March 1988 at a conference of 300 of the world's leading architects in Pittsburgh, a city whose environment is rotting in the wake of the collapse of the American steel industry, once its primary employer. He told them that much of the urban development of the last forty years had often been 'nonsense and thoroughly inhuman'. The solution, he said, lay in more cooperation between the public and private sectors, and more involvement of local communities in redevelopment planning. 'It is the anonymity created by post-war urban design which seems to have produced a breakdown in the normal functioning of a community. Let us bring life back to areas of our cities, which have become deadly and dangerous places at night.

'In the United States and the United Kingdom we have had forty years of practice at urban design and comprehensive planning and redevelopment. The results have been pretty disastrous, but people have felt this sense of disaster subconsciously. Having been told so firmly what was fashionable and intellectually acceptable, what was artistically correct and contemporary, most of us were cowed into feeling that we were imbeciles even to consider that what was being produced was thoroughly inhuman. Now, however, there is a growing awareness that it is all right not to be ashamed of such feelings.'

He has been accused of idealism – as though idealism were a crime – and of naïvety, as when he urged builders to put up new houses in inner cities rather than on green-field sites in the country; he does not seem to appreciate that green-field sites in the country are where a great many people want to live. He has been accused of being 'hijacked by the loony green brigade', but his opinions do not come solely from corduroy-clad academic architects in the newer universities; in his public life and travels he meets a very great many people of all backgrounds, and he believes, not without justification, that he is airing the genuine voice of the common man against the monstrous regiment of those who claim to know better.

Visiting a project to revive some especially ghastly housing in the east end of Glasgow late in 1987, to see tenants attempting to improve their environment and lack of employment with some community self-help schemes, he was asked by radio interviewer Brian Redhead if, in learning about other people's problems, he learned something about himself in the process.

'Well, I hope so, yes . . . I mean, clearly it would be much easier to lead a quiet life. I don't need to do all this, you know. I mean nobody's ordering me to go and do it, there's no set royal function; it's just that I feel strongly for better or worse about a lot of these things. I mean, if you go round the country in my position, I've learnt a lot, I've listened, I've looked a lot. I can't just sit there and do nothing about it. But if, you know, they'd rather I did nothing about it, I'll go off somewhere else.'

He practises what he preaches, when he is allowed. He hired a firm of community architects to work on Duchy of Cornwall property at Curry Mallet in Somerset. He sold a run-down Duchy tenement block in south London to a housing association so that tenants could work with community architects on its renovation. He commissioned a community architect, Ted Cullinan, to design new gates for Kensington Palace; unfortunately, nobody liked them.

At other times he has not been allowed, and harsh reality has filled in gaps in his worldly education. Seeing so many homeless youths on the streets of London, he proposed to house some of them in empty flats on the Duchy estate in Kennington, south London. Other tenants and the local council objected so strongly that he had to withdraw, puzzled at the strength of opposition. 'You,' he was subsequently told, 'don't have to live next door to a bunch of punks and weir-dos.'

8

The Mentors

CHARLES was on a fishing expedition in Iceland in August 1979 when he received the message that stunned, shocked and dismayed him more than any other piece of news in his life, up until then. Earl Mountbatten of Burma, his beloved Uncle Dickie, had been assassinated by a terrorist bomb while on a boat trip near his holiday home of Classiebawn Castle in the Republic of Ireland. At Mountbatten's subsequent funeral service in Westminster Abbey, Charles read the lesson from Psalm 107: 'They that go down to the sea in ships, that do business in great waters; these see the works of the Lord, and his wonders in the deep . . . He maketh the storm a calm, so that the waves thereof are still. Then are they glad because they be quiet; so he bringeth them unto their desired haven.'

It was an inhumanly cruel way for Mountbatten, who had survived so much wartime battle, to be brought to his own desired haven, particularly as two young boys in the boat perished with him. Charles was utterly devastated, wept openly, and as he stepped to the Westminster Abbey lectern he wore the grief plainly on his face for all the watching millions to see on television. His wreath by the graveside at Romsey, near Mountbatten's Hampshire home at Broadlands, bore a simple message: 'To HGF from HGS' – To Honorary Grandfather from Honorary Grandson.

Four months after Mountbatten's death, Charles was eventually able to articulate in public his feelings for the man who meant so much to him, in an address to a memorial service in St Paul's Cathedral:

'Although he could certainly be ruthless with people when the occasion demanded, his infectious enthusiasm, his sheer capacity for hard work, his wit, made him an irresistible leader among men. People who served under him or worked on his various staffs invariably adored him. And why? Because I believe that above all else he was honest. He was devastatingly frank with people. There was never any doubt as to where you stood – you always knew what he thought of you, whether it was complimentary or rude. That quality of real moral courage, of being able to face unpleasant tasks that need to be done – and yet to be fair and consistent – is a rare quality indeed. But he had it in abundance and that, I think, is one of the reasons why people would have followed him into hell, if he had explained the point of such an expedition. It is also one of the reasons why I adored him and why so many of us miss him so dreadfully now.'

Many people have influenced the course of Prince Charles's life and thinking at various stages of his development, but none was more constantly in the immediate background than Mountbatten; his role was to take Charles out of the close hothouse atmosphere of his own family and guide him in the ways of the wider world. By position, temperament and experience, he was singularly well fitted to do so. Mountbatten's family tree was thoroughly entwined with those of both the Queen and the Duke of Edinburgh. His mother, Princess Victoria of Hesse, was a granddaughter of Queen Victoria, one of seven children of the Queen's second daughter Princess Alice. His sister, Princess Alice of Battenberg, married Prince Andrew of Greece, and the only son of that union is Prince Philip, Duke of Edinburgh. Strictly speaking, therefore, he was Charles's great-uncle.

Mountbatten was intensely proud of, and passionately interested in, his royal lineage; indeed passion and intensity seemed to govern his every endeavour. Nothing was ever done by halves, no interest merely toyed with. Only a man of his stature and unshakeable self-assurance could have shouldered the task of giving India back to the Indians in 1947. Yet he was a flawed genius whose weakness was an immense vanity, a weakness which was undoubtedly responsible in large measure for his obsession with his royal role. The other factor at work was a continuing desire to clear the family name and to re-establish it in good standing and in the highest possible social position after the hounding his father, Prince Louis of Battenberg, had suffered at British hands during the First World War. Prince Louis had come from his native Germany and settled in England, rising to become First Lord of the Admiralty; although he had never been shown to be anything other than patriotically British, public opinion would not stand for a German commanding the British Navy in a war with Imperial Germany. He was removed, and given the title Marquess of Milford Haven in 1917 as a consolation, anglicising his name to Mountbatten.

His younger son, Lord Louis Mountbatten, always believed that it was his father's Battenberg blood, rather than his mother's line through Queen Victoria, which gave him what he perceived to be his own immense talents. Until Prince Philip injected some Mountbatten blood into the line, he believed, the British royal family were in serious decline. Richard Hough, the more flattering of his two principal biographers, quotes him as declaring once: 'Prince Philip is an absolute Mountbatten and not a bit Hanoverian, and his children have a degree of intelligence quite lacking in King George V, King George VI or any of those people at all. Prince Charles, too, is an absolute Mountbatten. The real intelligence in the royal family comes through my parents to Prince Philip and the children.' But not even the supremely egotistical Lord Louis could bring himself to besmirch the name of the reigning sovereign, and he backpedalled somewhat: 'The Queen, of course, is a marvellous person. She is extremely sound – not brilliant – and that comes from her mother. There was great worthiness in King George VI, King George V, and even Edward VII, but that old Hanoverian line was becoming dimmer and dimmer so that they could not even pass their exams.'

Such were Mountbatten's ambitions for his family name that he put considerable pressure on the Queen to add it to the name of the royal house of Windsor. The Queen relented, and by an Order in Council in 1959 announced that her children would henceforth bear the surname of Mountbatten-Windsor. The wording was unclear, and the precedent was properly established only in 1973 when the Queen's daughter signed her marriage certificate 'Anne Mountbatten-Windsor'.

Back in the 1930s, Mountbatten had assumed a role of father-figure to his nephew Prince Philip following the latter's banishment from Greece with his family while still an infant, and the subsequent decay of his parents' marriage. The young Philip became something of a high-born gypsy, roaming between distant relatives in various European royal houses and being properly cared for by none of them. Philip developed the greatest admiration for the uncle who had taken him under his wing and had, inevitably, set him on course for a successful and deeply satisfying naval career. It was therefore entirely natural that when Philip had a son of his own he should encourage a close relationship between the child and Mountbatten.

The relationship flourished from the beginning. Mountbatten always had a winning way with children, relishing their company, endlessly amusing them, treating them as equals, and displaying with them a patience in startling contrast to the short-fused ruthlessness that characterized most other departments of his life. He seized on the chance to mould Charles, and saw him whenever he could, which was at least as frequently as he saw his own grandchildren. His was one of the loudest and most persistent voices in discussions on Charles's education; he counselled Gordonstoun and the Navy in the footsteps of Prince Philip, which Charles's father thoroughly approved of, but in addition recommended a full degree course at Trinity College, Cambridge which Prince Philip would perhaps not have advocated so strongly. It should be no surprise that in the event Mountbatten's scheme was followed more or less to the letter.

As he grew older Prince Charles, for his part, found the atmosphere of the Mountbatten home both relaxing and stimulating. It is perfectly common for children to form a particular bond with relatives one step removed from their own parents, where they can find a peace and understanding that parents, in the everyday front-line battle of trying to knock the child into shape, often cannot easily give. Charles found that relationship with his grandmother Queen Elizabeth, and with Mountbatten, whose family home at Broadlands became a wonderful refuge from the stuffiness of Buckingham Palace and the sometimes intolerable pressures of family life. Prince Philip has always had a reputation for intolerance, short temper, and a strong dislike of introspection, tears or failure. Mountbatten, although in many ways cast in the same brisk, no-nonsense, action-man mould, with an enthusiasm and drive that many would regard as sheer naked bullying, could afford to be far more understanding with Charles, to listen and to sympathize, to advise without hectoring, and to encourage without threatening. At the same time Charles found the atmosphere at Broadlands, or wherever Uncle Dickie happened to be at the time, exceedingly lively. There was always laughter, and there was usually good-natured argument for argument's sake, particularly if any of Mountbatten's large pool of sharp and witty Battenberg relatives from Germany were present. Charles always found the Mountbatten family atmosphere deliciously relaxed and amusing, in sharp contrast to the pressures and predictability of life at home.

Charles used Broadlands as a frequent refuge throughout Mountbatten's life. He would go there on school holidays from Gordonstoun, to voice a dislike of the place that he would hardly dare admit to his father. He would drive down from Cambridge to talk of the pressures of preparing for his investiture as Prince of Wales at Caernarfon, which so cut into his academic career. In the Navy he would drive the short distance from Portsmouth to Broadlands for dinner, a night's bed, and conversation with the most eminent living old seadog on the trials of a very junior officer's life. If Charles had to make a speech there was always sound advice from Mountbatten – not always heeded by his pupil – for he had a long perspective of history. He instructed Charles in the finer points of fly fishing and of polo, but more importantly he discussed at great length with the Heir Apparent the role of monarchy and the duties of kingship.

Mountbatten was strong on the notion of duty, if only because he demanded it in full measure from all those beneath him. But he was also an unashamed elitist whose views on how the United Kingdom should be governed were thoroughly right-wing; he strongly supported what were to all intents and purposes the plans for a military coup to dislodge Harold Wilson's mildly socialist government in the 1960s. Nor was he universally admired by those who saw him at war; Frank Gillard, the distinguished BBC war correspondent, recalled recently his profound distaste at returning from covering the disastrous Dieppe raid, his uniform caked in the blood of dead comrades, to hear Mountbatten on the Portsmouth dockside in spotless naval whites congratulate the survivors on an absolutely splendid job.

But at least Mountbatten's elitism was not of a narrow, insular British kind; his perspective was international. Nothing better encapsulated his view than his agreement in 1968 to become chairman of Atlantic College, a highly unusual school on the shores of the Vale of Glamorgan in South Wales. Occupying the fourteenth-century St Donat's Castle, which had been owned briefly by the megalomaniac American newspaper baron William Randolph Hearst, Atlantic College was another brainchild of Kurt Hahn, the founder of Gordonstoun.

The project suffered from a chronic shortage of money until Mountbatten became its figurehead; with typically ferocious enthusiasm he assumed the role of chief fundraiser, and wherever he went in the world he unashamedly bullied and browbeat presidents and prime ministers of all colours and religions in his efforts to gain their support, both moral and financial. He was so successful that during his chairmanship not only did the original Welsh college flourish, but also additional schools on the same model were opened in Canada, at Victoria, British Columbia, and in Singapore, and plans for another were being drawn up in Venezuela. The original Atlantic College operates as a sixth-form college, taking 300 pupils at a time for two years from as far away as the People's Republic of China, and preparing them for the International Baccalaureate.

The Baccalaureate is an examination pioneered by the Colleges themselves, and is now being increasingly used by international schools throughout the world. It is recognized by nearly 500 universities including Oxford, Cambridge and the Sorbonne, and its syllabus covers the six areas of mathematics, languages, literature, the arts, experimental sciences, and a broad, vague category known as 'The Study of Man'. By contrast, no entrance examination is required for admission to the colleges; selection is by interview, previous academic performance, and 'personal qualities'. Most come on scholarships, and although no one is turned away for want of the fees, the school nonetheless unashamedly picks only the extremely able, who if they were not at one of the schools in what has now been renamed United World Colleges (to reflect the international dimension), would be receiving a superior education at some other exclusive establishment. Mountbatten would have seen absolutely nothing wrong in such elitism, which he regarded as the operation of the perfectly acceptable principle of meritocracy, and nor does Prince Charles.

There was never a clearer signal of the pair's regard for each other than when, in 1978, Mountbatten asked his great-nephew to take over as World President of United World Colleges, and Charles accepted with enthusiasm. In his first speech to the governing council he said: 'My acceptance of the presidency was based really on a deep and personal conviction of the intrinsic merits of the UWC concept which I think in many ways is close to the Gordonstoun ideal, which essentially is the belief in the importance of human relationships in world affairs.'

Charles has continued to embrace wholeheartedly the ideals of United World Colleges. He is a much less aggressive fundraiser than his great-uncle, but he nevertheless loses few opportunities to spread the word, especially when visiting Third World countries, and a great many of his overseas tours include in their schedule a meeting with UWC old boys, who are expected to act as missionaries for Hahn's ideals when they return to their own countries. If he is in a country where there is no associated college, he will often explore tentatively the possibilities of setting one up. Such was the case in Venezuela in 1978, where he learned the same sorry tale from a great many sources – the lack of proper agricultural training in a country which, despite its oil revenues, was essentially a rural economy. Charles asked for a meeting with the country's president, Carlos Andres Perez, explained at length the merits of UWC, and offered him a deal: if Venezuela would put up the money for an agricultural college, UWC would find the necessary staff of international experts, and a proportion of foreign students. The deal was struck, but the reality was a long time coming, delayed by bureaucracy and changes of government. The college was finally due to be fully operational in 1988, functioning rather differently from the others and less open to charges of elitism. Rather than grooming already-favoured youth for university, the Simón Bolívar Agricultural College aims, by means of high-grade instruction, to put farmers back on the land of Venezuela, and to disseminate its teaching throughout the Third World. Every UWC student is regarded as a 'multiplier', a disciple who will spread the word.

One final cameo illustrates the bond between Mountbatten and Charles. Like his parents had done in 1947, Charles spent the first night of his honeymoon in 1981 in the Mountbatten family home at Broadlands, not so much for reasons of sentiment as for the fact that it offered excellent privacy and security. The following morning an alert estate worker saw

Charles leave the house and make for the banks of the River Test; in his hand was one of his late mentor's favourite fishing rods. It was an indulgence that his young bride of less than twenty-four hours may have found hard to understand.

The death of Mountbatten at the age of seventy-nine at the hands of IRA terrorists left Charles bereft, disconsolate and confused. His father was equally shocked, for he too had been exceptionally close to his uncle, but Prince Philip's great attributes are not those of sympathy, introspection and soul-searching. Charles, in his bleakest hour, turned first to his grandmother Queen Elizabeth, a woman of immense kindliness and understanding who had herself experienced premature bereavement with the death of her husband King George VI. He turned second to a more unlikely comforter, a man he had known slightly since childhood, with whom he was beginning to feel a growing affinity, and who would come to exert a significant influence on Charles's thinking as the Prince sought to make some sense, and to find some positive way forward, from Uncle Dickie's death. He began to find what he was looking for in the sometimes curious and unconventional wisdom of Laurens van der Post.

Van der Post, a gentle, soft-spoken, silver-haired philosopher and writer born a white Afrikaaner South African in 1906, would appear at first sight to have little or nothing in common with the aristocratic, vain, loud, all-action Mountbatten. But such appearances would be quite wrong. During the last war van der Post was a colonel in the British Army, effectively serving under Mountbatten in the Japanese campaign in the Far East. His views of the world were at least partly forged during his spell as a Japanese prisoner of war on the island of Java in Indonesia. In addition the outlook of both men, although radically different in style and expression, was based on a fundamental premise that they hated socialism, communism or any other form of collectivism that threatened the essential freedom of the individual.

For that reason, if no other, van der Post has long been an admirer of Mrs Margaret Thatcher, and she of him; philosopher and Prime Minister have been friends for years, and have held many a soul-searching conversation. They were introduced by the late Airey Neave, a celebrated prisoner of the Nazis in Colditz and subsequently the Conservative Government Secretary for Northern Ireland until he too was assassinated by an IRA bomb, within the very precincts of the House of Commons. Such is Mrs Thatcher's regard for van der Post that it was she who recommended the knighthood conferred on him in 1981.

Van der Post and Mrs Thatcher share a wide spectrum of political beliefs. He, like she, believes the West must 'stand fast' against the Soviet Union which, he is convinced, would have invaded Poland during the 'Solidarity' crisis had it not been frightened off by Britain's decision to take arms against Argentina over the Falkland Islands.

He has said that he sees in the Soviet Union a similar collectivist peril to the Nazi Germany of the 1930s, and he believes that the Soviet Union will change from within only if the West stands firmly in defence of its own values. Van der Post also seems to have supplied the Conservative Government with some of its thinking on the problem of how to deal with his native South Africa. He is on record many times as an implacable opponent to apartheid, but he does not believe that it will be eradicated by the rest of the world taking sides; the only way South Africa will change, he believes, is from within, through reconciliation between black and white. Mrs Thatcher, in announcing her opposition to sanctions against South Africa, might almost have been listening to Sir Laurens the previous night.

But there is a wider dimension to his political beliefs, and one which perhaps more directly concerns his influence on Charles. Van der Post, when young, was a close friend and disciple of the philosopher and psychoanalyst Carl Jung, from whom he absorbed the view of the collective unconscious, that evil is a tangible force and not merely an absence of good. Later, he travelled widely in the deserts of southern Africa, developing an understanding of, and a profound respect for, their nomadic native bushmen, documented in *The Lost World of the Kalahari* and other books of distinction. His two overriding impressions of the bushmen, regarded by the less comprehending as among earth's deepest primitives, were their ability to live in perfect harmony with the world around them, and their immense intuition, enabling them to speak little but to understand volumes.

The sum total of van der Post's immense lifetime of experiences has led him to at least two important philosophical conclusions: that man must live in harmony with all around him, be it fellow man, animals or the land; and that he will find truth only by listening to his inner self rather than to the urgent political expediencies of an essentially capitalist world – a point at which, one suspects, he and Margaret Thatcher begin to travel different roads. Twenty years ago a reviewer in *The Times Literary Supplement* said of him: 'He is preoccupied with man's continual awareness of a lost inheritance. There is a strong undercurrent of regret for the primal opportunity to establish a proper balance between man, God and environment.' Much more recently, the author himself said in an interview: 'Part of our human problem today is that we are governed by the attitudes of the city. We need the country mind to appreciate the importance of time – seasons, growing, flowering and harvest, good years and bad years. Yet politicians want immediate solutions.'

There is no shortage of people ready to treat van der Post the philosopher with great reserve. The unkind brand him an eccentric, the kind a mystic – a term the man himself detests, with its overtones of muddled thinking and deliberate obfuscation. A sympathetic reviewer said of his writing recently that it consisted of 'dark impenetrable swirling fogs of words, broken at times by sunbeams of insight, black storm clouds piling up, punctuated by lightning flashes which momentarily illuminate for us vast tracts of unfamiliar landscape.

'Patience is required, and the humility to recognize and profit by them – two qualities especially rare in those narrowly urban and rationalistic Western minds which are anathema to Sir Laurens.'

No one, however, has accused Sir Laurens of being anything other than a thoroughly good man, although his logic is sometimes obscure and he occasionally teeters towards self-importance. He is a believer in a whole world, and shies away from easy and instant solutions to its problems. Problems, indeed, he believes to be man's greatest asset. In this holistic, low-key view of the world, Charles found comfort and justification for life after the death of Mountbatten. It would be entirely wrong to suggest that the Prince, in his hour of need, suddenly discovered Sir Laurens; they had in fact known each other slightly for many years, and Charles's inquiring mind and essentially religious nature had always been intrigued by van der Post. Now, however, he embraced the concepts of intuition and oneness with nature a great deal more warmly. His debt was recognized in 1982 when he asked Sir Laurens to be a godfather to the infant Prince William.

The van der Post influence has manifested itself in many of Charles's public utterances ever since. Sir Laurens wrote of the bushmen in *The Lost World of the Kalahari*: 'It seemed as if Nature was for them a mirror, where they learned to recognize and understand aspects of themselves.' Compare that with Charles, addressing a puzzled small-town audience in Canada in 1986: 'I rather feel that deep in the soul of mankind there is a reflection of the beauty and harmony of the universe. Through the outer manifestation of that reflection, we can attain the kind of peace for which we yearn.'

That he had absorbed the van der Post doctrine was shown much more fully in 1984 when he gave a lengthy interview to the London *Evening Standard* newspaper following his controversial address to the British Medical Association in which he stated in no uncertain terms that conventional doctors by no means held a monopoly of healing. He told the paper's interviewer, Anne de Courcy: 'The knowledge that man is capable of harnessing nature to his own ends to such a fantastic degree – that he even has the capability to destroy the entire planet with the deadly weapons he himself has designed – has given us the feeling that *we* are masters of our fate. Which is so far from the truth it makes one cry sometimes.

'The denial of the intuitive, listening side of our natures is one of the most negative aspects of civilized life. It is trained out of us from childhood – children are naturally aware – but our whole educational pattern is one where we knock it out of everybody's lives. We are a left-brain society, we concentrate on organizing the denial of the "intuitive" right half of the brain.

'To me it is very interesting to see how primitive societies – though I think primitive is a complete misnomer anyway – are the whole time subconsciously far more aware of their instinctive relationship with the things and people round them than we are in the so-called civilized world. Look at the problems we get into as a result, when we deny this important aspect of ourselves and merely rely on intellectual analysis.

'It's still there, but buried under a mountain of – what? Anxieties, fears, worries, a feeling that it's something we should be ashamed of, as though rational thinking is the only acceptable process. Yet I believe instinct, sensitivity, call it what you will, is enormously important. But one has to grit one's teeth because you still think, "My goodness, I may be talking absolute rubbish here – how do I know it's right?" But slowly you learn to trust and develop this vital quality.'

Charles permitted this baring of a small part of his philosophical soul shortly after delivering the speech to the British Medical Association on its 150th anniversary in 1984 which took that essentially conservative and protective body considerably by surprise. What shook the doctors was his suggestion that conventional medicine and its heavy reliance on drugs might not be the only route to healing, a view which the traditional medical establishment is coming to accept only with great caution. He said, in part, 'I have often thought that one of the less attractive traits of various professional bodies and institutions is the deeply ingrained suspicion and outright hostility which can exist towards anything unorthodox or unconventional. I suppose that human nature is such that we are frequently prevented from seeing that what is taken as today's unorthodoxy is probably going to be tomorrow's convention.

'Perhaps we just have to accept it is God's will that the unorthodox individual is doomed to years of frustration, ridicule and failure in order to act his role in the scheme of things, until his day arrives and mankind is ready to receive his message ... I would suggest that the whole imposing edifice of modern medicine, for all its breathtaking successes is, like the celebrated Tower of Pisa, slightly off-balance. It is frightening how dependent upon drugs we are all becoming and how easy it is for doctors to prescribe them as the universal panacea for our ills. Wonderful as many of them are it should still be more widely stressed by doctors that the health of human beings is so often determined by their behaviour, their food and the nature of their environment.'

Charles was in effect making a plea for the wider recognition of holistic medicine, and the overall outlook expressed in his address was in direct line of descent from van der Post. But it would be most unfair on both the Prince and Sir Laurens to suggest that Charles merely swallowed the old man's teachings and regurgitated them. For one thing, alternative medicine has for long had a certain stamp of royal approval; the Queen is a firm believer in homeopathy, as were both her parents. For another, Charles is quite capable of formulating his own thoughts. He revealed how he had come to make the speech.

'I agonized over what on earth I was going to say, because although I had vague ideas over the area I wanted to approach – well, was I going to pluck up enough courage to launch into it? There's a lot of scepticism in the world of orthodox medicine.

'And it was the most extraordinary thing – I was sitting at my desk at the time and I happened to look in my bookshelf and my eyes suddenly settled on a book about Paracelsus [the sixteenth-century healer]. So I took the book down and read it

154

and as a result I tried to make a speech around Paracelsus and perhaps a re-look at what he was saying and the ideas he propounded; wasn't it time to think again about the relationship between mind and body, or body and spirit?'

He was astonished by the response to the speech. 'I have never *ever* had so many letters. I was riveted by this because while I was pretty sure I was going to stir up a hornet's nest – which I did, I think – I also realized there was a great deal more interest in and awareness of this aspect than I'd imagined, particularly among lay people – although many doctors, especially the younger ones, also seemed to feel the same way.'

He also admitted that there was another important influence on his views about alternative – he prefers the word 'complementary' – medicine, and that was Gordonstoun. 'Kurt Hahn, the founder, was a great believer in the Platonic ideal of a healthy mind in a healthy body, and the whole structure of the Gordonstoun educational system was geared to this aim, so you learned a lot about how to look after yourself there.'

Critics of Charles have pounced on van der Post as having been an undue influence on the Prince's outlook converting him into a potential Buddhist or at the very least a drifting mystic who has abandoned the realities of life in favour of dabbling in fringe medicine and the paranormal. A story surfaced at one stage that his suite at Kensington Palace was crammed with hundreds of photographs of Earl Mountbatten, and that he had tried to communicate with his dead uncle by means of seances and an ouija board. On reading the stories, Charles had to have it explained to him exactly what an ouija board was.

It would take a great deal more even than the considerable persuasions of Sir Laurens van der Post to cast Charles entirely adrift from the immense anchor of his royal background and upbringing; the influence of his family and his position are so all-pervasive that there is little chance of him abandoning all that has gone before and emulating another wealthy prince

of an earlier age. Gautama Siddhartha left all behind and
became a wandering ascetic. At the age of 35, seated under
a banyan tree, he experienced at last his sought-after state of
oneness with the universe and thereby laid the foundations of
Buddhism.

In 1987, at the end of a tour of southern Africa, Charles
retreated with Sir Laurens into the Kalahari Desert of Bot-
swana for four days, accompanied only by a policeman and
a doctor. It was assumed that this would be a major religious
experience, a finding of the state of oneness. They were
expected by the Press to make contact with the bushmen,
to live as guru and acolyte, and to stumble upon the secret
of the universe.

Charles was talking about it soon afterwards to a group of
interested listeners, including myself. No, they had not met
the bushmen, nor had they intended to; it was the wrong part
of the desert. The highlight for him was not the discovery of
the secret of the universe, which appears as elusive in the
Kalahari as it does in Fleet Street, but the night two lions
stole into their camp and made off with a plastic bucket.
And his principal concern seemed to be that, in the middle
of the expedition, the batteries of his razor had run out.

Nevertheless the influence of van der Post has undoubtedly
enriched Charles, and although it may not have separated him
entirely from his traditional English aristocratic background,
and the great weight of history he must carry on his shoulders,
it has undoubtedly broadened his mind far beyond the narrow
strictures of the dark corridor of monarchical succession
into which he was born. Although the influence may be
easily dismissed as cranky it is essentially of a high moral
tone; it has, for example, bolstered Charles's concern for
the underprivileged, a concern which extends far beyond
any *noblesse oblige*. Those who criticize his efforts to alleviate inner city problems, to create employment, and to
improve housing, as being mere inconsequential tinkerings
with a massive problem, seem to forget that Charles is not a
politician, and that in his unique and unenviable position it

can be exceptionally difficult to achieve anything concrete at all. The previous Prince of Wales evinced great concern for the Welsh miners, but his concern never created a single job.

Should anyone ever think that Charles is on the verge of giving away all his worldly goods and abandoning his privilege to become another Buddha or St Francis of Assisi, they need only listen to him beating the drum for the elitist United World Colleges. At a fundraising dinner in the United States in 1985 organized by Dr Armand Hammer, the remarkable octogenarian industrialist, to which the minimum entrance fee was £10,000, Charles told the guests: 'What is wrong with being elite, for God's sake? How on earth does anyone expect anything to get done in life unless there is some effort to educate people's characters as well as their minds? How are we to have any hope of balanced and civilized leadership in the future unless there are some people who have learned about service to others, about compassion; about understanding, as far as possible, the other man's religion, the other man's customs and his history; about courage to stand up for things that are noble and for things that are true? After all, there is so much to be done in this world – so much famine exists, so much disease, so much poverty, so much conflict, bigotry and prejudice, and there are so many people who are crying out for help, for their own simple dreams to come true.'

The elitism of the colleges would seem to be irreconcilable with the gentle, holistic egalitarianism of van der Post. But Charles would not think so; in his view, rightly or wrongly, the first can be a means of achieving the second.

One of the great advantages of Prince Charles's own elitist position is that he can call for advice, guidance or help from virtually any quarter, and few if any will refuse him. Spiritual mentors like Mountbatten and van der Post have exercised a great influence on him, but the great majority of his mentors advise him on a more worldly, day-to-day level. Even some of those, like the architect Rod Hackney and the late secretary of the Duchy of Cornwall, Sir John Higgs, both discussed elsewhere, have been powerful influences, others less so. Their common factor is that they are all pre-eminent in their own fields, if not always representing the mainstream.

In the world of global politics Charles has benefited from the vast knowledge, and his charities from the even more vast wallet, of Dr Armand Hammer, founder of Occidental Petroleum and a man equally acquainted with the highest corridors of power of both Washington and Moscow. On the domestic political scene Charles has learned much from, and formed a close friendship with, Lord Tonypandy, who as George Thomas MP was for many years the gifted and mellifluous Speaker of the House of Commons. His love of nature and conservation has been encouraged and developed by Dr Miriam Rothschild, a descendant of the great banking family and an outstanding botanist with particular expertise in butterflies and wild flowers; Dr Rothschild helped Charles to plant the gardens of Highgrove, seeding a former dandelion meadow with dozens of species of Britain's fast vanishing wild plants. On her advice, Charles has seeded strips of wasteland and roadside verge all over the Duchy of Cornwall estates with wild plants that would otherwise be in danger of extinction.

Critics who think that van der Post has had too much influence on Charles, turning his mind to the metaphysical at the expense of the practical, need only look at the people he chooses for his advisory board at the Prince's Trust. George Pratt, former deputy chief probation officer for London, was invited to participate after Charles had heard him talking on the radio about the problems of rehabilitating young offenders. 'It seemed to me to be more appropriate if the Prince were to help prevent youngsters getting into trouble in the first place,' Pratt remarked at the time. 'The Prince put forward his ideas and we dealt with them. We decided to test our theory that young people, if trusted to do their own thing, could be encouraged to do something worthwhile with their lives.'

Other advisers picked by the Prince for the Trust's work include Dr June Paterson-Brown, the Chief Guide, for her knowledge of youth work, the rock singer Phil Collins both for his knowledge of rock audiences and his experience with major fund-raising events like the Band-Aid concerts, and James Gardener, former chief executive of Tyne and Wear Metropolitan Council, which governed an area of particularly high and stubbornly persistent youth unemployment.

The elitism of Mountbatten, the metaphysics of van der Post, and the idealism of both, have been turned by Charles, within the frustratingly narrow confines of his constitutional position, to unusually practical effect.

9

'In Love – Whatever That Is'

ONE EARLY MORNING in June 1977 Charles was listening once again to his favourite radio programme *Today*, when he was stopped in mid-shave by a startling news item. The *Daily Express*, using a type size normally reserved for declarations of war, splashed across its front page the headline: 'Charles to marry Astrid – Official'. The story, by the paper's usually reliable political editor John Warden, stated without any shadow of doubt that the Prince would marry Princess Marie-Astrid of Luxembourg, and that the formal announcement would be made the following Monday. The fact that she was a Roman Catholic would be overcome by 'a novel constitutional arrangement' – any sons of the marriage would be raised in the Anglican faith to preserve their eligibility for the British throne, while any daughters would be raised as Catholics. The Queen and Prince Philip, it was stated categorically, had assented to this procedure.

'Prince Charles, who is 28, first met 23-year-old Astrid about a year ago. Although their association has been kept secret by the Palace – even to the extent of denying they have ever met – a close friend said last night: "They fell for each other at that first meeting." ' It was the word 'Official' in the headline that lent the story a certain veracity, and indicated that the *Express* believed it. Charles, finding no mention of it in his copy of *The Times*, sent out for an *Express* while he racked his brains to remember if and when he had ever met his supposed bride-to-be.

The reason for the absence of this earth-shattering announcement from *The Times* was its complete fabrication;

there was not a word of truth in it, and not the remotest possibility that the heir to the British throne would marry the granddaughter of King Leopold of the Belgians. Warden, who had written the story in good faith, had been the victim of a plot to trap the indiscretions of a member of the Privy Council, who was suspected of being the source of some top-rate and highly accurate political gossip that was appearing regularly in the *Express.* Downing Street, with the help of police Special Branch officers, fed the suspected leaker the fictitious and faintly plausible nugget of Charles's engagement, and when it duly appeared the mole was confronted, confessed, and discreetly retired.

Charles was at first amused, and then annoyed that Marie-Astrid should be put in such an embarrassing position. Unusually, he authorized the Queen's then press secretary, Ronald Allison, to issue a formal denial: 'There is no truth at all in the report that there is to be an announcement of an engagement of the Prince of Wales to Princess Marie-Astrid of Luxembourg.' But even that did not entirely kill off the speculation, and the following day Allison was obliged to make another statement: 'They are not getting engaged this Monday, next Monday, the Monday after, or any other Monday, Tuesday, Wednesday or Thursday. They do not know each other and people who do not know each other do not get engaged. The Royal Family do not go in for arranged marriages. If the Prince and Princess Marie-Astrid have met at all then it has been briefly at official functions.' The suspicion that there may have been something to it after all rumbled on for several years, to the extent of some newspapers wondering whether the 1701 Act of Settlement was about to be changed to allow a Catholic to marry the Heir Apparent.

The Marie-Astrid affair was one of the highlights of an energetic guessing game which kept the gossip columns busily amused during Charles's courting years between Navy and marriage. Any girl who came within a mile of him ran the risk of being named as a candidate for the role of future Queen of England, although in truth very few indeed got beyond even the first rung of that impossibly steep and slippery ladder.

The public portrayal of Charles was that of an energetic ladies' man and the string of girls whose names were associated with him became known as 'Charlie's Angels' after a television series popular at the time. Charles himself, in reality and in his occasional public musings on the subject of marriage, was infinitely more circumspect. In an interview in the mid-1970s he talked at some length on the matter.

'Marriage is a much more important business than falling in love. I think one must concentrate on marriage being essentially a question of mutual love and respect for each other. Creating a secure family unit in which to bring up children, to give them a happy, secure upbringing – that's what marriage is all about, creating a home. Essentially you must be good friends, and love I'm sure will grow out of that friendship. I have a particular responsibility to ensure that I make the right decision. The last thing I could possibly entertain is getting divorced. I've fallen in love with all sorts of girls and I fully intend to go on doing so. But I've made sure I haven't married the first person I've fallen in love with.

'The right age for marriage is around thirty. By this time you have seen a great deal of life, met a large number of girls, been able to see what types of girls there are, fallen in love every now and then and you know what it's all about.' A very traditional view, and hardly the credo of a philanderer.

In his bachelor days Charles never let women rule his life, nor disturb his pre-ordained routine. No official visit, no polo match, was cancelled on their behalf; they had to fit in with him, not he with them, and in his life's priorities they often appeared to stand in third place after his work and his sport. In that he could be regarded simply as a straightforward male chauvinist who liked to make the running and who liked girls to be at his convenience, not he at theirs. Some of his former female associates have reported that, while he liked to telephone them, he did not at all care to be called back. That, of course, may be entirely due to the ladies in question having an unfortunately inflated view of the importance of their relationship.

Charles has certainly never shown much sympathy with ideas of women's liberation or even of female equality; his views about a woman's place are distinctly old-fashioned. But his love life was equally governed by its extreme difficulty; the need for discretion was paramount and by no means easy to achieve with the Fleet Street cavalry in full and constant pursuit, and the ever-present danger that ladies who had enjoyed his company would fall prey to the blandishments of a reporter. Those who did found their royal association instantly terminated.

Discretion was achieved, when necessary, by the hospitality of trusted friends at weekend house parties, and by the use of a 'safe house' in London not far from Buckingham Palace, whose address was never discovered. His former valet Stephen Barry, who subsequently fell foul of his erstwhile master for writing a mildly indiscreet book, recorded: 'The relationships he did have were arranged with the most enormous discretion. In all those twelve years that I worked for him, if he was meant to be in his bed in the morning when I went to wake him up – he was in bed. Alone.'

Power and position may be potent aphrodisiacs, but the girls invited into Charles's company often found a considerable obstacle course in the way of romance. There was, firstly, the lack of privacy; even if no Press were lurking behind the lamp posts, there was always a detective or some other member of the Prince's personal staff not far away. Then there were the rigours of the Balmoral test. Girls with whom Charles became at all serious were often invited to spend a few days on the Scottish estate, a prospect they viewed with great excitement until they discovered the distinctly unromantic reality, the surprisingly spartan existence and the male chauvinism of shooting and stalking parties which traditionally leave the women behind with little to do except dwell on the boredom and the rain. Women who failed the Balmoral test generally destroyed any chance of the relationship being taken further.

The overall impression of Prince Charles that his girl friends formed was of an incurable romantic in love with the idea of being in love, who enjoyed giving red roses and candlelit dinner parties, but whose full attention was rarely with them for long. His work schedule came first, if only because it had been laid down months in advance, and his sports came a close second. His action-man activities, in which he developed a reputation for pushing himself to physical limits, seem in retrospect to have been a compensation for the difficulties and strictures he faced in conducting a normal love-life with the eyes of the world constantly upon him and the permanent perils of publicity. He was hidebound too, as he admitted himself, by the overriding need not to make a mistake, which much of the time seemed to make him cautious and even distant. At the same time his position and upbringing meant that his life followed very much a set pattern with set routines, and he showed little desire to break the mould. He has often displayed in no small measure the overriding characteristic of the male chauvinist, which is selfishness.

The great majority of Charles's liaisons were distinctly casual. A handful were more serious, but in only one or at most two cases was marriage ever considered. His caution, his shyness and his inborn uncertainty made him a dilettante and a ditherer.

Charles's first public date was at the age of fourteen, when he splashed out thirty shillings on a stalls seat at *The Sound of Music* for Marilyn Wills, daughter of one of the Queen's closest friends. At Cambridge he became friendly with Lucia Santa Cruz. Still at Cambridge, he holidayed on Malta with the Governor-General's daughter, Sybilla Dorman; the liaison was brief. A clumsy attempt was made to pair him with Princess Caroline of Monaco, then aged only fifteen, but the meeting was disastrous; she found him unbearably boring, and he found her irritatingly superficial, as he did Tricia Nixon, who was also pushed in his direction by her hamfisted father in the White House.

Another American fared better. Charles met Laura Jo

Watkins at a California yacht club while his ship *Jupiter* was visiting the West Coast in 1975. He liked her because, being American, she was different and refreshingly uninhibited by his high position; she came to London to listen to his maiden speech from the Strangers' Gallery of the House of Lords, but the ardour soon fizzled out as Charles's attention wandered elsewhere, as it often did. Sabrina Guinness, a member of the brewing family, was favoured for a while, until Charles invited her to a ball at the Earl of Pembroke's home in Wiltshire, except that he invited her twin sister Miranda as well. Charles departed alone, leaving both sisters and the entire gossip column industry mystified.

Various partners fell rapidly from grace for various reasons. The Countess Angelika Lazensky, an exotic Czech beauty, was invited north for the Balmoral test, but succumbed to the cardinal sin of talking to the Press about it; she was never heard of again. Fiona Watson, daughter of a Yorkshire landowner, was briefly favoured until it emerged that she had posed nude for a men's glamour magazine; she too was instantly dumped. Jane Ward, who worked in the office at the Guards' Polo Club at Windsor, suffered from being a divorcee and then for talking to the Press. After a brief and seemingly close association in 1979, she vanished from Charles's life at great speed on the day that, having chosen to end it, Charles sent over his detective who asked her to leave the polo ground at once. With nothing left to lose, she spoke on the record: 'He has a very strong sense of duty and he is a very moral person. It worries him that so many of his friends have been divorced. I am sure it has put him off marriage, because he has certainly become wary.'

Earl Mountbatten, who took it upon himself to be such a guiding influence in all aspects of his great-nephew's life, could not resist dabbling in the affairs of Charles's heart. He pressed very strongly the suit of his granddaughter Amanda Knatchbull, seized with enthusiasm and egotistical hope that a Mountbatten might once again marry directly into the British throne. But he failed; Charles and Amanda had known each other too long as friends for any romance to blossom.

One partner who seemed to pass all the tests was Davina Sheffield, whom Charles met in 1976 at a dinner party in Fulham. Her qualifications were excellent; the daughter of an Army major, she was tall, blonde and extremely attractive with a wide and ready smile. She was 25 years old, faintly aristocratic, loved the country, and never betrayed a confidence to the Press; so she was invited north for the Balmoral test. Unlike so many lesser southern softies more at home on the pavements of Chelsea, Davina relished wet Scottish heather, indeed too much so for Charles's liking. When the men went off stalking, she wanted to come too, and was not content with Charles's explanation that the ladies stayed behind and met up later for lunch from the back of a Range Rover. Davina refused to be left behind, so Charles, an exceptionally fit man, deliberately walked her all day through the roughest gorse and boggiest heather he could find. By evening she was so exhausted that she could not even come down for dinner, and left for home the following morning. But what finally killed the romance was the Sunday newspaper revelations of one of her previous lovers, who described in detail how they had shared a cottage in the West Country for six months. Any whiff of a past life meant automatically that a relationship could go no further; Charles, imbued with a strong religious and moral sense, clung rigidly to the ideal, if not of a virgin Queen, at least of a virgin Princess of Wales. But there was more in the departure of Davina than that; in truth she was too wilful for Charles, and did not know her place sufficiently. She departed to care for orphans in Vietnam.

Another wilful spirit was Lady Jane Wellesley, daughter of the 8th Duke of Wellington and another friend of Charles's from childhood, her father being a close acquaintance of the Queen. She and Charles were close for four years, and although she was not put through the Balmoral test – which she would probably have failed through boredom of her alert and active mind – she was invited to Sandringham for the 1975 New Year holiday. She appeared to pass muster on most counts, being aristocratic, lively, attractive and thoroughly discreet, but Charles was never entirely sure about her. He found her emancipated, tough and radical in her views; indeed she went on to work in the highly competitive world of television, and combined her BBC researcher's job with being her office representative of the National Union of Journalists. For Charles, in the end, she was too outspoken, too articulate, and too unwilling to accept a subsidiary role, although had she married the Prince of Wales her effect on his outlook would have been fascinating to behold.

Some of Charles's companions hurt him publicly by more than mere indiscretion, even though they might not have intended to. Lady Sarah Spencer appeared at one time as a serious contender for marriage, and when she accompanied the Prince on a skiing holiday to Klosters in 1978 the Press naturally followed. Klosters was relatively informal in those days, and there was little to prevent reporters walking up and knocking on the chalet door. Some did, and when Lady Sarah answered they posed the inevitable question.

To which she replied: 'Charles is a fabulous person but I am not in love with him. He is a romantic who falls in love easily. I would not marry a man I did not love, whether it was a dustman or the King of England. If he asked me, I would turn him down.' If Charles indeed had any thoughts of asking her, they could hardly have had a larger bucket of colder water poured on them. And to be mentioned in the same breath as a dustman, indeed! Exit rapidly from his innermost affections Lady Sarah Spencer although, as he managed to do with the majority of his cast-offs, he remained on friendly terms with her.

One woman perhaps more than any other came close to marrying Charles. Anna Wallace was the daughter of a Scottish landowner whom Charles met at a hunt in 1979; she was attractive, extrovert, and known as Whiplash Wallace, more for her strong temper than her love of hunting. She was not aristocratic, but she was certainly county, quite self-possessed and at home in Charles's circle. She was spirited, but not in the radical, feminist way that Jane Wellesley was. She shared Charles's love of country pursuits, and passed the Balmoral test with flying colours. They dated for a year, and Charles is widely rumoured to have proposed marriage to her. But the knot became irrevocably untied when he took her to a ball at Windsor Castle in the summer of 1980 to celebrate the Queen Mother's 80th birthday. She became infuriated by the way Charles ignored her all evening while he circulated among the many guests, an act he would have regarded as perfectly natural given his upbringing and his perceived duties as a host.

But it was no way to treat a lady. Like some crossed Cinderella she stormed from the ball at midnight, exasperated by her escort's behaviour, never to take the arm of her prince again. Charles's conduct was perhaps not very different from that of the average man unschooled in the mysteries of the female mind, but the sins of the male tend to be magnified tenfold in one with so high a public profile. Shortly afterwards she married another, only to experience separation and divorce in rapid succession. The scene at the ball left Charles a much sadder but somewhat wiser man, chastened in the ways of a woman scorned, but now aged thirty-one with the feeling that life might be passing him by. He had failed, either by choice or by inertia, to acquire a partner from the enormous range to which he had access, and he began to observe wistfully how many otherwise eligible women were already spoken for. He still feared the spectre of divorce, and saw it all around him. He had already passed his own appointed target date of thirty, and although caution was of necessity his watchword, he was also a ditherer who could not make up his mind about what and whom he wanted. Big fish are caught partly by patience, partly by luck, but also largely by determination.

His father was beginning to agitate that it was time his son settled down. In fairness to Prince Philip there is nothing to suggest that he ever tried to push Charles towards any particular partner, and the most that he would ever commit himself to in public was to say: 'You will find that people tend to marry within their own circle. The advantage perhaps is that there is a certain built-in acceptance of the sort of life you are going to lead.'

Charles had known Lady Diana Spencer since her childhood as a vague bit-part player on the far edge of his social stage. They had been neighbours at Sandringham, where the Spencer family had a house, but she was thirteen years younger and had impinged upon his life barely at all. The first meeting that either can remember occurred in 1977, when Charles was paying some attention to her elder sister Sarah and had been invited to join a shooting party at the Spencer family seat, Althorp in Northamptonshire, a stately home which claims to have one of the finest private art collections in Europe, but which to the casual visitor is a stultifyingly tedious family album of Spencers in oils. The two met casually in a ploughed field while Diana was at home on holiday from boarding-school, an unsophisticated and seemingly guileless sixteen-year-old clothed in puppy fat. The meeting appeared at the time to mean little to Charles, but Diana was star-struck, smitten by the vision of a handsome prince. For the next year and more, nothing of significance happened; Diana bided her time and nursed her outrageous dream.

As 1978 drew to a close and the royal family moved in their ordained orbit to Sandringham for the New Year holiday, the Queen invited the Spencer sisters Sarah and Diana as house guests out of concern for their welfare. Their father Earl Spencer had suffered a massive brain haemorrhage which almost killed him, and he was still in hospital under intensive care. That New Year weekend Charles began to take a little more notice, but the relationship was still insignificant; he enjoyed her company, not least because she was unaffected, bright, and laughed at his jokes.

He began to invite her to join parties for dinner or to visit shows in the West End, if only to make up the numbers. Still he paid her only passing attention, but discreet plots were afoot in an attempt to concentrate his mind.

Diana's maternal grandmother was Ruth, Lady Fermoy,

lady-in-waiting to the Queen Mother, a contemporary and one of her oldest and closest friends. The Queen Mother in turn was perhaps Charles's closest confidante, a woman of great kindness, wisdom and good sense to whom the Prince had regularly turned since childhood in moments of personal difficulty. There is of course no record of any conversation between these two elderly and highly influential ladies, but it seems inconceivable that Lady Fermoy, aware of her granddaughter's hero-worship of the heir to the throne, did not bring the matter to the attention of the elder Queen Elizabeth, who in turn was well aware that her grandson was having an outstanding lack of success in attracting a marriage partner.

In spite of the apparent disability of a thirteen-year difference, Diana had a great deal in her favour. She had had no serious boyfriends, and therefore no murky past to be raked up by the Sunday papers; even her uncle went on record in a tabloid newspaper on the day of her engagement to swear that she was a virgin. She was an academic dunce, having failed to pass any O levels or CSEs whatsoever, but she was otherwise bright, witty, kind, healthy, honest and loved children.

The popular image that was subsequently built up of her was of a Cinderella from Bedsit Land who tried on the glass slipper and won her prince. Certainly she had lived in the real world of bus queues, supermarket shopping and baked beans for supper, but her blood was impressively blue. She descended five times over from Charles II by one of his mistresses. She was the Prince of Wales's seventh cousin once removed. They had a common ancestor in William Cavendish, 3rd Duke of Devonshire (1698-1755). Cavendish's son the 4th Duke was the great-great-grandfather of Nina Cavendish-Bentinck, mother of the Queen Mother. Meanwhile Cavendish's daughter Elizabeth had a direct descendant who married the 6th Earl Spencer, Diana's great-grandfather. The Spencers had in the past grown to be one of England's richest families on the back of the country's once pre-eminent wool trade, although none of them had ever before married into royalty. Clearly if such a marriage could now be engineered the family honour would be immensely enhanced. But the engineering must be discreet, low-key, and no more than a gentle encouragement, well-timed. Arranged marriages for royalty are a thing of the past.

Diana had the further advantage of being quite worldly behind her apparent innocence, and it was not acquired solely through flat-sharing with three friends.

When Diana was only six years old her mother had walked out of the family home leaving four children and ending a failing thirteen-year marriage which had begun in Westminster Abbey with the future Queen Elizabeth II among the guests. Although facing accusations of marital cruelty, Diana's father Johnny Spencer had fought, and eventually won, a long and bitter battle in the courts to retain custody of the children. Her mother subsequently married Peter Shand-Kydd, an industrialist who had made a fortune out of wallpaper, and they moved north to run a newsagent's shop in the Scottish west coast holiday resort of Oban and a sheep farm on the nearby island of Seil. Johnny married a divorcee, Raine Countess of Dartmouth; she was the daughter of the larger-than-life romantic novelist Barbara Cartland, who on Diana's engagement gleefully seized the opportunity to extol on television and in newspapers the virtue of virginity. Charles held a terror of divorce in his own eventual marriage, but divorce in his future wife's family was not regarded as any barrier at all. Times had changed, and those who had abandoned marriage no longer carried the mark of Cain on their brow; in the 1950s the Queen's sister had been prevented from marrying a divorced man, but in the 1970s her own divorce went through without the world falling in on her head.

Whatever machinations took place between the two elderly and powerful family ambassadors, Diana's presence in the royal circle became increasingly more evident in the summer of 1980. She turned up to watch Charles play polo at Lord Cowdray's home at Midhurst in Sussex. Her presence was noted by watching pressmen, but no conclusions were drawn; they did not even know who she was. Soon afterwards the Queen invited her aboard the Royal Yacht *Britannia* for Cowes Week, a perfect cover away from prying eyes; again she went unnoticed, indeed unseen. Diana was patiently biding her time. Then, in August, she happened upon a perfect excuse to travel to Balmoral. Her sister Lady Jane Spencer had recently married Robert Fellowes, an assistant private secretary to the Queen, who had the use of a holiday cottage on the Balmoral estate; the couple had retreated there with a new-born baby, and it seemed perfectly natural and inconsequential that Diana should join her there to assist in the chores of early motherhood. Her timing was perfect; family pressure on Charles to marry was growing even greater, and his self-esteem was still stinging from the slap administered to it at the Windsor ball by Anna Wallace. Diana the vestal virgin was ready to sacrifice herself to the Balmoral test.

The test might have been conducted in complete secrecy had it not been for a routine patrol to see how Charles was spending his holiday conducted by James Whitaker, a Fleet Street royal reporter who boasts that he never leaves his own front door without a pair of binoculars round his neck.

The girl sitting on the river bank watching in adoration as Charles fished was rapidly identified, and thereby began six of the most bizarre and hectic months in which even Fleet Street has ever indulged. Reporters and photographers camped day and night on Diana's doorstep and pursued her wherever she went, including to Sandringham for the New Year holiday. But for all the harassment and nuisance she was almost never anything other than calm and charming, even giving the impression at times that she rather enjoyed the thrill of the chase and the subterfuge she employed to throw the hounds off the scent. The newspapermen loved her, and as a result she enjoyed an extremely flattering Press. Other members of the respective families were at times less amused. Significantly, the Queen was furious that the Balmoral test had been rumbled; she clearly knew that a serious romance was afoot. Diana's mother also despaired of the Press attention, and wrote to *The Times* appealing to the newspapers at least not to make up statements which Diana had never uttered. Charles, for his part, managed to conduct the subsequent romance with immense discretion; he never went near Diana's flat, but obliged her to drive hundreds of miles in her own car to secret destinations all over southern England.

During the great paper chase the question often posed, but never satisfactorily answered, was whether Diana had in fact passed the Balmoral test that so many others had failed. The truth seems to be that during that August she was never subjected to its full rigours, and even if she had been she was too determined to catch her man to let it trouble her.

The romance was encouraged – no doubt discreetly – by the Queen Mother and the Queen, both of whom thoroughly approved of Diana, and more openly by two married women with whom Charles was particularly friendly, with whom he felt secure and unthreatened, and with whom he shared confidences, Camilla Parker-Bowles and 'Kanga', Lady Tryon, so nicknamed by Charles after the familiar marsupial of her native Australia. There was no shortage of friends to dispel doubts about the age difference; Diana was at the peak of her childbearing years, and the ability to produce healthy heirs was of paramount importance in a hereditary monarchy. Some friends did however sound a mild alarm over the lack of common interests; Charles was an introverted, solitary, well-read countryman with a love of books and classical music, a thinker whose bachelor ways, at the age of thirty-two, were in some danger of becoming set in concrete, while Diana had absorbed little formal education and took her enjoyment from shopping in the high-class stores of Knightsbridge or from pop music through a personal stereo regularly clamped to her ears.

But the lack of education belied a formidable native wit and perspicacity in the young girl. She knew that to be sure of winning Charles's approval she had to appeal not only to his family – a battle already won – but also to his private secretary Edward Adeane, who was in a position to exert considerable influence on the Prince, even if it was not strictly within the terms of his employment to vet prospective brides.

The sharp-tongued Adeane had been scathing to his master about some of his previous girlfriends, and had taken a particular dislike to Anna Wallace, who reciprocated by disliking Adeane for being an apparently committed bachelor. Diana, however, teased him, flattered him, made him laugh and convinced him of her determination to become Princess of Wales. He was won over, and another barrier fell.

Charles proposed, in traditional old-fashioned style with a request for permission from Diana's father, in his private sitting room at Buckingham Palace, and was immediately accepted. Well aware of what he was asking a young girl to take on he urged her to go away and think about it; Diana went off on a holiday to Australia, where the pursuing Press were fended off by the simple expedient of a straight lie by members of her family claiming that she was somewhere else. She returned with her certainty unshaken, and a decision was taken to announce the engagement at 11 a.m. on 24 February, 1981. By a sweet irony after the frenzied antics of the popular Press, it was *The Times* which had made an exclusive advance announcement of the news earlier that morning, the result of a tip-off to one of the paper's well-connected senior executives.

With Diana flashing her £28,000 diamond and sapphire ring from Garrard, the Crown jewellers, the couple subjected themselves to the obligatory engagement interview conducted by the Press Association's heavily pregnant court correspondent, Grania Forbes. Both declared themselves thrilled; Charles described how he had proposed and had given Diana time to think about her answer. 'Oh, I never had any doubts about it,' she chipped in confidently. It had been settled there and then, said Charles, and the real difficulty had been keeping the secret. He confirmed that the romance had begun in earnest at Balmoral the previous August: 'We began to realize then that there was something in it.' Of their casual meeting in the ploughed field in 1977 he said: 'I remember a very jolly and amusing and bouncy sixteen-year-old. She was very attractive. She was great fun and full of life.'

Diana confirmed that her first impression of her Prince had been 'pretty amazing'. Charles said that they both loved the country, and that he would prefer to spend much more time there.

One thing on which they both agreed was that the age gap did not matter. She said: 'I have never thought about it,' and he said: 'Diana will certainly keep me young; you are only as old as you think you are. But I shall be exhausted.' They also thought that they had a lot in common, a fond hope not subsequently borne out. 'Diana is a great outdoor-loving sort of person,' said Charles. 'She's a very energetic character as well.' Diana said: 'We both love music and dancing and we both have the same sense of humour.' Diana, the Prince acknowledged, was 'a great skier'.

To a television interviewer who asked how they fell in love, Charles said: 'It was gradual. I began to realize what was going through my mind and hers in particular. These things happen; it was a gradual business.' To Miss Forbes they repeated that they were 'thrilled'. And were they, she asked them, in love? 'Of course,' said Diana instantly. Charles, as though still plagued by uncertainty, added the curious coda: 'Whatever "in love" means.' Cautious to the last.

Everyone who could be found who had ever known Diana was also interviewed that day. Her father Earl Spencer declared: 'Diana is a giver, not a taker. She was always a delightful child, and as a baby she could have won any beauty competition. Publicity doesn't worry her. She'll take it all in her stride. She's very practical and down to earth, and a very good housewife.' Her flatmate Carolyn Pride described how Diana broke the engagement news: 'There was a lot of shouting and we all burst into tears. It was all very emotional. We knew about the engagement soon after Prince Charles proposed. But it wasn't hard to keep the secret; we never dreamed of telling anyone. It's not the kind of thing one does to one's friends. We have been ever so discreet; that's the way we were brought up.' Charles's former companion Lady Sarah Spencer, by then herself married, could barely contain herself. 'I'm Cupid; I introduced them,' she burbled, adding more sternly that her own relationship with Charles had been 'totally platonic' despite the fact that no one had believed her.

Simon Berry, a Spencer family friend who occasionally joined Diana's skiing parties, recalled that as long ago as 1979 Diana had confessed to him that her ambition was 'to be a successful dancer – or maybe the Princess of Wales'. He disclosed that she had lowbrow tastes in television viewing, including the frightful soap opera *Crossroads*, and he added: 'She has broken the hearts of dozens of young men. Chaps would meet her and instantly fall in love. Many have tried to win her – sending her flowers and begging for a date. But she always politely declined.'

The nation was so awash with secondhand sentiment that at times it felt as though it was raining cream buns. Only William Hamilton, the veteran anti-royalist MP, had the bravado to dismiss it all as 'mush', and the Communist Party's *Morning Star*, alone among daily newspapers, struck a sour note under the headline *Don't Do It, Diana*: 'Lady Diana Spencer is to sacrifice her independence to a domineering layabout for the sake of a few lousy foreign holidays. As the future Queen of England she can expect a fair bit of first-class travel and a lot of attention, but with a £100,000 home of her own and a steady job as an exclusive nursery nurse, who needs it? *Morning Star* readers may find it hard to sympathize with the daughter of a millionaire earl with a Buckingham Palace future. But the "suitable bride" treatment she has received at the hands of the press and even her own family degrades not only her, but all women.

'Most obnoxious have been the delicate assurances of her virginity. Any illusions Lady Diana may have about being a person, the owner of her own body and sexuality, should have been sharply shattered by her father and uncle who have publicly guaranteed their valuable commodity will be delivered to the Prince in a state of unsullied innocence.' The paper quoted genealogists who enthused at Diana bringing Stuart blood back into the royal line, and at her ability to have a large number of children if necessary.

'Perhaps we are carping,' said the *Morning Star*, 'but surely even she deserves to be regarded with more dignity than a pedigree Friesian cow.'

10

A Princely Marriage

ON 29 JULY, 1981 the newspaper writers reached for their copies of Walter Bagehot, the nineteenth-century theologian of the British monarchy, to find suitable quotations to decorate their descriptions of the wedding of Charles and Diana. 'A princely marriage,' wrote Bagehot, 'is the brilliant edition of a universal fact, and as such it rivets mankind.' One million of mankind lining the processional route, and a further 750 million worldwide watching on television, were riveted by the spectacle, particularly when it was reduced to intimate and human scale by the couple stumbling over their lines. Diana vowed to take in matrimony Philip Charles Arthur George rather than Charles Philip Arthur George who in turn, fully intending to share all his worldly goods, promised instead that 'all thy goods with thee I share.' When the couple kissed on the balcony of Buckingham Palace, the vicarious pleasure of the crowd was complete, and they roared 'Nice one, Charlie!' No couple could have stepped out on the marriage road with a greater fund of goodwill behind them, and the bridegroom said afterwards that the day's events had made them extraordinarily proud to be British.

Few couples ever did so well for wedding presents, the glittering haul insured for £4 million when it went on public display at St James's Palace but more accurately valued at nearer £11 million. Arab princes vied to outshine each other in the ostentation of their gifts; the Amir of Qatar gave a set of diamond earrings, ring and necklace for Diana, while the Emir of Bahrain countered with a solid gold diamond-encrusted model of an Arab dhow. Ronald and Nancy Reagan gave a £40,000 cut glass vase which now adorns the hall of the Wales's Kensington Palace apartments. John Broadwood, piano manufacturers, gave a £7,000 boudoir grand in spite of being cautioned that Charles plays barely a note. Two rival German manufacturers each gave a fitted kitchen, one of which ended up in the Kensington Palace nursery. Pearls descended from Fiji, ivory from Nigeria, carpets from India. But wedding gifts often fail to include basic necessities; the Queen led Diana to the vaults of Buckingham Palace, which are stacked to the roof with the spoils of a hundred royal tours and past anniversaries, and invited her to help herself to any furniture and knick-knacks that she desired. A groaning vanload of booty subsequently made its way to Highgrove.

Charles was not content to leave the wedding arrangements in the hands of the Lord Chamberlain, the traditional producer, director and stage manager of all royal ceremonials (except for coronations and state funerals, which are the province of the Earl Marshal). He had very firm ideas on what he wanted, and the concept and overall planning was largely his own.

He conceived the wedding ceremony as a joyful, populist musical extravaganza; he chose the music programme himself in consultation with Sir David Willcocks, Director of the Royal College of Music, and assembled three orchestras, the Bach Choir, and the New Zealand opera singer Kiri Te Kanawa to perform it. He made the Lord Chamberlain's life difficult by insisting that the ceremony be held, not in Westminster Abbey as was traditional, but in St Paul's Cathedral. The Abbey is Gothic, and harbours a certain sepulchral gloom; Wren's cathedral is a triumph of post-Renaissance light and airiness, with better (although far from perfect) acoustics for musical performance, and room for many more guests. The Abbey seemed additionally inappropriate to him on the grounds that, less than two years previously, it had played host to the funeral service for his beloved Mountbatten, and the memory of that tragic day had not left him.

The problem with St Paul's against the Abbey was that it was three times further from Buckingham Palace and Lord Maclean, the Lord Chamberlain, doubted whether, in those days of savage cuts in defence expenditure, he could summon a sufficient number of soldiers to line the route. 'Well,' said Charles with irrefutable logic, 'stand them further apart.'

Charles's instincts were quite right. The soldiers stood further apart, and the longer route made room for hundreds of thousands of additional sightseers, who cheered everything that passed including the dustcarts on the trail of the Household Cavalry horses, to watch the procession.

The day was a triumph, and the world gasped when Diana stepped from her carriage to reveal her ivory silk taffeta wedding dress designed by the Emanuels, its creased train not entirely hiding the fact that tension and worry had shed more than a stone (nearly four kilograms) from her tall frame. At least some of the tension was released by the time the couple made their return drive to the Palace in an open landau; Diana was seen to be singing, and lip-readers watching the television close-ups deciphered the song as a popular ice-cream commercial, *Just one Cornetto*. The wedding, in the form insisted on by Charles, had cost some £150,000 to stage, but sales of the souvenir programme raised £500,000 for charity work with the handicapped, it being the International Year of the Disabled, and the tourist revenue to London doubtless far exceeded even the value of the wedding presents.

As mentioned earlier, Charles and Diana spent their wedding night at Broadlands. It was a rather inevitable choice, given the Prince's liking for tradition, order and routine. His own parents had begun their honeymoon there in 1947, and besides, Mountbatten's old home was such a treasure house of happy memories for Charles. Any bride would have relished the romantic setting of the large four-poster bed in the Portico Room, but not perhaps the events of the following morning. Charles left his bride, picked up one of his late great-uncle's rods, and made for one of the finest salmon beats in southern England on the River Test that flows through the estate. It was a fitting nemesis that he caught nothing.

Two days at Broadlands were followed by two weeks cruising the Mediterranean in *Britannia*, which steamed a secret and evasive course lest any photographers harboured thoughts of pursuit. Great efforts were made to ensure privacy, to the extent that the entire crew, with the exception of an official Royal Navy photographer who could be relied on to perform only when ordered, were forbidden to bring cameras on board. The crew was all-male; indeed Diana's dresser Evelyn Dagley was the only other woman on board. The cruise did Charles and Diana a great deal of good, unwinding them from the immense strains of such a grand and public marriage ceremony and all the stresses of the preceding months. They returned looking exceptionally brown, fit and well and, more significantly, looking happy. Charles was obviously delighted with his wife, touching her, holding her and gazing at her in a way that he had not done in public, and does increasingly rarely nowadays.

The second half of the honeymoon was less idyllic. Diana had escaped the sternest rigours of the Balmoral test during her period of courting there the previous year, but it could not be put off for ever, and the time had come to face it. To rejoin his family there for their summer holiday seemed perfectly natural to Charles; he had always done it, and saw no reason to break the habit of a lifetime. His family thought it a good idea too; it would give Diana a settling-in period with her in-laws, absorbing more of the royal routine she would perforce have to acquaint herself with, and would provide several more weeks of privacy for the couple before they launched into a public life.

Balmoral is among Charles's favourite places in the entire world, a retreat ideally suited to solitude and contemplation, and in late summer and autumn the heavily wooded slopes of Deeside exhibit a rare beauty, vibrant with muted colour that is peculiarly Scottish. It was the creation of Victoria and her consort Albert, a man of considerable artistic energy and talent. The couple fell in love with Scotland on their first visit to Edinburgh in 1842, and their affection grew on subsequent forays as guests of various landed gentry in Perthshire and the Western Highlands, fuelled by their acquaintance with the romanticism of Sir Walter Scott who had done much to rescue the nation's sense of identity after languishing in post-Jacobite disgrace and referred to in polite London society simply as 'North Britain'. Victoria and Albert bought the Balmoral estate sight unseen in 1848, and were not disappointed. They relished the clear dry Aberdeenshire air and the intensely cultivated, rich and grand Deeside scenery because it reminded them of parts of their ancestral Germany. The estate had a small and inadequate castle; it was demolished and replaced by the present much larger one, designed by Albert with the help of William Smith, the Aberdeen City Architect, in an elaborate copy of the traditional Scottish Baronial style. When Victoria heard that trees on the neighbouring estate of Ballochbuie were to be felled for timber she bought that as well to preserve it, and the present estate covers an immense moorland swathe of 50,000 acres (20,000 hectares), from the banks of the Dee to the 3,876-foot (1154-metre) peak of Lochnagar, whose 'steep frowning glories' so stirred Byron.

After Albert's death in 1861 Victoria remained deeply attached to her Scottish home and to her servant John Brown, who personified her romantic vision of Highlanders. Her son Edward VII did not much care for Balmoral, but George V, George VI and the present Queen have all fallen for its scenic beauty, its peace, and its distance both geographical and spiritual from the strictures of official London life.

Not so Diana, who found its atmosphere so removed form the bustling city sociability of the world of the Sloane Ranger that it might as well have been on another planet. In late summer the moors come alive with sport, when grouse and deer go in danger of their lives and hillwalkers find their accustomed free access impeded by warnings not to intrude on the stalking. She grew restless and bored; tramping all day

The dress that launched a thousand gasps, its ivory silk taffeta train spilling down the steps of St Paul's. *(Eric Shaw)*

ABOVE The wedding-day reception that the couple said made them 'extraordinarily proud to be British'.

BELOW On honeymoon aboard *Britannia*, the newlyweds entertain President and Mrs Anwar Sadat of Egypt. Sadat was assassinated soon afterwards. *(MOD)*

RIGHT First-born. Proud parents leave the Lindo Wing of St Mary's Hospital, Paddington, with the newly arrived Prince William. *(PA)*

BELOW Family and godparents at the christening of Prince William in the Music Room at Buckingham Palace, 1982. Standing behind the baby's mother, grandmother and great-grandmother are (l to r): Prince Philip, Princess Alexandra, Princess Anne (seated), King Constantine of Greece, Lady Susan Hussey, Charles, Lord Romsey, the Duchess of Westminster, Earl Spencer, Mrs Frances Shand-Kydd (seated), Ruth Lady Fermoy, Sir Laurens van der Post, and Prince Edward. *(Syndication International)*

LEFT Landlord meets tenant on a Duchy of Cornwall farm at Yardworthy, near Chagford, Devon, in 1983. *(Western Morning News)*

BELOW You'll never walk alone, at least not in Australia. Arriving at the Civic Hall, Brisbane, during the 1983 tour, surrounded by detectives, private secretary Edward Adeane (behind Charles, with glasses), lady-in-waiting Anne Beckwith-Smith (behind Diana) and assorted Australians. *(Roy Letkey)*

RIGHT The next Supreme Governor of the Church of England wanted to join Pope John Paul II at Mass during the 1985 Italian visit, but had to be content instead with a Vatican private audience.

BELOW Reunited with William and Harry on the Royal Yacht *Britannia* at the end of the 1985 tour of Italy. *(Kent Gavin)*

ABOVE The Mounties always get their man to dress up. Recapturing Klondike days at a restored Hudson's Bay Company fort near Edmonton, Alberta, in 1983.

BELOW 'You put your right foot out . . .' Well, you have to, really, when you are created Tench Lord of Manus, Papua New Guinea, 1984.

ABOVE An award for gallantry at polo, Smith's Lawn, Windsor, 1984.

BELOW Polo prizes at Windsor, 1985. Other winners only get a cup.
(Kent Gavin)

RIGHT Australia loved the new Fred and Ginger in 1986. But Ginger never thought to wear her necklace as a headband. *(Kent Gavin)*

BELOW 'Darling, he's got more teeth than Harry.' Warily inspecting a two-year-old at the Darwin Crocodile Farm during the Australian bicentennial tour, 1988. *(J S Library)*

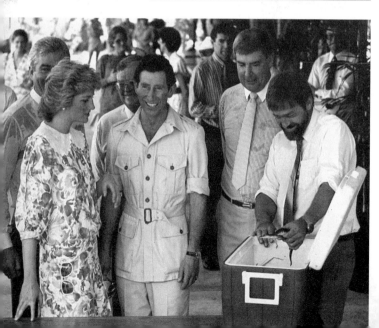

through tussocks of ankle-breaking heather and thigh-high bracken for the purpose of killing wildlife held no appeal for her. Charles's assertion in their engagement interview that both were country-lovers might have held in the tame domestic setting of Gloucestershire, but it was being severely strained beneath Byron's wild and majestic crags. It was a stern lesson in what her future life would hold, for her in-laws and to some extent her husband carried on with their accustomed lives while making little concession to her presence. She invited one or two of her old friends to join her, but the opportunities for shopping or night-clubbing were seriously restricted. She knew well enough, however, that to leave early would invite torrents of speculation on marriage difficulties, and her only escape was a brief visit to London, supposedly for shopping but in fact to have her pregnancy confirmed by George Pinker, the Queen's gynaecologist.

Thankfully back in London at last, she had to overcome a creeping dismay that as a wife she was in many respects redundant. Charles had always had staff to dance attendance upon his every need: to cook his meals, wake him in the morning, bring him his breakfast, lay out his shirts and even choose his clothes for the day, clean his shoes, run his bath, answer his telephone, keep track of his appointments. He had been a bachelor, and a deeply conservative one, too long readily to change his ways. However, Diana determined that he must be transformed into a married man.

She bought him mildly adventurous shirts from chainstores to alleviate his dull squareness, and brighter ties to accompany them. She even persuaded him to break from the tradition of black lace-up shoes and appear in public in his first pair of slip-ons. He remains essentially conservative in dress, clinging to trousers with turn-ups so long that they returned to fashion, and insisting on a shirt and tie even when attending rock concerts.

Soon after her arrival in Charles's life the first of a long list of his staff began to leave. Among the first was his outrageously homosexual valet Stephen Barry, who had been with the Prince for twelve years and who subsequently died of Aids in the United States. Rumour was rife at the time that he and Diana had had a row, and that she had objected to him entering the bedroom to open the curtains while she was still in her nightdress. Barry's own version was that he resigned of his own free will and on good terms, having found that the arrival of a wife in his master's life had made many of his own duties superfluous.

Many other departures followed, including that of Diana's detective Chief Inspector Paul Officer, who had served Charles as his bodyguard for many years beforehand and had become a close friend. Another royal protection officer took early retirement; John Maclean was a hilarious, uninhibited Glaswegian, a man of such legendary dishevelled untidiness that beside him Bob Geldof resembled Fred Astaire. Domestic staff left, and Diana's brother, Viscount Althorp, admitted in a women's magazine interview that she had 'weeded out some of the hangers-on'. But it is nonsense to suggest that she sacked staff by the dozen, or even that she directly drove them out. Many simply found, as Stephen Barry did, that the old familiar order had changed somewhat; there were new practices and new routines. Many had been there for years, and felt it was time to move on. Some left for the cast-iron reason that wages in the royal households are notoriously mean; even the Wales's butler has to take on outside contract work on his days off to supplement his income.

Diana was certainly not the prime mover in the most significant departure of all, that of Edward Adeane, although the bachelor Adeane is reputed to have once exploded that if he saw just one more knitted bootee he would go quite mad. Charles and Adeane had long been out of sympathy, and the impeccably correct private secretary found his advice and guidance being listened to less and less as Charles found guides and mentors outside his immediate circle and broke away from the suffocation of tradition. The two began to disagree quite openly, until Adeane felt that there was no point in continuing in the job. He left suddenly late in 1984 to return to his more lucrative practice as an eminent libel lawyer, without even waiting for a successor to be appointed.

His departure left a serious gap in Charles's staff which David Roycroft, an assistant private secretary, struggled to fill for some months. There was no obvious candidate of whom Charles approved to fill a post whose reputation had been somewhat tarnished by a poor salary and a difficult master who was not always willing to heed advice. Charles wanted someone who was at once efficient in administration and business – he has a Scotsman's interest in money – but who would not order him about unduly, or attempt to smother him with his influence. Yet it had to be someone who, when the order to jump was given, jumped without question. A professional headhunter was set to the task, and came up with three possible names. Of these, Charles eventually chose Sir John Riddell, a fifty-one-year-old merchant banker with First Boston Credit Suisse in London and a part-time deputy chairman of the Independent Broadcasting Authority. He had the right background, being a baronet from an old and vaguely aristocratic Northumberland family and educated at Eton and Oxford. He had no previous experience of royal employment, but he was a well-regarded professional financier. He was also sociable, with an easy manner, and unlike Adeane was a family man with two young children and a house in a fashionable part of Kensington in addition to his northern family seat.

Sir John was frankly astonished to be offered the job, a position he had never contemplated in his life, but he was flattered and intrigued by the challenge. Since moving to Kensington Palace in 1985 he has kept his head firmly down, but it is difficult to resist the impression that his influence over the Prince is no greater than slight.

With the departure of David Roycroft to become an executive at Independent Television News, Charles acquired two new assistant private secretaries: Humphrey Mews, a bachelor and career civil servant from the Foreign Office, and Rupert Fairfax, a young City financial expert from the aggressive Hanson Trust conglomerate, who was initially hired for his business expertise to help Charles run his burgeoning portfolio of trusts and charities, but who now accompanies him on most of his foreign visits as a general organizer and factotum. Today the Prince's staff is almost entirely cleansed of the old-style courtiers who still surround the Queen, a further indication that the Wales roadshow is run very much as a production independent of Buckingham Palace.

Charles had moved his quarters from Buckingham Palace in 1979, after a decaying and abandoned wing of Kensington Palace had been restored by the Government's Property Services Agency at a cost to the taxpayer of £900,000. Built as a private residence in 1605, Kensington Palace was bought for 18,000 guineas in 1690 by King William of Orange, who decided to escape from the damp of London to the sweeter, drier air of Kensington. He commissioned a major reconstruction from Sir Christopher Wren, and the result was substantially what remains today, pleasing in proportion and scale, elegant and inviting with warm red brick and deep windows. Besides the Waleses, its apartments house Princess Margaret, the Duke and Duchess of Gloucester, and Prince and Princess Michael of Kent. The interior decoration of the Wales's quarters shows the influence of Diana, who commissioned her South African-born designer friend Dudley Poplak to alter some of the Government's colour schemes after he had carried out similar work at her request at Highgrove.

In spite of patient coaching in the niceties of royal behaviour at the practised hand of the Queen Mother, Diana's early months on the public stage as Princess of Wales were a severe trial, largely because of the unremitting Press attention. The Queen became so alarmed at the effect it was having on her daughter-in-law that she summoned newspaper editors to Buckingham Palace and requested them to lay off. One editor, he of the *Sun*, declined to attend on the grounds that he would not be a party to any deals. Another, he of the *News of the World*, offered the Queen the advice that, if Diana wished to go shopping for a packet of wine gums, she should send a servant instead. He was rewarded with one of the monarch's iciest stares, and dismissal from his post soon afterwards. The worry and pressure kept Diana painfully thin, although rumours that she was suffering from the slimmer's disease of *anorexia nervosa* were greatly exaggerated; she had simply surrendered her appetite to tension.

Yet she was a great public success from the beginning, although photographers cursed her habit of wearing wide-brimmed hats and constantly staring at her feet. Meeting crowds on walkabout initially terrified her; she began to overcome her fear by always making for the children in the throng. Charles began to notice, with some dismay, that it was her the crowds had come to see, and not him. Not that he was vain, but he found that if he made a speech when they were together at a function, his message was entirely ignored by newspapers and television which were obsessed with Diana. His self-confidence, never strong at the best of times, was being further undermined.

Press attention plumbed the deeper abysses of intrusion in February 1982 when the Princess, by now obviously pregnant, refused on the grounds of her condition to undertake the traditional royal skiing holiday, and persuaded her husband to take her instead to the relaxing sunshine of the Bahamas. Unfortunately two newspapers learned of their destination and pursued them to the tiny island of Windermere, where they snatched pictures of her on the beach wearing only a bikini which made no attempt to conceal her bulging abdomen. Charles was furious, and even the Queen was moved to issue a statement that they were 'in the worst possible taste'. Diana was said to have been much less concerned; pregnant or not, she has never really minded having her body admired.

The birth of Prince William on 21 June, 1982 brought the determination of Diana into full view. She was adamant that the birth should be natural, with no administered inducements to suit the convenience of hospital staff, and she refused to have any truck with traditional royal nannies with their strict Presbyterian ways and starched white aprons. She hired instead, on the recommendation of Princess Margaret whose friends the Tennant family had spoken highly of her, Barbara Barnes, a nanny of no formal training but considerable practical experience. Diana had wanted the birth to be at home, but for once she had to bow before the insistence of George Pinker, who had booked a bed for her in St Mary's Hospital, Paddington, before she even had a chance to object. Home births were fine, Pinker explained, until something went wrong.

Charles was delighted to be a father. He had always had a particular empathy with children, and had taken a close interest in his brothers and sister from the moment he was first allowed to see them. Children were the perfect people with whom to be uninhibited and goonish. He was present at the birth of William – and subsequently Harry – after suitable instruction from a teacher of the National Childbirth Trust, and declared to the massed reporters outside the hospital: 'I'm obviously thrilled and delighted. Sixteen hours is a long time to wait. It's rather a grown-up thing, I find – rather a shock to the system.'

When the choice of godparents was announced, it was clear that whatever determination Diana might have had to include her friends and family had been almost entirely squashed. Only one of the six was her choice: Natalia, Duchess of Westminster, an old personal friend. The others were obvious Windsor nominees: Lady Susan Hussey, lady-in-waiting to the Queen; Laurens van der Post; the deposed King Constantine of Greece, who lives in London and is a distant relative but close friend of the royal family; Mountbatten's heir Lord Romsey; and Princess Alexandra, a royal family member of whom Charles has always been fond. A similar pattern prevailed when Prince Harry's godparents were announced; only one, her former flatmate Carolyn Pride (by then Mrs William Bartholomew), was the obvious choice of the child's mother.

Apart from the natural pleasure that a firstborn gives its parents, the birth of William did Diana a particular piece of good; it made life a great deal easier for her in her public appearances, giving her an inexhaustible topic of conversation which, six years later, remains largely undiminished. Her self-confidence grew, and with it Charles's feeling that he was being ever more overshadowed. She also learned to stop reading, and fretting over, every last one of the millions of words the newspapers publish about her.

When, in 1983, the couple were scheduled to make their first major overseas tour together to Australia and New Zealand, Diana once more exercised her mother's rights against the might of Palace precedent; she decided that William should go with them. It had not happened before; royal children had always been left behind when their parents made long and arduous visits to the Colonies. But William went, looked after in a well-guarded house near Sydney while his parents criss-crossed the continent and flew back to see him every few days. The tour was an exceptionally gruelling one lasting all of six weeks, and exhausted them both. It was largely drawn up by Edward Adeane, who appeared to think that his master had been slacking in his duties. Charles was tired and irritable by the end of it, not least because the Australian media had more or less ignored him and had concentrated almost exclusively on 'Di and Will'. Diana, however, was an immense success, and set back the cause of Australian republicanism by several years. They liked her because she was glamorous, entirely natural, and always spoke to children, giving uninhibited answers to endless questions about the number of Will's teeth and the state of his crawling prowess.

Australians have mixed feelings about royalty. Their Head of State is a woman who lives on the other side of the world, and who by the summer of 1988 had paid them a mere dozen official visits during her entire reign. Their economic and political ties with the old country have become a great deal weaker since Britain joined the European Community, and as the Royal Navy no longer rules the waves enforcing the *Pax Britannica*, Australia's defence treaty is now with the United States. The stream of young Australians making the obligatory two-year pilgrimage to London has declined as new regulations have made work permits harder to obtain and the American west coast has proved a more enticing lure for the adventurous. Nearly forty per cent of Australia's population now has roots outside the British Isles, and Melbourne claims to be the largest Greek-speaking city in the world outside Greece.

Republicanism is constantly discussed, but has never quite arrived. Too many Australians still feel they are an essentially white, Christian, democratic island in the sea of foreign cultures like those of Indonesia, China and Japan, for the ties to be broken entirely. As the political links have slackened, their relationship towards the British monarchy has even become easier and more tolerant in some ways, as it no longer has so many political overtones in Australia. For that reason if for no other, the Waleses are exceptionally popular there, even if they are now regarded more as soap opera megastars than representatives of the Australian Crown.

As time wore on, Prince Charles naturally wished to spend as much time as possible with his children, a desire perhaps compounded by his frustration at being ignored while his wife stole all the limelight. His diary of official engagements became a great deal thinner, which was one of the reasons for Adeane's departure. Another was that the schedule being drawn up for the Waleses' tour of Italy in 1985 indicated that it was going to be a visit of almost unalloyed pleasure, lasting for three weeks but unusually light on the worthy tasks of opening trade fairs, inspecting the work of the British Council, and other such solemn duties that Charles is expected to perform when abroad. It was in fact the Grand Tour that he had always wanted to undertake, to soak up the music of Donizetti and Verdi in its natural surroundings, to drink deep of the fountain of classical architecture, the glories of Rome and the Renaissance. And he wanted to introduce civilization to his wife, to wean her away from her personal stereo and her other uncultured tastes.

But the tour was not without controversy. Charles, who

had corresponded with Pope John Paul II for some time on wide-ranging issues of world peace and unity among the Christian churches, felt no qualms at all about calling at the Vatican, as heads of state and other notables regularly do; he felt that it was a reciprocal gesture after having met the Pope during his British tour in 1982.

He also had a further purpose. He saw his visit as an opportunity to make an attempt at bridging the ecumenical chasm that divides the Church of England and the Church of Rome. It was a popular theme of the moment, given impetus by the Pontiff praying with Robert Runcie, senior clergyman of the Anglican church, at the altar of Canterbury Cathedral during the 1982 visit. Through Runcie, Charles had asked if the Pope might say public mass for him in St Peter's Basilica; Runcie reported back that the Vatican thought such a public gesture towards the inheritor of the throne of the heretic Henry VIII might be politically unwise, and suggested instead the compromise of an early morning mass with the Pope in his private chapel, followed by breakfast. Runcie could see no objection.

However, the Queen could. As Head of the Church of England she might herself have no objection to this gesture of compromise between her own church and that of Rome, but she was well aware that several million of her subjects, particularly those living in Northern Ireland, were members of much less compromising Christian faiths than her own, and that many of them regarded the head of the Roman Catholic Church as being on a par with the Scarlet Woman of Babylon. Certainly Protestants in Northern Ireland, and to a lesser extent in some areas of Scotland, would have regarded the heir to the Protestant throne of Great Britain participating in a Roman Catholic mass as an immense betrayal.

It was a dimension which Charles, in his well-meaning naïvety, had seemingly not thought of, although to be fair to him the Archbishop of Canterbury had regarded it as perfectly feasible. Six days before the Italian tour began, the Vatican received a letter from Buckingham Palace cancelling the mass. Charles was frustrated and angry at having to make do with an uncontroversial audience with the Pope for himself and his wife. At least the furore, when it broke, diverted for a day or two the Italian obsession with Diana's clothes.

There was no such souring when, later in the same year, Charles and Diana visited the United States; only the manic cries of those nearly killed in the rush to lay hands on tickets for a charity dinner. The dinner, at Palm Beach, Florida, had been arranged by Charles's friend and benefactor, Dr Armand Hammer, with entrance at about $20,000 a head. It was royal soap opera at its glittering, ludicrous height; the actress Joan Collins, who loses no opportunity to upstage the Princess of Wales or anyone else, secured herself admission and insisted on dancing with Charles. He was too much of a gentleman to refuse. No Florida hostess dared admit that she had failed to acquire a ticket; excuses varied from: 'We booked a cruise and it was too late to cancel' to 'My husband had to have his gall bladder out and the surgeon said it just couldn't wait.' At the end of the dinner Hammer handed over a cheque for the benefit of United World Colleges, written out for $1,000,000.

Armand Hammer has been a friend of Charles's for some years, and an exceedingly generous benefactor to a great many of the Prince's causes, including the raising of the Tudor warship *Mary Rose* from the bed of Portsmouth harbour, and the Transglobe Expedition of 1979-1982 led by Sir Ranulph Twistleton-Wickham-Fiennes, described by Hammer himself as 'perhaps the oddest of Prince Charles's enthusiams for which he lassoed my support'. The remarkable Dr Hammer is a great admirer of Charles, and has kept him informed on a wide range of issues with which he is familiar, from North Sea Oil to the Soviet Politburo; but he has never graduated to the position of guru, and is not one of those who has left a deep philosophical imprint on the Prince.

Hammer wrote in his autobiography: 'It is said that Prince Charles was inhibited by shyness and uncertainties in his adolescence. I never knew him then, but there remained, when I first met him in the late Seventies, some subtle but obvious signs of uneasiness in his attitude to himself. His manner was unfailingly warm, his sense of humour keen and his intelligence as shining as a beacon. But his constant fiddling with his cufflinks and with the signet ring on the little finger of his right hand and his curious sudden gestures of hand and arm suggested that he was not fully comfortable with himself. Perhaps – I am guessing – he seemed less than sure that he was entirely worthy of the immense prestige and privilege of his birth; perhaps he did not know exactly what he should be doing with himself while he remained heir to the throne.'

Lunching with Charles and Diana at Highgrove some years later, Hammer found a somewhat changed man. 'When we were about to leave, Prince Charles suddenly disappeared and returned to present us with several boxes of plump, sweet strawberries which he had picked himself as a present to us. I think his pleasure in those strawberries tells you all you need to know about him. He was more delighted to give us berries he had grown, and picked with his own hands, than if they had been jewels from the family vault.'

Certainly Charles would rather be picking strawberries from his Highgrove garden than being the centre of attention – bar one – at a glitzy show business carnival. He appeared to endure his American tour through clenched teeth, putting up with it only because United World Colleges were to benefit so handsomely. Occasionally on foreign tours, even prosaic ones to places like Portugal to commemorate the anniversary of Britain's oldest alliance, he can look lost, bored, and distinctly puzzled as to why he is there at all. His preferred place of work is his study at Kensington Palace, seated amidst an unholy clutter of paper and in front of a packed Georgian bookcase heavy with works of philosophy, with an open fire burning in winter. Family photographs jostle for space with treasured personal mementoes, including the flag of the Polish trade union Solidarity, a model of the American space shuttle, and a small silver replica of the wooden minesweeper he briefly commanded, HMS *Bronington*. The room is reminiscent of a professor's study, its donnish air reinforced by the view from its windows into the quiet Palace quadrangle.

No secretary nor servant would dare move any piece of paper in Prince Charles's study. He is fussy, pernickety even, about details; everything must be right and to his liking, and he will yield easily to moodiness, irritability and even brief flashes of temper if his path is crossed or his desires frustrated. He is the Prince of Wales, and others are not. He will frequently leave pained notes for staff, heavy with underlining, if he finds a familiar object has been moved from its accustomed place, or even a radiator turned up in the bathroom without his approval. He works hard, even obsessively, when he is not on holiday, travelling abroad, or weekending at Highgrove, and he is quick to make it known that even the smallest spanners in his works are most unwelcome.

When at Kensington Palace, which is most weekdays when he is not travelling to a public engagement, he will often be at his desk before 8.30, and is sometimes still there until late into the evening. His working days are regularly broken by informal lunch parties, to which he invites a wide and eclectic cross-section of guests in order to pick their brains, much as the Queen and Prince Philip do at Buckingham Palace.

After a period, when his children were very young, of winding down his public life and withdrawing into himself and his family, he has become revitalized. He earned the disapproval of his father for dropping close to the bottom of the league table of the royal family's public engagements published annually in *The Times*: Philip has always maintained the strong belief that the family firm should be seen to be earning its keep. During 1987 Charles was fourth in the family league table with 276 engagements, after the Queen with 432, his energetic sister Anne with 367, and Philip with 322. Diana, by comparison, clocked up 180 appearances.

A more valid reason for Charles's return to a high public profile is his wholehearted espousal of a cause and a crusade, that of improving the lot of the inner cities, their residents and their architecture. He is gratified that once again he is being listened to and reported, without the serious message being smothered by his wife's frocks.

Sometimes, however, the popular Press seems wilfully determined not to understand him. During the summer of 1987 he spent three days in secret on the island of Berneray in the Outer Hebrides learning at first hand about the hard marginal subsistence life of a Scottish crofter, which for a man who is landlord to dozens of English farms might seem a perfectly reasonable thing to do. But, under the headline 'A Loon Again', it was taken as evidence that he was well and truly away with the fairies.

Sharply – but not always painfully – conscious that his own world is one apart, he has an insatiable curiosity about how other people live, and feels it relevant and proper to find out. He said himself of his Hebridean expedition: 'I went to try to find out what it's actually like to be a crofter, and also to find out what problems people have in life; it's easier to do that in somewhere like an island than it is to do it in the middle of Glasgow.'

Press interest in Diana has abated, but not much. Predictions by some editors that the reading public was sated with her and that the Duchess of York would replace her as the star of the media have not come to pass. Diana has carved out her own public niche; although her workload is much less than that of her husband and, when at home, not much greater than that of the average Lady Mayoress, and although she may never win awards for public speaking, she has gained widespread approval and respect for her manner.

She is particularly at home with children and the sick, and has brought precious moments to the dying in her visits to hospices; she does not shirk from visiting a ward of Aids sufferers. She has a knack of being entirely unaffected, always interested, and never condescending. Her conversation is of the everyday, of children, television and embroidery, and those who meet her appreciate her the more for it. Her natural defence is self-deprecation; she will quite happily tell people that she is as thick as a plank, and they know at once she is not. The truly stupid are as thick as *two* short planks. It is no part of her duty to weep in public, but she was reduced to tears by a dying young woman who told her: 'I want to live long enough to see the flowers of spring.'

Charles and Diana have earned much approval for their spur-of-the-moment visits, usually conducted on Charles's initiative, to the victims of accidents or natural disasters, and their presence certainly proves uplifting to those who have suffered. Yet they often seem to function best in public when they are apart and pursuing their own interests; Charles frequently looks uneasy when accompanying his wife, as though still afraid that he is no more than an irrelevant appendage to her glamour. They have in fact reached an accommodation of pursuing separate lives to some extent; Charles will often travel abroad alone, sometimes for business and sometimes for pleasure, and with the royal family calender deeply ingrained in his soul he will still not give up his precious time at Balmoral, even if that means being there alone.

Charles was exceptionally distressed when, in the autumn of 1987, some newspapers noticed that he had spent upwards of a month at Balmoral without seeing either his wife or his children, who remained in the south. Rumours of a failing marriage and the possibility of divorce were fuelled, but as Charles himself has said often enough, divorce is not really an option for him. Nor was it for a moment contemplated, and anyone who imagined that it was fails to understand the mores and lifestyle of the English aristocracy, who can pursue quite separate lives, with long periods of separation, and still remain perfectly firmly married. To name but one, Prince Philip was hardly a slippers-and-pipe man himself at the same stage of his married life. Yet the ghost of a suspicion remained over Charles that it was an odd family man who did not even wish to see his children, of whom he was once so fond, for such a long period.

The speculation hurt Charles, who regards his married life

as an exceedingly private affair. Not long afterwards, reading an overblown account of a minor shotgun incident which happened some distance away from him when he was out with the Belvoir Hunt, he told one of his companions: 'It's inevitable that I get this sort of publicity, and I don't really mind. I just wish they would not write about my marriage.'

Unfortunately, they probably always will. They will note that Diana has learned the lesson of a million wives before her, that marriage is 100 per cent hard work, only twenty per cent of it from the man. They will note too that she has faced additional problems of which ordinary wives are mercifully free. She shares her husband to an unusual degree with her mother-in-law; because of their unique positions, monarch and heir are tied by a bond that goes beyond that of mother and son. Diana's reaction has been to keep her distance from the Queen, who is said to complain that she is rarely invited to visit her grandchildren. The Princess of Wales also faces the strictures of immovable tradition; however much she might like to spend Christmas just with her own husband and family, Christmas will always be at Windsor, because it always has been. Within those strictures she has fought to establish her own life, home and identity; she appears to have won, helped by the arrival of an influential ally in the person of the Duchess of York with whom she can confide and clown to her husband's mild disapproval.

She is doing no more than continuing an established trend. Queens Alexandra, Mary and Elizabeth were all women of strong personality, as was Wallis Simpson; the Windsor men seem attracted by dominant females. Diana's future role will consist partly of keeping her husband in touch with the real and ordinary world outside his own rarefied circle, and to keep him from too much introspection. On both counts, she still has much to achieve.

His close personal friends are few, although his acquaintances are many. He has a small number of friends among the aristocratic families, like the Duke and Duchess of Westminster and his cousins the Romseys. He has a handful of friends from polo, from hunting and from his days in the Air Force and Navy. The circle is entirely predictable, discreet, and each compartment rarely makes contact with any of the others. Except at traditional family gatherings like Christmas at Windsor, he sees little of his father, his sister Anne, or his brothers Andrew and Edward, for he no longer has much in common with them. Among his immediate family, only his mother and grandmother enjoy his company with any frequency. Among his immediate neighbours at Kensington Palace, he has few dealings with Prince and Princess Michael of Kent, but enjoys the architectural company of the Duke of Gloucester and maintains a kindly relationship with his aunt, Princess Margaret.

He is happy with his own company, as can be seen from his enjoyment of solitary pursuits like fishing and painting. On at least two foreign tours in recent years, to Italy and to Saudi Arabia, he has taken an established artist with him as tutor, and he was rewarded in 1987 with a hanging at the prestigious Royal Academy summer exhibition. The painting, a tiny watercolour of a Norfolk farm scene, was entered in the name of Arthur George Carrick (from two of his names and one of his titles); the address given for Mr Carrick was in fact the private address of his private secretary Sir John Riddell. The ruse was rumbled by Lynda Murdin, the perceptive arts correspondent of the *London Daily News*, but at least the picture got in on its own merit.

Charles has displayed some talent for painting from his earliest years, and seems to have inherited it from his father. But whereas Philip's efforts have been mainly bold attacks of oil on canvas, Charles prefers the gentler tones of watercolour.

Painting has taken over the role occupied in his earlier life by music. Presented with the chance to play a cello in full public gaze during the 1988 bicentennial tour of Australia, his fruitless effort to coax melody from it showed that his once-favourite instrument is now long abandoned. In a delicious little cameo of upstaging, the Princess of Wales, who is supposed to have as much brain as the average vacuum cleaner, then sat down at the piano and delivered a recognizable rendition of part of the Rachmaninov Piano Concerto No.2. 'Well done, darling,' said Charles. Diana smiled sweetly and said nothing.

Any frustrations Charles may have had at not being taken seriously, and any difficulties he may have encountered in his marriage, paled suddenly into insignificance one tragic day in March 1988 during his annual and much-enjoyed skiing holiday at Klosters, the picture-postcard resort high in the Swiss Alps near Davos which has quietly prospered from more than a decade of regular royal patronage.

Charles is a highly competent skier, which in a man with little natural physical grace is a triumph of dedication over a lack of natural ability. He is, above all, a brave skier, who has never shirked from the most terrifying downhill runs. It was his twelfth visit to Klosters, and conditions seemed good; the season had begun with a depressing lack of snow, but fresh falls within the previous few days had made the off-piste runs powdery and inviting. After a morning's unexceptional sport with Diana and the pregnant Duchess of York, Charles decided to spend the afternoon seeking fresh challenge off-piste, on a precipitous slope of the Gotschnagrat which was not a recognised ski run; it lay a little to the right of the celebrated Wang run, one of the most testing in Europe on which those who attempt it frequently cross themselves before launching off the crag at its top. Avalanche warnings had been posted that day, as warm sunshine beat down on fresh snow that had not yet bonded to the season's earlier falls.

Skiing off-piste – away from the recognised runs – is a perfectly normal practice among experienced skiers, who are well aware of the dangers. Charles had with him Charles Palmer-Tomkinson, a former British Olympic skier, his equally proficient wife Pattie, Major Hugh Lindsay, a regular skiing companion and former equerry to the Queen, Bruno Sprecher, the leading ski guide of the Klosters area, and Stefan Kadruvi, a Swiss policeman. The party had skied more than halway down the slope when a wall of snow 600 metres (2000 feet) wide and 70 metres (230 feet) high broke free above then and hurtled downwards. Charles, who was leading the party Charles Palmer-Tomkinson, and the two Swiss managed by a matter of seconds to steer clear, but Pattie and Major Lindsay could not get out of the way in time and were engulfed Charles and the others dug frantically in the snow with a shovel and with their bare hands, guided by electronic bleepers which all the party were wearing. Pattie was brought out with badly broken legs and a collapsed lung; Lindsay had died instantly from a severe blow to the skull from a block of ice.

The skiing holiday was abandoned, and a desolate royal party flew home the next day with Major Lindsay's body in the royal aircraft, to be met by his widow Sarah, an assistant press officer at Buckingham Palace who was expecting their first baby. Major Lindsay's funeral, conducted with military honours at the Royal Military Academy, Sandhurst, had the largest representation of the royal family at any burial service since that of the Duchess of Windsor.

When Charles returned to Klosters the following week to visit Pattie in Davos hospital, his features had assumed a colour that was almost grey. He spent hours by Pattie's bedside, and went for a long walk in the snow with the two Swiss who had been in his party; his hotel bedroom had an unimpeded view of the fateful mountainside across the valley.

Although protected by diplomatic immunity from any possible prosecution by the Swiss authorities, Charles made a full statement to the local investigating magistrate immediately after the accident, and had his press secretary Philip Mackie read out a full account, written in the Prince's own hand with a blue felt-tip pen on Prince of Wales crested notepaper, to reporters at Zurich airport. It was entirely in character that he should be so open, almost as though a full public statement were part of his process of coming to terms with himself. His discomfiture was made no easier by a statement from the director of the Swiss Federal Avalanche Institute that the party had probably set off the avalanche themselves by skiing over the fresh snow.

Certainly, in subsequent weeks, he appeared by his demeanour to take full responsibility upon his own shoulders, although Major Lindsay's mother publicly absolved him from any blame, dismissing the tragedy as an unfortunate accident. But Charles is not the man to accept excuses and escape routes from his own actions; he was utterly mortified by his own role in the unhappy event.

Skiing off-piste may be foolhardy at times, but it is in no way uncommon; every dedicated skier will seek out the delights of virgin, powdery snow away from the crowds, and even avalanche warnings are treated to a large extent as a caution rather than a prohibition. Charles acted no differently from, and no more foolishly than, any other dedicated and accomplished skier. But the question raised at the time, which will be asked for years to come, is whether the heir to the throne should place himself in such danger; his own death was only a matter of seconds away.

It will take a long time to know what the long-term effect will be on a man who wears honesty and responsibility so openly on his sleeve. It will, perhaps, have convinced him at last that it is both unnecessary and undesirable for him to pursue dangerous physical challenge in the middle years, and that he has no need to prove himself, either to himself or to others. His crusades on behalf of a better society are worthier endeavours in which he ought to be able to find fulfilment, and for which his public will think the better of him. But he will not come to terms easily with such a view, and the tragedy of Klosters is just as likely to compound the frustrations of his life, in which physical challenge was always a safety valve to its pressures. The Queen, whom he saw at Windsor as soon as he returned home, will doubtless have reminded him that it is not part of the function of the heir to the throne to place himself voluntarily within a few inches of death.

11

Duke of Cornwall

MARTIN EUSTACE, who farms 320 acres (129 hectares) with 500 head of beef cattle near Wadebridge in Cornwall, was visiting the Royal Cornwall Agricultural Show one day in June 1984 when he chanced to meet his landlord. Farmer Eustace was mightily displeased and said so, for his farm rent had just been increased by 25 per cent, requiring him to find an extra £2,000 a year, and that at a time when farmers, thanks to an agricultural overabundance in the European Community, were being urged to cut back on production.

Mr Eustace was by no means the only tenant of the Duchy of Cornwall to beard the landlord that day; some had even taken to telephoning his London home in Kensington Palace to register their dismay. This was made the greater by a fact which most of them were too polite and deferential to mention face to face; the Duchy had just published its accounts for the previous year, which already showed a healthy twenty per cent increase in profits, and the landlord's income had risen to a whisker short of £1 million.

Charles, Duke of Cornwall, landlord to 170 tenant farmers and master of 127,500 acres (51,600 hectares) in twenty-one counties, listened with concern, made several sympathetic noises, and tried to point out that rents were assessed fairly on the profitability of individual farms. And although some of the protesters subsequently benefited from minor adjustments, they could not escape the inevitable truth that the estate to which they were beholden for their land was a changed beast. The Duchy of Cornwall, for generations a slumbering,

202

old-fashioned, unprofitable, inefficient and on the whole thoroughly benevolent English landowner, had suddenly succumbed to the epidemic infection of profitability.

Although in total size it falls well short of the properties administered by such institutions as the Forestry Commission, the British Railways Board or the Commissioners of the Church of England, the Duchy of Cornwall is nevertheless among the largest private estates in Britain, and the dukedom which goes with it is the oldest in the English peerage. It was created by decree of King Edward III on 16 March, 1337, a scattered parcel of the monarch's lands at a time when the Crown personally owned as much as one-fifth of the land area of England. Edward's ostensible purpose was to provide a comfortable income for his first-born son and heir, Edward of Woodstock, the Black Prince, but by the terms of his charter, which still exists (in the British Museum) as does its provisions, he appeared to be striving for other more obviously political ends, in an age when the throne was under regular threat from usurpers and counter-claimants.

He was particularly specific in his condition that the Duchy be held by the first-begotten son of the monarch and by no other; the Duke of Cornwall has always therefore been automatically the natural heir to the throne. If the monarch had no sons – as, most recently, was the case of King George VI who had only daughters – the Duchy and its revenues would revert to the monarch himself, and the dukedom would lie in abeyance. The result has been that for approximately half of its 650 years' existence, the Duchy has been without a duke. At this distance King Edward's intentions can only be guessed at, but his purpose appears to have been to establish more clearly the line of succession, and to give the rightful heir an additional bulwark against the claims of lesser princes, foreigners, schemers and upstarts. The iron rule has at times been bent; Prince George, second son of Edward VII who subsequently reigned as George V, assumed the dukedom after the early death of his elder brother the Duke of Clarence. But the principle remains, that he who assumes the dukedom will ultimately ascend the throne, provided he survives that long. Charles is the 24th Duke, and well aware of the salient historical fact that ten of his twenty-three predecessors never made it.

The Duchy was once a great deal more extensive than it is now; over the centuries successive dukes sold off bits piecemeal to keep the whole viable. But because of its peculiarity and its more or less inviolable charter, the estate survived intact when, in 1760, King George III surrendered the great majority of Crown lands to the government in return for the annual royal salary of the Civil List.

In the middle years of the nineteenth century the Duchy benefited from the enormous energies and talents of Prince Albert, who in his unhappily brief span as Victoria's consort managed to reorganize and modernize a great many stagnant backwaters of the British royal house, usually to impressive effect. He instituted wide-ranging reforms in the way the Duchy was run and made it a great deal more productive and efficient, to the extent that when his eldest son Edward, Prince of Wales, later Edward VII, achieved the age of twenty-one and became eligible to draw on his inheritance, he found that the Duchy could provide him with a capital sum of £600,000 (out of which he bought the royal estate of Sandringham) and an exceptionally handsome income of £50,000 a year. It went a long way to financing the life of fleshly delights that filled his interminable wait for the throne.

With the death of Prince Albert from typhoid in 1861 at the age of forty-two, the Duchy had to wait well over a century before it again experienced such a smack of energetic management. Edward, Prince of Wales, remained Duke of Cornwall until he ascended the throne in 1901, and for much of that time his mind and body were occupied elsewhere. Prince George had nine unspectacular years as Duke until his accession as George V in 1910. His eldest son, who subsequently reigned briefly as Edward VIII, enjoyed twenty-six years as Duke, and was a frequent and enthusiastic visitor to the Duchy and its properties. But in truth, during his long tenure, little of great substance happened. He enjoyed the thought of being a landowner, but never seriously came to grips with the work and responsibilities it entailed. He was more at home in café society than on the land.

On Edward's accession in 1936 the Duchy and its revenues reverted to the monarch, for he had no eldest son to claim it. Nor did his brother George VI, who therefore took the revenues for himself and used them largely to support his younger brother the Duke of Gloucester. The three-year-old Charles became Heir Apparent and Duke of Cornwall on the accession of his mother in 1952, but he was not entitled to draw the revenues until he attained the age of twenty-one; during the intervening years the Queen used the revenues chiefly to subsidize the Civil List and thereby to reduce the royal family's demands on the Treasury. When he reached the magical age he found that he had fared poorly by comparison with his great-great-grandfather Edward VII, for his accumulated nest egg was almost half, at £300,000. A great deal less than half, indeed, if inflation is taken into account. Even if Charles had been inclined to follow the path of a wildly sybaritic life, such a sum would not have taken him very far along it.

Charles's relatively paltry inheritance was party a result of his mother drawing on substantial amounts to keep the Civil List within bounds and to allay political sniping that the royal family were costing the country far too much; but it was equally a result of the great estate falling once again into a kind of rudderless sloth, an enterprise without a dynamic chairman to give it impetus and direction, to drag it out of the nineteenth century where Prince Albert had left it, and to fire its governing council with the notion of substantially increasing its revenues.

Not that things were all that bad. During most of Charles's twenties the Duchy was each year able to produce an average surplus of about £250,000 for his benefit, half of which he dutifully handed to the Exchequer as a token payment of taxes, only right for a Prince of Wales who enjoys the greatest possible privilege for a British citizen – exemption from income tax.

For some years after he was first able to draw on the Duchy revenues, Charles was much too busy, either with his university studies or with his full-time career in the Navy, to be much bothered with the running of his great estate. In 1973, however, he did make a token appearance amid the ruins of Launceston Castle to receive his traditional dues as Duke of Cornwall: one load of firewood; one grey cloak; two greyhounds; one hundred silver shillings; one pound of pepper; one hunting bow; one pair of gilt spurs; one pound of herbs; one three-pronged salmon spear; and one pair of falconer's gauntlets.

After the presentation they were all returned to the Launceston Museum whence they came to await presentation to Prince William as next Duke of Cornwall at some far-future date. With the exception, of course, of the greyhounds, which were returned to their owner. Such ancient rituals have their foggy origin in the Black Prince's hunting expeditions around his vast western domain.

Charles first began to take a serious interest in the running of the Duchy in 1979, after he had completed his naval career, had spent a further year involved in the charitable trusts set up to mark the Silver Jubilee of his mother's reign in 1977, and then, for the first time, had been seriously obliged to confront the inconvenient truth that he had no proper full-time occupation. That he should turn to his estate was entirely natural; landowning and estate management are, after all, the regular profession of the aristocracy, and the English aristocracy have over the centuries made a very fair job of it despite all attempts to frustrate them by rapacious tax gatherers. The Duke of Cornwall surveyed his inheritance and rapidly came to two conclusions. The first was that the returns on such an apparently huge estate were so small that no commercial property entrepreneur would tolerate them; the second was that improving that position, both for the sake of the Duchy, its tenants and employees, and for the sake of enhancing his own income, would be a very worthwhile occupation indeed. It was certainly the nearest he was ever likely to come to earning his own living.

It was far from easy. The Prince of Wales cannot act like a heartless commercial landlord; the adverse publicity would be immense, the political reaction damaging, and besides it is not in his nature. But quite apart from that Charles inherited an estate which by its very nature had an exceptionally limited ability to make money.

More than half of the Duchy's 127,500 acres (51,560 hectares) lie on the high Devon heathland of Dartmoor; they are occupied by small hill farms that lie within the area of a National Park with all its planning strictures, and their capacity for development is therefore strictly limited. Another 4,000 acres (1,620 hectares) cover most of the Isles of Scilly off Land's End, and they too are largely protected. In Greater London the Duchy owns forty-five acres (eighteen hectares) in Kennington, south of the Thames, containing some 600 houses, in one of which the great Charles Chaplin spent his first year of life until his family were evicted for arrears of rent. But Kennington is on the wrong side of the tracks, much of the housing stock is in poor condition, and the returns are paltry compared with those enjoyed by landlords like the Duke of Westminster who own quite startlingly valuable swathes of the most desirable West End areas.

As if that were not enough, there were further constraints on profit. The Duchy was prevented by Act of Parliament from investing its money outside the estates, except for an account at the Bank of England, and as if to ensure it complied, it was obliged to report each year's net profits to the Treasury. There was little money to invest, and not much scope for investing it. Through what appears to have been a combination of benevolence towards the tenants, and lack of incentive to invest, the Duchy missed out almost entirely on the wave of major rent rises that swept the rest of the country in the 1960s, something of a disaster for an organization whose sole business at the time was that of landlord.

Charles began to be a regular visitor at the Duchy's London headquarters in an elegant block at Buckingham Gate, just round the corner from the front gates of Buckingham Palace, taking his seat at the head of the Prince's Council and letting it be known that he had every intention of being an active, 'hands on' chairman of the committee which, were the Duchy a commercial company, would be its board of directors.

The changes were discreet, but swift and far-reaching, none more so than his appointment of a new Secretary and Keeper of the Records, in effect the managing director of the enterprise. John Higgs was an unusual choice, but in the event an inspired one. He had begun as a farmer, become a bursar running the extensive estates of Exeter College, Oxford, and had spent much of his working life as an adviser to the United Nations Food and Agriculture Organization. He and his master immediately struck up a close rapport; Charles warmed to his enormous enthusiasm, his sense of humour, and his breadth of knowledge from practical farming to the politics of agriculture. They enjoyed each other's company, and Higgs shared and nurtured Charles's developing concern for conservation and for the problems of employment in rural areas; the Prince was quite devastated when Higgs died in harness in 1986, after being knighted on his deathbed.

Concern for the environment was one thing, but the need to generate more money was paramount. Charles wasted no further time; he brought in as advisers on finance Sir John Baring, the head of Barings merchant bank, and Lord Franks, a former British ambassador to Washington. Two things then happened in quite rapid succession. First, Charles married in 1981, and as was his due he increased his income from the Duchy from half to three-quarters of his entitlement, and he now pays only one-quarter of the net proceeds back to the Treasury in lieu of income tax. Second, the Duchy watched with satisfaction the passage through Parliament of the Duchy of Cornwall Management Act 1982, its best aid to profit enhancement for well over a century.

The Act removed some of the ancient fetters on the Duchy's finances; suddenly, it was allowed to borrow money and to invest in the City. This latter it did with alacrity and gusto; after only one year of the new regime it had built up an investment portfolio with a book value of £9 million, largely financed by selling off some of its traditional stock of property. This mainly blue-chip excursion into money-making brought Charles at the end of the 1984 financial year profits of £700,000, against less than £600,000 from the Duchy's traditional sources of land and rents. For the first time, Charles's Duchy income had exceeded £1 million; he drew £828,726 and handed the rest to the Treasury.

Selling the Duchy's unwanted properties brought Charles a good deal of unwelcome publicity. In the village of Curry Mallet, Somerset, middle-class residents complained that the rash of 'For sale' boards outside the Duchy's cottages was depressing their property prices. At Stoke Climsland in Cornwall, tenants, offered the chance to buy their homes, asked the Prince to intervene claiming that the prices being asked were far above what tenants of the local district council were being asked for their houses, and that they could be afforded only by middle-class outsiders who would change the nature of the village. 'Prince Charles as an individual is very well thought of, but the Duchy's name actually stinks with many of the tenants,' declared the local officer of the housing charity Shelter. And in Kennington, inner-city tenants took issue with the policy of leaving apartments empty when their occupants departed, in order that the entire block could eventually be sold. They even voiced fears that their royal landlord intended to fill the empty flats with vagrants.

Charles managed to deflect some of the criticism that he was deliberately running down his inner-city properties when he agreed that one particularly notorious Kennington apartment block, Newquay House, should be sold to a housing association and its running handed over to the tenants themselves. It was an act which, for once, seemed to equate with the Prince's preaching on the decay of inner cities; but behind it was the purely practical realization by Charles and the Duchy accountants that the ownership of property controlled by the Rent Acts was no longer a paying proposition in the 1980s.

John Higgs painted the picture with blunt candour in an interview shortly before his death. 'Without doubt, people over the years had seen the Duchy as a soft touch. Between 1936 and Prince Charles's coming-of-age in 1969, there had been no pressure at all on Duchy income. It was clear from the start that the Duchy had to divest itself of some of its less profitable interests and diversify generally if it was to carry out parliamentary instructions and operate as efficiently as possible.' The Duchy he said, was 'not a housing authority'.

Undue drains on the principal source of Charles's income were plainly no longer allowed. For centuries one of the Duchy's more burdensome properties has been the 4,000 acres (1,620 hectares) of the Isles of Scilly, a tiny, disadvantaged archipelago that stands thirty miles adrift from the Cornish coast in the Western Approaches to the English Channel, and whose treacherous rocks have claimed every manner of vessel from Armada galleons to oil tankers. The Duchy has for long helped to provide many of the island's essential services, baling out a local council whose meagre resources are stretched by having to send the children of its 2,000 inhabits to secondary school on the mainland, and by having to dispose of the refuse of its thousands of summer tourists. In the foreword to a report on the islands' future in 1984, Charles made it plain that he was keen to withdraw much of his beneficence. 'The islanders must become more self-reliant. The Duchy will continue to help, though I personally hope that it will gradually become less prominent as the reins of leadership are handed over to the community itself.'

The replacement of somnolent benevolence by a brisk, sharp-edged capitalism has certainly cast its spell on the Duke of Cornwall's balance sheet. The accounts for 1986 show the effects of selling off poor properties, investing money in the better ones, and handing much of the proceeds to the sharp money managers of the City of London. Income from estates stood at £4.5 million, and expenditure on them at £3.2 million, leaving a highest-ever profit from traditional sources of £1.2 million. The share investment portfolio, with a market value at the end of the year of £14.9 million, yielded dividends and interest of just under £1 million. Charles's gross income for the year, before he handed his quarter to the Treasury, was £1,739,238; the pay packet that he took home to support his wife and two children – and, it must be said, to cover much of the expense of his public and official life – amounted to £1,304,429.

To put that figure in context, Charles is still nowhere near as well-off as his mother who is assumed, without much supporting fact, to be numbered among the world's richest women. Like the Duchy of Cornwall, the monarch enjoys the proceeds of a large estate, the Duchy of Lancaster, for her own personal use. The Queen's estate, little of which is nowadays in the County of Lancaster, is less than half the size of the Duchy of Cornwall, but comprises much more productive farmland in pockets all over England, as well as a diamond-studded belt of real estate in central London that includes the Savoy Hotel.

The Duchy of Lancaster regularly returns more income to its beneficiary than does that of Cornwall, and in addition the Queen is funded by the taxpayer to the tune of over £4 million a year for her staff salaries and working expenses.

One major expense which Charles did not have to stand from his own pocket was the purchase of a house. He never has, and he probably never will. In 1974, while still serving in the Navy and with no place properly to call his own outside his mother's official and private residences, he accepted, with no great show of enthusiasm, the tenancy of Chevening. The house in question is a stately but heartless pile of 115 rooms set in 3,500 acres (1,400 hectares) of the North Downs of Kent, with a fine view over the Kentish Weald. Its previous owner, Lord Stanhope, decreed in his will that his house should be occupied by the prime minister, or failing that another member of the Cabinet. Should no government minister want it, its tenancy should pass to a lineal descendant of King George VI and Queen Elizabeth, and only after all those and several other less exalted avenues had been explored and exhausted should it be handed over to the National Trust.

Despite the incentive of a £250,000 covenant for its upkeep the Prime Minister, Harold Wilson, did not want it; he already had the use of Chequers in Buckinghamshire, the prime minster's traditional weekend retreat. No member of his Labour Cabinet seemed over-anxious to grace the splendour with a socialist presence. So it was offered to Charles, although what a bachelor spending most of his time at sea was supposed to do with 115 rooms was never entirely clear.

Charles never liked it, and rarely went there, although in an early burst of enthusiasm for gardening he put in motion the use of some of Lord Stanhope's covenant to restore and improve the grounds. Even when he left the Navy he spent much of his time and energy finding other places to lay his head, his particular fondness being for Earl Mountbatten's Hampshire home at Broadlands. Chevening's gloomy vastness, in which the single and sometimes lonely Charles would rattle around like a pea in a drum, was only one of its drawbacks; although only twenty-two miles from central London access was difficult, with no fast motorway scything through the interminably dreary south-eastern suburbs. But for Charles, its overwhelming disadvantage was that it was quite simply in entirely the wrong part of the country. Kent contained neither any of his relatives, nor a decent Hunt. In 1980, he gave it up.

His preference was for Gloucestershire, where his sister Anne and her husband had set up as farmers at Gatcombe

Park outside the pleasant little country town of Minchin-hampton. Charles too had a fancy for a farm; his new-found role as chairman of one of the country's largest private estates had sharpened his taste for real practical contact and experimentation with the land. He secured the Duchy's approval to buy a suitable house for him, the condition being that it remained Duchy property and not his own. It would therefore pass to Prince William when he in his turn assumed the dukedom, but if by mischance Charles should die early, his wife would, strictly speaking, have no claim to it.

The man charged with finding a suitable property was the Duchy's steward for the eastern area, who also happened by good fortune to be a partner in a large Gloucestershire estate agency. It did not take him long to come up with a selection of possibilities, and one in particular caught Charles's eye. The advertisement for Highgrove, laced with the usual house agent's hyperbole, described it as 'a distinguished Georgian house standing in superb parkland in the Duke of Beaufort's Hunt', set in 347 acres (140 hectares), with thirty rooms including nine bedrooms and six bathrooms, and having 'easily maintained gardens'. It was a plain three-storey block of no great architectural distinction but with the satisfying proportions of all good Georgian buildings. Built between 1796 and 1798, it had been extensively restored after a fire in 1894, and claimed some good interior features, including a fine central staircase and a selection of eighteenth-century fireplaces brought from other houses at the time of restoration. (Its new owner has since added a classical façade to the front which it never had before.)

The vendor was Maurice Macmillan, MP, son of the former Conservative Prime Minister Harold Macmillan; Macmillan junior was in failing health, and had decided to sell up to live with his father at the family home at Birch Grove, Sussex. He had bought Highgrove in 1965 for £89,000 and was now looking to a selling price of about £1 million. The Duchy managers sold off three mansions in the West Country to raise the money, and secured Highgrove for a price which has never been precisely revealed, but which is thought to have been a shade over £800,000.

The Duke of Cornwall and his financial advisers must be credited with the ability not only to bargain hard, but also to spot a shrewd investment; should the Duke and his family at some future time decide they no longer want Highgrove, a house once occupied by the Prince of Wales will surely command a substantial premium in the open market.

In buying Highgrove, Prince Charles fell for the garden and its potential as much as for the house, even though when he first saw it the grounds had been let go somewhat, and were largely given over to vegetables. 'It was a challenge to create something and I did rather fall in love with it,' its new owner said later. 'The big cedar tree in the front and the walled garden finally made up my mind.'

There were other advantages. Highgrove lay only ninety miles west of Buckingham Palace along the M4 motorway, in easy reach of relatives, hunting and many existing Duchy properties. Its disadvantages were that it could be easily seen from the main road, although that has since been cured by some dense tree and shrub planting, and that a footpath, much used as a short cut by residents of the town of Tetbury a short distance away, ran through the grounds; that too was cured by a simple diversion. It was also, frankly, too small, and today if the Waleses entertain, some of their staff have to put up at a hotel. But all these were nitpicking distractions: Charles had what he wanted – a farm and garden of his own.

His marriage the following year produced some useful wedding presents to make Highgrove more like a home, including a set of fruit trees from the Fruiterers' Company and a herb garden from a Sussex Women's Institute, both of which delighted the new gardener. Another gift was less appreciated by the local population: the Army decided to mark the wedding with a gift of a covered swimming pool for Highgrove, its £20,000 cost raised by a whipround among the muttering soldiery. Why, the residents of the nearby town of Dursley demanded, should Charles and Diana have their own private pool when the 600 pupils of the local comprehensive school, denied a pool of their own for lack of council funds, had to travel fifteen miles to Stroud for a swim?

'I was never a gardener before I came here,' Charles said soon after his move, seemingly forgetting that the basic pleasure of tending the earth had been instilled in him at a very early age by his green-fingered grandmother Queen Elizabeth. At Highgrove it was instantly reawakened; he found the simple physical tasks of digging and weeding a catharsis to his stressful public life, and he took delight in laying out the walled garden, which stands a fair distance from the main house and is reached by narrow mown paths through thigh-high grass and wild flowers; in the middle is an arbour hung with roses, wisteria and clematis which he uses as a haven in which to sit and write letters, or simply to think. He is in many ways a solitary and withdrawn man, but he is not so unlike a million other gardeners who seek occasional peace in the solitude of the greenhouse.

His walled garden is now one of his greatest pleasures, entered through a gate he designed himself, based on the arches of the Taj Mahal, the path leading through a tunnel of runner beans and sweet peas, another of his innovations to avoid bending to pick the flowers and vegetables. The garden is decorated with an Italian fountain, a pool full of carp given to him by the violinist Yehudi Menuhin, and a dovecot presented to him by the Sultan of Oman.

Proudly showing his work to the television camera for a documentary on his life, he made a now-celebrated and somewhat regretted revelation to the interviewer: 'I love coming in here and I potter about and sit and read. I just come and talk to the plants really – very important to talk to them. They respond, I find.' Tabloid newspapers seized on the nugget as a godsend to their view that the heir to the throne was a spineless wimp, entirely failing to mention that the remark had been made through one of Charles's wry, crooked smiles, and had been followed by a self-deprecating laugh. That even a joke was used as ammunition against him caused him to despair, and cemented one more brick in the wall he has slowly built between himself and almost all manifestations of the media, printed and electronic. What irks him most about the Press, however, are the photographers who snatch pictures of him on private land, or lie in wait for him behind bushes; they have seen outbursts of temper of which even his father would be proud.

One winter at Sandringham Charles was out riding when a photographer from the *Sun* newspaper sprang from behind a tree. 'What the hell do you think you're doing?' the Prince raged. 'I'm only doing my job, sir,' replied the photographer, a solidly-built east Londoner with voice to match who feared no man. 'And what kind of a job do you call that?' Charles spluttered, his colour rising. 'Well, at least I've got one, sir,' quoth the cameraman. Charles rode off in a fury direct to the messroom used by the Sandringham policemen, and swept the tea mugs of the assembled constables off the table with his riding crop. 'What are you doing sitting round here drinking tea?' Charles demanded. 'There's a *photographer* out there.' The cameraman in question, Arthur Edwards, subsequently became the Princess of Wales's favourite newspaper photographer, not least because he rescued her from some unpleasant mêlées during the days leading up to her engagement.

It is from the world in general, and such encounters in particular, that Charles feels protected within his walled garden at Highgrove. The estate was, however, not bought primarily for privacy, but for real-life farming; and for that its 347 acres (140 hectares) were really not big enough. In 1984 the Duke asked his Duchy to buy for him the 420 acres (169 hectares) of Broadfield Farm next door from its then owner, Mr Tony Keen. Mr Keen sold for a sum close to £1 million, and once again the Duchy sold off property elsewhere to pay for it.

With Broadfield and part of Highgrove combined into a viable mixed farming enterprise, Charles set about running it with vigour. He called in the advice of John Pugsley, a working farmer and member of the Prince's Council. Together they developed a system in which a herd of about a hundred Ayrshire cows produce milk with the emphasis on production from grassland and a minimum of bought-in feed. Some 420 acres (169 hectares) are given over to arable, and in 1985 a section of eighty acres (32 hectares) was set aside for a trial scheme of rotational farming without use of chemical fertilizers; in 1988 Charles harvested his first organic crop, a field of spring beans. Contrary to reports that its owner had gone wholly organic, the rest of the farm is run as a normal commercial enterprise, but a further 160 acres (64 hectares) have been set aside for future planting without chemicals. According to Charles, the long-term object is to run a profitable farm, but also to show that consideration can be given to the interests of wildlife, and to explore the possibility of a significant reduction in the use of chemicals, as well as contributing to the visual improvement of the countryside.

To this latter end Charles has invited the Duchy's Wildlife and Landscape Advisory Group to the farm on several occasions, and has begun an active programme of improving and extending the existing woodlands, planting new trees in the corners of fields and on waste patches, and encouraging the growth of the hedgerows. One problem which faced this particular farmer was his insistence that all farm machinery should, if possible, be British. But almost all his British machinery is second-hand; Charles was dismayed to find that the domestic farm equipment industry had all but ceased to exist.

Beyond the confines of his own farm, the Duke of Cornwall enjoys nothing more than visiting his own tenants, dropping in for a farmhouse lunch to discuss milk quotas or wheat yields. During the early years of his marriage Charles disappeared from public view for weeks. For much of that time, when he was not simply soaking up the new-found pleasures of family life, he was giving his attention to the Duchy – not because it especially needed his guiding hand but because he felt he had stumbled across a proper job, and felt that he could make a tangible contribution to its management.

Previous Dukes, particularly the last Prince of Wales, enjoyed the seigneurial pleasure of inspecting their estates and making small talk with the peasantry. Charles takes it all rather more seriously, to the extent that on at least three occasions he has slipped away unannounced for several days at a time to work as an ordinary agricultural labourer on Duchy farms, milking cows, mucking out byres and bringing in the hay; it is a hard existence when it is a lifetime's work, but a refreshing and fulfilling break in the life of a prince, particularly when he regards it as having some serious purpose beyond mere novelty. As a duke with definite ideas on how the Duchy should be run, he at least has the wit to ensure he knows what he is talking about. His high public profile demands that he act and speak with care.

Next to ensuring a reasonable financial return, Charles's principal ducal concern is for the conservation of the environment, a philosophy he learned partly from Sir Laurens van der Post, partly from reading E.F. Schumacher, but chiefly from the Duchy's remarkable secretary, John Higgs. Higgs not only nurtured a genuine concern for the land, but he was also well able to detect the shifting winds of public opinion. In a policy paper prepared for the Duchy, and heartily endorsed by Charles, Higgs wrote: 'The major problem facing all landowners at the moment is that of reconciling competing demands on land, namely the need to make an economic return against social and other demands. The need for integrated rural development is a modern phenomenon not yet well understood which could lead to much greater changes in rural management than anything we have had to face up to in the post-war period ... There is a growing awareness that agricultural management alone is insufficient if those who own the land are to give an adequate account of their stewardship.

'After years in which increasing agricultural output and maximizing rents were paramount, we are entering a period in which subjects like low-input agriculture, conservation, employment creation in rural areas, tourism and recreation, to mention but a few aspects, all form part of the equation which an estate owner must consider.'

Guided by Higgs, Charles initiated two important conservation studies on his estates. In 1983 the Duchy produced a major report setting out guidelines for the future management of Dartmoor, attempting to balance the needs of the farmers with the ambitions for the National Park, two areas of potentially conflicting interest. Charles wrote in its preface: 'I am not going to claim for one moment that the Duchy of Cornwall knows all the solutions to the main problems that beset modern Dartmoor, but I am seriously concerned that we neither try to preserve it, as it were, in aspic as a curiosity for future generations nor destroy its unique heritage by rash development. The moor is as it is today because men and women over many centuries have cared for it and have made it so. It is very important for me that the Duchy works closely with all those with a legitimate interest in Dartmoor to ensure its well-being as a living community into the twenty-first century.' More than fifty bodies were consulted in the report's preparation, and three years later the Dartmoor National Park Authority noted with appreciation in its own annual report the Duchy's 'increased cooperation noticeable over the last few years'.

Soon after the Dartmoor report, the Duchy, with Charles and Higgs at the helm, produced another, this time on future land use and community development in the problem areas of the Isles of Scilly. Its tenor was that the Duchy wanted itself to pay less, and the local district council to pay more, for essential island services. That report was less well received, the islanders feeling that their landlord simply wanted to shuffle off his more costly responsibilities.

Concerned at rising unemployment in the rural areas of the Duchy, as elsewhere in the country, Charles and Higgs, in collaboration with the Council for Small Industries in Rural Areas, launched a scheme to convert redundant farm buildings into small workshops in the hope of attracting one-person businesses and other small enterprises back into the country. By the middle of 1987 nearly 100 such workshops had been set up or were in the pipeline, creating over 150 jobs. The scheme uncovered a sizeable demand for rural workshops; one barn that the Duchy converted near Bath drew sixty applicants. Almost on Charles's doorstep at Highgrove, the Duchy carved five workshops, at a cost of £105,000, out of redundant buildings at Street Farm; at the last count they were occupied by a ceramic restorer, a textile tool sharpener, a woodcarver, a furniture maker and a graphic designer. The furniture maker was delighted to receive a commission to make a cot for Prince Harry. The Duchy scheme is one of the largest job-creation projects of its type in the country, and Charles shrugs off criticism that it attracts only 'arty-crafty' entrepreneurs; jobs, he believes, are jobs.

The death of Sir John Higgs in 1986 was a serious loss to the Duchy, which had benefited enormously from his energy and vision, and a great personal loss to Charles. During their brief, bright encounter Higgs implanted in the Prince of Wales a great store of knowledge, caring and love for the land. If in his concern for the environment Charles is a man of his time, it is in no small measure due to Higgs.

12

The Travelling Circus

HIGH ABOVE the terracotta roofs of the city of Lisbon, with the damp, insistent wind tugging at his hair, the Prince of Wales resembled the troubled Hamlet on the battlements of Elsinore as he gazed dutifully but glumly down on the Portuguese capital which, devoid of sun, was drained of life and colour. The Mayor droned his mechanical commentary, which had to be filtered through an interpreter, while the dark racing clouds threatened yet another raw squall of stinging Atlantic rain. Diana clutched her head in a hopeless effort to prevent the demolition of the morning's *coiffure*, while Charles turned to the attendant knot of reporters and muttered in quiet despair: 'Can anybody tell me what I'm supposed to be doing here? In Lisbon? In February?'

What he was supposed to be doing there was cementing relations between Britain and her oldest ally. The previous year President Mario Soares of Portugal had visited England to attend a ceremony marking the 600th anniversary of the Treaty of Windsor by which the two nations agreed to gang up on the Spanish and press the Lancastrian John of Gaunt's ambitions to the throne of Castile. Charles and Diana's presence in Lisbon was the return match, and it too fell on a convenient anniversary, that of the marriage of John of Gaunt's daughter Philippa of Lancaster to King Joao I of Portgual, a union which produced a child who grew up to become Henry the Navigator.

But there were more immediately political reasons for the visit beyond mere cosy historic reminiscence. Portugal had thrown off the right-wing dictatorship of the notorious Salazar

221

regime, had regained a government of democratic socialism, and had become a member of the European Community, its application actively supported by the British Government. The prime ministers of the two countries had exchanged visits, and the Queen had paid a State visit to Lisbon, a certain sign of the British Government's approval of Portugal's regime and policies. The invitation to Charles and Diana was a means of keeping the mutually beneficial political process rolling; not quite a full-blown State visit – which can be made only by a Head of State – but a prestigious official visit whose weight and significance were only marginally less.

The British Government actively encouraged the trip; since Portugal had attained full membership of the European Community, a flood of cheap textiles and shoes had tipped the balance of Anglo-Portuguese trade heavily in Portugal's favour, and any piece of public relations that might stimulate the Portuguese to buy a few more British cars and computers in return was to be warmly welcomed. A memorial service in Oporto cathedral on St Valentine's Day, precisely 600 years on from the marriage of Joao and Philippa, was an ideal peg upon which to hang a British promotion, and a number of British exporters combined to stage a trade fair, promoting a range of goods from Scotch whisky to mechanical road diggers. Which explains why Prince Charles found himself on the battlements of the Castle of Sao Jorge in the middle of winter, looking down on a chilly, rain-drenched city in which he was almost the only tourist.

Overseas visits are a major part of Charles's working life, and are generally a curious mixture of diplomacy, trade promotion and sightseeing. The serious business of the Portuguese visit – attendance at the cathedral and the trade fair, both in the same city – could have been comfortably achieved in a single day, but the invitation was for four days, and the programme was padded out with visits to the tomb of the explorer Vasco da Gama, a restored cod fishing boat, a new office for Lloyds Bank, a school, a centre for the care of young victims of cerebral palsy, several palaces, and the exquisite little hill town of Sintra, which Byron thought the most romantic place in all Europe and which was almost entirely obscured by mist and drizzle on the day of the royal visit.

In addition the couple attended several exceedingly grand banquets held in majestic surroundings, for Portugal is well supplied with palaces from its days as the hub of an empire. At each one the bejewelled Princess Diana drew gasps of admiration for her evening outfits. The hosts produced the finest Portuguese wines and ports for their distinguished guests, and at each one host and guest exchanged comfortably uncontroversial speeches praising the ancient alliance. Charles is something of a linguist, and will usually insert a few sentences in the local tongue to impress the assembled company.

Everywhere the royal couple went the crowds turned out in their thousands, braving the dreadful weather to catch a glimpse of the famous and glamorous visitors. The British generally reciprocate by ignoring any foreign royalty that comes to London, believing their own royal family to be superior to any other, although they have been known to make exceptions for the President of the United States, the General Secretary of the Soviet Communist Party, and the Pope, media stars all. Charles and Diana have the power to pull large crowds, alerted by gushing torrents of advance warning in local newspapers, almost everywhere they go. Almost everywhere. During their 1986 tour of Saudi Arabia there were no crowds at all, except for small knots of expatriate Britons at a few strategic locations. 'It is not the Arab way to stare at visitors,' the Saudi *chef de protocol* explained. It is also not the way of some host states to publish the royal itinerary in advance, for fear of a security breach.

Security obsessions, sometimes obsessive, conspire with the niceties of protocol to ensure that wherever Charles travels, he sees little of the real country. In Portugal he could have done a lot worse than spend a morning with Dom Duarte Pio de Braganca, pretender to the Portuguese throne and a man

223

after his own heart. Dom Duarte was not invited to any of the official banquets, and contact was restricted to his brief presence at an informal reception for the Waleses. Which is a pity, for Charles, with his interest in inner city decay and helping the dispossessed, would have found much to talk to him about.

Instead of pressing his by now somewhat unrealistic claim to the throne, Dom Duarte assumes the mantle of a Geldof, raising large sums through pop concerts, appeals and television spectaculars for Portugal's growing population of urban dispossessed. Lisbon has many thousands of such people from Mozambique, Angola and East Timor, wretched leftovers from its days of empire who live in shanty towns on the edge of the city, a surprising sight in a European capital. But on his travels Charles is kept largely insulated from such realities, and from such down-to-earth people with home truths to tell, and he has to rely for his picture of the host country on endless briefings with officials who are bound to apply a shiny gloss of varnish.

Even the sightseeing sometimes manages to omit the glaringly obvious. On their visit to Australia for the 1988 Bicentennial celebrations, Charles and Diana personally brought with them the Ashes, the most revered trophy in cricket. Yet they made no appearance at the Bicentenary Test Match for which the trophy was played, and which was one of the highlights of the entire birthday programme in a nation which elevates cricket to a kind of pagan religion, especially when the opponents are the Poms. The fact that Charles has never shown any overpowering interest in cricket is no explanation; he spends many a long hour abroad struggling manfully to appear interested in other things which in truth must bore him to distraction.

Royal tours are the result of months of meticulous planning, discussion, negotiation and the observation of protocol, but it is in the very nature of things that the best-laid plans of mice, men and Princes of Wales can go astray, as during the royal tour of Saudi Arabia. Crown Prince Abdullah, the most senior member of the ruling Al-Saud family next to King Fahd, who was to have been the royal couple's official host, suddenly went missing. At the last moment the royal party was told that he had had to go at short notice to a clinic in Geneva for urgent medical treatment of an unspecified nature. One of his sons, Prince Moutaib, averred that he had spoken to his father in Switzerland that very morning.

There was no apology on the Saudi side, and little more than amusement on the British side, when the following day the Crown Prince was unmasked by a Spanish news agency as having taken over an entire floor of a hotel in the Canary Islands with a group of friends, and was enjoying a variety of entertainments supposedly forbidden to followers of the Prophet. 'Inshallah,' said the Saudi protocol officials with a shrug of the shoulders. 'It is the will of God.'

The will of God had little to do with the absence of Crown Prince Abdullah, but the current state of Britain's diplomatic relations with the Arab world did. Saudi Arabia, a huge buyer of British armaments and technology, had no wish to disturb its good relations with the United Kingdom, a country it has generally considered to be less pro-Israeli than the United States. The visit of the Waleses therefore had to proceed unclouded by diplomatic incident. At the same time, the Saudis maintain a relationship with the Syrians, which Britain at that time did not; Crown Prince Abdullah was not only the Saudi government's principal contact with Syria, he also had a Syrian wife. His method of ensuring that neither side took offence was simply not to be there. Not that Charles would have, or indeed could have, taken offence; he represents the British government abroad, but only indirectly and in the most general terms, and has always taken great care not to step into the day-to-day political arena. Had Saudi-British relations been in any way tricky at that time, the man missing would have been Charles. The unmasking of Abdullah in Las Palmas gave the royal entourage no small measure of private amusement.

But Charles can have his diplomatic difficulties, too, in

spite of the care he and his advisers take to steer him clear of controversy. Visiting West Germany at the end of 1987, he delivered an address to trainee officers at the German Military University in Munich which pleased the Germans but which had some Members of Parliament back home jumping up and down. 'In Britain,' Charles began, 'Germany is well known, among other things (like football and fast cars) for the excellence of its military officers down through history.' How offensive, cried the MPs, to thousands of Second World War veterans who fought and died against those excellent officers.

Charles then ploughed on into the politics of Western European defence. 'I think people in positions of authority, in European governments, in the armed forces and in public life generally, have a constant responsibility to ensure that nothing obscures the fundamental nature of the American defence guarantee for Western Europe.' The MPs, mainly from the Opposition, howled again that the heir to the throne was allying himself openly to Mrs Margaret Thatcher's pro-American and pro-nuclear defence policies. Even the Germans sat up and took notice of that one; there is a substantial and growing body of opinion in their country opposed to the stationing of nuclear weapons, and even American troops, on their soil.

It is in fact not unreasonable that in the context of a speech to a military audience Charles should touch on European defence policy; nor is it entirely improper that when abroad he should support the policies of the British government of the day. His German defence speech, like all his major utterances when abroad, had been read and approved in advance by the Foreign and Commonwealth Office. But it is an indication of how careful he has to be if he is to preserve the Crown from the taint of party politics.

If Charles has to make an official tour abroad, he would on balance prefer to make it to a Commonwealth country, where he feels on safer and more familiar ground, and where there is likely to be a great number of relevant people and places to visit. One day, after all, it will probably be all his.

Senior members of the royal family devote the majority of their travelling time to the Commonwealth, and particularly the core of the old White Commonwealth that comprises Australia, New Zealand and Canada. Charles has now made ten official visits to Australia, eight to Canada and seven to New Zealand; Canada, being closer than the Antipodes, has received more royal visits than any other country, with fourteen by the Queen alone. Charles, having been to school in Australia, shows a slight bias towards that country while his brother Andrew, having attended a school in Ontario, is the more regular visitor to Canada.

Britain's connections with what were once the two principal dominions of its empire are now exceedingly tenuous. Almost the last links have been broken in recent years with the repatriation to Canada and Australia of their constitutions; until then, in both countries, the last court of judicial appeal when the local process of justice had been exhausted was to the Privy Council in London, but even that archaic link is now severed. All that remains is the monarchy itself.

The Britishness of Australia is diminishing; at least 37 per cent of the population now have roots outside the British Isles, and of the remainder a significant number are of Irish origin with no reason for allegiance to the British Crown. Yet the country is still predominantly white, western, Christian, with a strong streak of sentimentality, and it can sometimes feel hemmed in by the alien cultures of the Pacific basin. The last formal link with the mother country that gave birth to a penal colony is proving hard to break, and Australian republicanism is taking a remarkably long time to catch a proper hold.

Those who advance that republicanism believe that the realistic moment for its introduction is at the end of Queen Elizabeth II's reign, for there is more widespread respect for the Queen of Australia than for the institution she represents.

Republicanism or no, the Bicentenary birthday celebrations attended by Prince Charles, Princess Diana and two million Australians on a January morning in Sydney was the most spectacular royal extravaganza yet seen Down Under. Australians need little excuse for a party, and this was their biggest; thousands of small craft packed the world's largest natural harbour to welcome the nine square-riggers that had sailed from England in memory of the 1788 convoy which landed the first batch of a thousand Europeans, most of them English convicts.

The edge was taken off the birthday junketing by the well-publicised plight of the Aboriginals, who had been living on the southern continent for many thousands of years before Captain Cook happened by. There was a distinct hint of embarrassment in the air. As a gesture to Aboriginal feeling, the crews of the replica convoy stopped short of actually making a landing, and some of them even read out a declaration calling attention to 'acts of history of which none can be proud'.

Charles himself caught something of the mood when he referred to the Aboriginals' plight in modern Australia in a speech from the steps of the Sydney Opera House: 'If they said their predicament was not ended, who could argue with them? But a country free enough to examine its own conscience is a land worth living in, a nation to be envied.' Thus did the possible, but far from certain, future King of Australia at once acknowledge the political issue, and diplomatically sidestep it.

Canada too clings determinedly to the last apron string, in spite of a significant and influential French element in its population, history and culture. Even the French-speaking Quebecois now accord the Queen of Britain (and, of course, of Canada) a civil welcome, unlike twenty years ago when, at the height of the Quebec separatist movement, she was booed in the streets of Montreal.

To the Canadians the monarchy is a bulwark against fears that their giant and powerful southern neighbour will swallow them up economically and culturally and turn them into little more than the fifty-first state of the Union. The fears have been stirred again with discussions on a free trade area between

Canada and the United States. A hereditary monarchy makes them distinctively different from their republican neighbour, and it remains an important element in Canada's long struggle to find a national identity.

If Prince Charles goes to Canada, or Australia, or New Zealand, or any of the sixteen Commonwealth countries of which the Queen remains heads of state, he is strictly speaking not visiting a foreign country at all, for he is heir to the throne of Australia as much as he is heir to the throne of Britain. When he and Diana visited Australia for the 1988 Bicentennial, the Royal Australian Air Force sent a Boeing 707 to London to fetch them; Australia and Canada always do so when Charles or his mother is paying an official visit, and it is the host country which foots the bill. If the visit is to somewhere far-flung and indisputably foreign, he will travel by a British scheduled airline, sometimes on a specially chartered aircraft but just as often in the curtained-off first-class section of a normal commercial flight. If the destination is within range, as is most of Europe, he will travel in one of the two British Aerospace 146 jets recently bought for the Queen's Flight at a cost of £20 million each, a bill paid by the Ministry of Defence.

Travel can be subject to last-minute changes of plan. It had been the intention that the Waleses should embark on their nine-day tour of friendly states on the Arabian Peninsula by a scheduled flight of British Caledonian Airways, taking over the first-class compartment to insulate them and their party from the inevitably curious eyes of the fare-paying passengers at the rear. But three days before departure the Prime Minister's office intervened, voicing concern for the aircraft's safety. Britain had recently broken off diplomatic relations with Syria, and in such a volatile area of the world the possibility had to be considered of a retaliatory strike against a civil aircraft.

It is difficult, even for royalty, to argue with the Prime Minister's office. The Ministry of Defence was ordered to tell the RAF to produce one of its VC10 passenger jets equipped with anti-missile devices and advanced radar, and normally used for flying the highest military personnel around the world; it was an order with which the RAF naturally complied, but not without some difficulty given that its fleet is in constant use. Somewhere across the Atlantic, a party of NATO generals suddenly had to alter their flight plans; their VC10 was diverted to Brize Norton air base in Oxfordshire, where it picked up the royal party and conveyed them in superb comfort (no commercial airline can better the standard of service on RAF VIP flying) to Muscat on the Gulf, accompanied for part of its journey by a Nimrod reconnaissance aircraft and two Phantom jet fighters.

Charles's official forays abroad consume the time and energies of a large number of people, not only during the visit but also during the months of planning which precede every one. Because of Charles's crowded diary invitations have to be received at the very least six months, and preferably a year, in advance. Then the Foreign Office has to be consulted on the desirability of Britain sending one of its most powerful diplomatic weapons to the country in question; if the government says no, the visit does not take place. But that rarely happens, as informal feelers will have been put out through the normal channels of diplomacy before the official invitation is issued.

There then follows six months of intensive planning, with the host country sending proposed itineraries to Charles's office, and the local British Embassy acting as a go-between and adviser on what the royal visitors might or might not like. On the whole, Charles will go where his hosts want him to, but proposed programmes sometimes have to be severely curtailed as, in their enthusiasm to show the royal visitors everything, the hosts barely leave Charles enough time to visit the lavatory. Even in their final form, after much discussion and compromise, tour schedules tend to be punishingly exhausting, especially in hot countries.

They also tend to be singularly unimaginative. During their tour of West Germany at the end of 1987, Charles and Diana seemed locked into an endless round of Golden Book ceremonies, signing the distinguished visitors' book and making strained conversation with the burgomeister of every town they passed through. At least their hosts in Bavaria took them to the opera.

There are certain immovable feasts which can safely be predicted to appear on every itinerary. They will always be obliged to visit a museum. There will be a banquet with local dignitaries almost every night. In a non-Commonwealth country Charles will always be shown the local office of the British Council, the quasi-official body charged with spreading the gospel of British culture and the English language, and he will inevitably be told that the British government is acting with criminal irresponsibility in cutting the funds for its work. There is always an underlying and highly impertinent presumption that Diana, poor little brainless bimbo, is incapable of understanding the serious world, and invariably there will be a children's school for her to visit. There will always be a fashion show – sometimes a trade show of British clothing and sometimes a display of local designers' efforts – to which both are invited and at which Diana becomes animated while Charles has a tendency to nod off. And there will always be a reception at the British Embassy for leading members of the expatriate community, at which British wives can twitter and coo and wear their best hats. The Embassy staff will have spent months of excruciating effort compiling the guest list.

Charles can veto any programme he is asked to undertake, but on the whole he goes along with what is proposed. What he does like included is a visit to a British trade fair, which makes him feel that he is doing something tangible and useful in using his media stardom to draw attention to British exports. Unfortunately the British are notoriously bad at coordinating their export efforts, and foreigners are constantly surprised to learn that if a British trade promotion is in town it is generally no thanks to the British government, but as a result of individual enterprise and the efforts of private exhibition contractors.

One of the more successful trade promotions was staged by a major Hamburg department store to coincide with Charles and Diana's visit to the city at the end of 1987. The shop stocked up with more than £1 million of British merchandise, from Scotch whisky to Royal Doulton china, from Burberry raincoats to English marmalade. The store was decked with British flags, and when the royal couple arrived to tour the counters a crowd of thousands in the street outside fought for a sight of them. Their single day's visit to Hamburg reputedly generated orders for £10 million worth of British merchandise.

The largest British trade fair ever mounted abroad was held in the Red Sea port of Jeddah to coincide with the Waleses' tour of Saudi Arabia; no fewer than 170 British companies had been persuaded to take stands. Charles arrived without his wife, who had been given the afternoon off, and made straight for the Jaguar cars stand where the new XJ40 model was on display. 'My brother already has one, and he's delighted with it,' he told Barrie Felton, the company's representative in Saudi Arabia. Felton beamed from ear to ear, praying that the sheikhs crowding round the stand had overheard. 'We are in with a great chance; the rich Saudis are becoming bored with Mercedes. Our problem is that we cannot get enough from the factory to satisfy the demand,' he told Charles, who immediately offered to telephone Sir John Egan, Jaguar's chairman, on his return to London, to ask him to divert more of the scarce models to Jeddah to satisfy a hungry market. The hapless Felton told Charles that he had 2000 advance orders for the XJ40, and only two cars in stock. It must be assumed that if Sir John Egan had had a single XJ40 to spare, it would not have needed a telephone call from the heir to the throne to get it to market.

Asad Mahmood, the local Jaguar importer, chimed in. 'Members of the Saudi royal family now drive Jaguars, so they are very fashionable. Women may not be allowed to drive here, but they have a great influence on their husbands' car buying. Women love the sensuous, stylish Jaguar lines compared with the solid Mercedes.' Charles nodded sagely, thinking no doubt of his own elderly but sensuous blue Aston Martin DB7.

Charles was so engrossed in the motor stands that he missed the best export story of the whole show. As the royal entourage ploughed its way down the aisles between stands it was followed by an anxious Asian clasping a package, who eventually managed to grasp the immaculate white naval coat tails of Commander Richard Aylard, Diana's equerry. He gave Aylard the package and urged him to give it to Charles; the ever-courteous Aylard agreed. The package contained twelve tubes of toothpaste – Islamic toothpaste said by the Asian, who was its importer, to be the first of its kind, which satisfied Muslim law by containing no animal fats. The good news was that it was made in England.

One item which used to appear on every royal tour itinerary has been quietly dropped by Charles. The cocktail party for the Press, both local and travelling British, at the beginning of each visit, avoided the need for the royal couple having to talk to the reporters again for the rest of the trip. It was intended as a purely social occasion, about which nothing could be repeated – especially conversations with the host – and all notebooks, cameras and recorders had to be left at the door. The royal Press entourage used to be a small and select band of accredited court correspondents from the main broadcasting media and one or two of the serious quality papers. But since Charles and Diana's marriage it has grown into a large, rowdy and unmanageable scrum, chiefly of photographers whose trademarks are a pair of sharp elbows and a small set of aluminium stepladders to see over the heads of the crowd. A travelling pack of 150 from Britain is not uncommon on the major tours, with as many again from local media.

Looking after the Press is a major organizational feat in itself, usually left to a hapless second secretary at the local British Embassy who wishes he had been put in charge of the table plan at the official banquet instead. The journalists and photographers have to be given positions at every function from which they may observe and photograph, and they have to be moved in buses, often with police escort, several steps ahead of the royal party wherever they move. A television and camera corral is a most entertaining sideshow, as the cameramen fight each other for the best view, and the air is loud with strong language and the tinny clatter of the infernal stepladders. They are barely recognizable in their best suits and party dresses when they arrive at the cocktail party, revealing themselves to be an amusing and companionable crew with a strong camaraderie and an almost obsessive dedication to their trade.

It was not they who brought the cocktail parties to an end, for the British travelling Press know the rules, respect their quarry even if they are sometimes somewhat intrusive in pursuit of their jobs, and have no wish to queer their pitch in what is already a difficult enough business. The guilty party was a Spanish woman television reporter, who heard as well as everyone else the stern lecture, in English and Spanish, before they entered the party salon, that all conversations were definitely off the record. The convention had been generally well observed in the past, and both Charles and Diana had unbent a little, chatting quite freely and amiably with the pressmen.

The Spanish reporter cornered Charles and asked him if he were not afraid of an assassination attempt by Basque terrorists while in Spain. Charles shrugged his shoulders and intimated that, if a bullet had his name on it, there was very little he could do about it. If he was going to worry about terrorists, he said, he would be much more concerned about the IRA than the Basques. Before the party was over the reporter had gone out into the courtyard where a live television camera was set up, and she went straight into the main Madrid evening news bulletin with a breathless verbatim account of her conversation. Charles was furious, and there have been no more cocktail parties. But Buckingham Palace cannot bring itself to admit outright the reason why; instead they offer transparent excuses, like a lack of time, or too many cities to visit and not wishing to hold the party in one city for fear of offending the others.

Charles will not greatly miss the parties; he never much enjoyed talking to the Press, even socially, although he has himself said that the time to start worrying is when they cease covering him. Even he has apparently accepted the idea, which could be a dangerous one, that at least part of the reason for his existence is as a media event.

Press arrangements are a major concern of the 'recce' which precedes every foreign visit. A month or two before each tour begins a small party from Charles's staff will go out to pace and time every step of his planned itinerary and go through the arrangements in minute detail. The party will usually consist of Sir John Riddell, a Royalty Protection Group police officer to inspect security arrangements, and Philip Mackie, the retired Edinburgh newspaper executive who has taken over as Charles's Press secretary since the return to his native Canada and subsequently untimely death from cancer of the bluff Victor Chapman.

The party which undertakes the actual tour will be a great deal bigger, and on the Bicentennial tour of Australia early in 1988 no fewer than twenty travellers from the household managed to hitch a ride on Charles's coat-tails. A more normal party will consist of Charles and Diana, Sir John Riddell, one of Charles's two assistant private secretaries Rupert Fairfax or David Wright (who replaced Humphrey Mews), Richard Aylard to act as Diana's equerry, secretary and scooper-up of official gifts, Anne Beckwith-Smith, Diana's lady-in-waiting, Philip Mackie, two personal police officers, Charles's valet, Diana's dresser and hairdresser, two lady clerks from Buckingham Palace to process the paperwork, and Ronald Ferguson, who tags along if there is the slightest chance of a game of polo.

If it is a polo-playing country, there will be a match. Charles is obliged to play in the middle of a hectic official schedule, without the benefit of mental and physical preparation which any serious player would consider necessary. That in itself is a credit to his ability. Perhaps the most exotic match he ever played was in Muscat on his Arabian tour of 1986. Fears that he might dissolve in a puddle of perspiration were dispelled when a cooling breeze took the edge off the fierce sunshine beating down on the hard-packed sand pitch of the Royal Oman Polo Club, whose team had managed to thrash the Prince's side at Windsor the previous year. The loudspeakers played Handel's *Water Music*, a curious choice for the desert, and the Arabic commentator constantly referred to the royal player as 'Amir Charles' and his most ardent spectator as 'Amira Diana'. Light relief was provided during the interval by the Royal Oman Police Mounted Camel Pipe Band, an unlikely spectacle if ever there was one, rendering an eclectic programme that encompassed the only known bagpipe version of the *Ode to Joy* from Beethoven's Ninth Symphony, and *God Bless the Prince of Wales*.

Charles was joined in his team by two local players and Ronald Ferguson. The Prince, looking exceedingly flushed, played an aggressive game and scored one goal, while Major Ferguson scored another to end the match 3-3 level with the opposition of two Omanis and two expatriate Britons. It was not Charles's happiest game. At the end of each chukka he was inspected by a doctor for heatstroke; he received a hefty smack on the wrist from an opposition mallet; and his stirrup broke, causing him to slide from the saddle and sit beating the ground in frustration with his fist. The prize of a Waterford crystal vase, inevitably named the Sultan Qaboos Trophy after the ruler of Oman, was awarded to the home team despite the draw, on the grounds that they had won it at Windsor and therefore retained it. But in polo everyone gets a prize, even the two umpires. Major Ferguson was presented with a khanjar, a traditional silver curved dagger, while Charles received from his wife a silver coffee pot and a kiss. Kissing in public is not done in Arabia, and the moment was pointedly missing from that evening's local television coverage of the event. Within an hour Charles was showered, changed, and attending a reception at the British Embassy.

How much these foreign tours cost, and who pays, is a difficult matter to establish. Naturally the host country bears the brunt of the expense. If transport is by aircraft of the Queen's Flight, then the bill is ultimately footed by the Ministry of Defence. If it is by commercial airline, the Foreign and Commonwealth Office may step in with travel funds, provided the tour in question has some hint of diplomatic purpose. The man who pays least is Charles himself; he has no income from the Civil List to cover his working expenses, and he lives almost entirely off the income from the Duchy of Cornwall. From that he will have to pay for Diana's extensive wardrobe, a not inconsiderable item in itself, and for the official gifts he hands over to his hosts. The gifts are generally modest by comparison with what he receives; a small piece of silver, perhaps a painting, or, in the case of his present to Sultan Qaboos of Oman, an Appaloosa mare foaled in England. He and Diana collect in return offerings that are sometimes embarrassingly opulent, in spite of an instruction in the advance protocol guidelines that they should be modest. On their Arabian tour Diana received some spectacular jewellery in spite of Palace denials that she had been given any such thing. One especially fine set of matching diamond necklace, earrings and brooch did not make its first public appearance until almost a year later, when Diana wore it to a banquet in Munich.

Whether or not overseas tours are worth all the effort is an unanswerable question because there is no clear balance sheet of effort and result that can be drawn up. As media events they are generally a triumph in the host country, and British television will usually add to nightly news coverage with a half-hour end-of-week compilation of the prettiest footage. They are, therefore, a generally successful public relations exercise on behalf of the British monarchy. On the diplomatic front they certainly do no harm, and although royalty no longer has the power to make or break international alliances, they certainly play their part in cementing good will. As a boost to the export effort they are a unique and useful piece of advertising for Britain, and the ambassadors and trade counsellors at British embassies abroad, while dreading the mountain of organization that royal tours present them with, certainly welcome them. But it would be exceptionally hard to prove that a single extra British construction contract, or Jaguar car, or tube of English-made Islamic toothpaste, was sold because of the presence of the Prince of Wales.

Charles has mixed feelings about them. He loved Italy, because to all intents and purposes he was the traditional English aristocrat making the Grand Tour, albeit a little late in life. He is prepared to undertake them if he can be persuaded that his presence will make some contribution, however indefinable, to British exports. Diana has no great love of them; they are extremely exhausting, and they separate her from her children.,

Standing on that wet and windy rampart above the city of Lisbon on a foul February morning, Charles certainly had the look about him of a man who would rather have been standing in the rain in Brixton trying to find an unemployed black youth a job. Or perhaps it was simply that polo was out of season.

13

King Charles III

EDWARD GIBBON, in his majestic chronicle of the decline and fall of the Roman Empire, dwelt with approval on the concept of a king who reigns by birthright, and considered that Imperial Rome might have been the better for embracing it longer. 'Of the various forms of government which have prevailed in the world, an hereditary monarchy seems to present the fairest scope for ridicule. Is it possible to relate without an indignant smile, that, on the father's decease, the property of a nation, like that of a drove of oxen, descends to his infant son, as yet unknown to mankind and himself, and that the bravest warriors and the wisest statesmen, relinquishing their natural right to empire, approach the royal cradle with bended knees and protestations of inviolable fidelity?

'Satire and declamation may paint these obvious topics in the most dazzling colours, but our most serious thoughts will respect a useful prejudice, that establishes a rule of succession, independent of the passions of mankind; and we shall cheerfully acquiesce in any expedient which deprives the multitude of the dangerous, and indeed the ideal, power of giving themselves a master ... The superior prerogative of birth, when it has obtained a sanction of time and popular opinion, is the plainest and least invidious of all distinctions among mankind. The acknowledged right extinguishes the hope of faction, and the conscious security disarms the cruelty of the monarch.'

What Rome abandoned after seven kings and 243 years, Britain still retains. Queen Elizabeth reigns in conscious security, and is disarmed of all cruelty. Now and again her family are incautious enough to offer some modest scope for ridicule, but the barbs of present-day satirists are hopelessly blunt in comparison with the knife-blades of their Georgian ancestors, and the person and institution of monarchy are wounded barely at all. The portrayal of Charles as a transcendental meditator who talks to flowers is bordering on the kindly.

The portly and dissolute King Farouk of Egypt predicted, at about the middle of the present century, that by the year 2000 there would be only five monarchs left in Europe: the four kings in a pack of cards and the king of Great Britain.

With only a dozen years to go his prediction seems unlikely to be fulfilled, for although in the intervening years Greece has lost a monarchy, Spain has regained one. But Farouk was speaking at a time when, after two world wars which reshaped the continent, the resorts of Europe were littered with deposed monarchs – all of them living proof, as Oliver Cromwell could have told them, that no king reigns by divine right.

Since the French toppled and topped the Bourbons in 1789, the great majority of the world's thrones have fallen to revolution, republicanism or invasion. At the beginning of the twentieth century almost every country in Europe except France and Switzerland had as its head of state a hereditary monarch. Even Norway, a nation born only this century, chose hereditary monarchy rather than elected presidency when it declared independence from Sweden in 1905, and sent over to the well-stocked royal house of Denmark for a suitable candidate. The decision was born of political reality; the Norwegian Prime Minister remarked that the country was more likely to win friends in predominantly monarchist Europe if it introduced a new member to the 'trade union of kings', and went on to note that a crowned head would be a more effective focus for the loyalty of the infant nation, well above the level of mere squabbling politics. In a referendum the Norwegian people voted 259,000 to 69,000 in favour of

Prince Carl of Denmark, who sailed into Oslo harbour bearing the new name of King Haakon VII.

Now, a handful of tiny and eccentric principalities apart, only Great Britain, Norway, Sweden, Denmark, the Netherlands, Belgium and Spain remain as European constitutional monarchies. Some of those once and former monarchs were swept away by revolution, war and the westward advance of Soviet Communism. Others crumbled under their own weaknesses of political ineptitude or sheer arrogance.

Spain has restored its monarchy, but in truth it never fully went away, for General Franco saw himself more as a caretaker than the founder of a dynasty. King Juan Carlos was not long back in power in Madrid when he had to fend off an attempt by the Army to dethrone him, a crisis he defused by skilful political judgement. He had the support of a majority of Spaniards, who had perhaps heeded the further words of Gibbon: 'The temper of soldiers, habituated at once to violence and to slavery, renders them very unfit guardians of a legal or even a civil constitution. Justice, humanity, or political wisdom, are qualities they are too little acquainted with in themselves to appreciate them in others. Valour will acquire their esteem, and liberality will purchase their suffrage; but the first of these merits is often lodged in the most savage breasts; the latter can only exert itself at the expense of the public; and both may be turned against the possessor of the throne by the ambition of a daring rival.'

When King Charles III ascends the throne he will reign, according to his full titles, By the Grace of God. He will also reign by the grace of the Act of Settlement. Were heredity the only criterion, we in Britain might well now be reigned over by Prince Franz of Bavaria, who instead lives the life of a minor German aristocrat in one wing of the splendid Schloss Nymphenburg outside Munich. Charles, in jovial mood, recognized this improbable fact when he visited Franz during his 1987 tour of Germany: 'Were it not for the Act of Settlement, the present head of the royal house of Bavaria would probably have a better claim to the British throne than myself. His claim comes through the daughter of King Charles I, who was careless enough to lose his head through an argument with Parliament. I only hope that the Prince of Bavaria does not press his claim too hard during lunch.'

James II of Great Britain was the last Roman Catholic king of a predominantly Protestant nation. His flight and subsequent defeat by the Protestant William of Orange at the Battle of the Boyne in 1690, an event remembered with undue obsession by the Protestant community of Northern Ireland, persuaded Parliament to take steps to ensure that his descendants never again occupied the British throne.

They tried, of course. In 1715 the Old Pretender James Stuart, and thirty years later the Young Pretender Prince Charles Edward Stuart, attempted to recapture the throne from a base of Scottish support, but both were soundly defeated by force of arms and public apathy. James II's second daughter Queen Anne did in fact occupy the throne, but she was tolerated for her profession of the Protestant religion. The 1701 Act however, ensured that she was the last Stuart.

The Act declared that in the event of Anne leaving no lawful heirs – which she did not – the British Crown should pass to the Electress Sophia of Hanover, a descendant of James VI of Scotland through his daughter Elizabeth of Bohemia, the so-called 'Winter Queen'. In the line of succession, far down it though she was, she was the first available Protestant. In the event Sophia died shortly before Anne, and the British Crown passed to Sophia's son the Elector of Hanover who arrived in London speaking not a word of English to reign as King George I. From him all succeeding British monarchs are descended in a relatively direct line.

After the vicissitudes and sideways leaps of past history, the line has become remarkably direct. When Charles ascends the throne he will follow Victoria, Edward VII, George V, George VI and Elizabeth II as the sixth generation of a direct line from parent to child, dented only by the abdication of Edward VIII when the throne passed from brother to brother. Such an uninterrupted run is unmatched since the days of the early Plantagenet kings, but the Act of Settlement is nonetheless proof beyond doubt that British monarchs reign, not by divine right not ultimately even by descent, but by the will of Parliament and people.

The Act of Settlement remains in force, and even today it occasionally surfaces to wag an admonitory finger at the British Crown's dealings with the Roman Catholic church. Prince Michael of Kent and the Earl of St Andrews, son of the Duke of Kent, have surrendered their admittedly lowly places in the line of succession by their marriages to Roman Catholics; had there been any truth in the 1977 rumour that Charles was to marry the Roman Catholic Princess Marie-Astrid of Luxembourg, it would have provoked a constitutional crisis which, taken to its logical conclusion, could have obliged Charles to give up his claim to the throne. The Act was waved under Charles's nose in 1985 when, from the best of ecumenical intentions, he desired to join Pope John Paul II in the saying of early morning mass in the Vatican. There is much of Protestant Britain that still will have no truck with Rome, and would oppose vigorously any attempt to repeal the 1701 Act.

Much of the history of the British monarchy is a history of its wings being clipped and its power being nibbled away – chiefly as a protection against bad kings – from the Magna Carta through the Bill of Rights to George III's surrender of the Crown lands in return for a salary from Parliament, still in existence as the Civil List. Erosion of the absolute power of monarchy began with King John's accession to the demands of his barons at Runnymede in 1215, reaffirming the rights of the church and preventing the king from extorting unlimited feudal dues without the agreement of his tenants-in-chief.

The present-day constitutional position of the Crown was largely determined by the Bill of Rights of 1689, presented to William of Orange and his wife before they ascended the throne in 1690 as William and Mary. It made illegal the suspension of laws, the levying of taxes or the keeping of a peacetime standing army by the Crown without the consent of Parliament, while enshrining the right of any citizen to petition the Crown. Since then the monarchy has gradually retreated from the political arena, and the fulcrum of government has shifted from Crown to Prime Minister.

The present house of Windsor, which would prefer us to forget that it is in fact the German house of Saxe-Coburg-Gotha under another name, has been a dynasty of benevolent philistines whose principal talent has been for survival, by keeping out of the political bear-pit altogether. There is no King's Party – except briefly during the 1936 Abdication crisis – and the days are definitely gone when the heir to the throne could, as the Prince Regent did in the reign of George III, act as a focus for the aspirations of the Parliamentary Opposition, encouraging it by the hope of eventual power. That was fine when the choice of a prime minster and his Cabinet colleagues rested largely with the sovereign; then there was something to be said for the heir making it his business to consort with those who for the moment were out of political favour. The historian Macaulay certainly thought so: 'Nothing is more natural than that, in a monarchy where a constitutional Opposition exists, the Heir Apparent of the throne should put himself at the head of that Opposition.'

Prince Charles, by contrast, in his public espousal of alternative causes like complementary medicine and the evils of unbridled property development, is a long way from being a spokesman for the Labour Opposition, and the issues he chooses are not ones which obviously divide parties. He would be extremely foolish if they were.

Today the emperor is truly without clothes, but it is to the credit of the Windsor dynasty that it recognizes that fact exceedingly well. The direct power of the Crown is almost entirely emasculated. By the definition of Walter Bagehot, the popular constitutional theorist of the Victorian age, the monarch retains only four rights: the right to be consulted, the right to encourage, the right to advise, and the right to warn. All government is carried out in the name of the Crown; all the judiciary and the armed forces swear allegiance to it, but the Crown can effectively do nothing to bend the will of elected government.

And therein lies the secret of its success. Because it can do so little, there is little it does that can be opposed. Yet, though its power may be minimal, its influence is enormous. It is firmly entrenched in what would otherwise be a dangerous vacuum; its strength does not lie in the power it has, but in the power it denies to others. Its purpose is not to do, but to be.

Its mere existence, with all its grandeur and weight of tradition, exists as a check on the power and pretensions of the prime minister of the day, whose office is decorated with no such pomp or privilege. Even the socialist George Orwell, writing in 1944, approved: 'It is at any rate possible that, while this division of functions exists, a Hitler or a Stalin cannot come to power.' It is perhaps significant that relations between the current sovereign and the most presidentially-inclined occupant of 10 Downing Street for many a year are said to be decidely cool.

The Crown draws its appeal from a stability and continuity that must remain unruffled by the shifting winds of the prevailing political climate, and yet it must appear relevant to its times. It must uphold currently held values, and it must be seen. The last serious bout of republicanism occurred in Britain when the widowed Victoria withdrew almost entirely from the public stage, while her son became a philanderer of very considerable reputation.

There is little danger in these present times of the monarchy withdrawing from public view. Television transmits its pomp and ceremony to the entire world, engendering envy in younger nations who see on their screens the State Opening of Parliament or Prince Charles's wedding, of which latter event an American newspaper commented: 'The Royal Family of England pulls off ceremonies the way the army of Israel pulls off commando raids.' At another level the British popular Press – and to a much worse extent the continental – is constantly raking over the family's domestic coals in search of inconsequential titbits or of moral laxity, real or imagined. We set them up as paragons, yet revel in their failings.

Interest in the royal family as a *family* has for long been at the core of monarchy's appeal. Bagehot, writing soon after the marriage of the future Edward VII in 1863, observed: 'A family on the throne is an interesting idea also. It brings down the pride of sovereignty to the level of petty life. No feeling could seem more childish than the enthusiasm of the English at the marriage of the Prince of Wales. They treated as a great political event what, looked at as a matter of pure business, was very small indeed. But no feeling could be more like common human nature as it is, and as it is likely to be.' The passage could almost have been written about the marriage of the present Prince of Wales except that, instead of being treated as a great political event, the 1981 version was treated as a major production of show business. Thus has public perception changed.

Public exposure is now so great that it brings the danger of destroying the mystique that Bagehot thought so essential to the survival of the institution. The Queen has managed to remain largely aloof, allowing only strictly limited and controlled glimpses into her private life, and thereby escaping with her dignity and reputation commendably unblemished. There are many times when she wishes the media would take *more* interest in her; she has been known to be quite put out when television and Press have largely ignored some of her worthy but less exciting overseas visits. But she detests intrusion into her privacy; her agreement to the BBC/ITV film *Royal Family* in 1969 was not entirely altruistic; it was partly a public relations exercise to launch Prince Charles on his public life at Caernarfon.

She has been able to exercise rather less control over members of her family and their appearance in the media. Much of it is harmless enough, but not all; the sight of two of her sons, her daughter and her daughter-in-law making fools of themselves in a charity edition of the television game show *It's a Knockout* caused her considerable disquiet. There is no point in members of the royal family trying to pretend they are just like other people; if they come to be perceived just as other people, then why should they be accorded their position of privilege?

For some years Charles was open with and accessible to the media, but he has grown wary and sceptical even of television, in spite of always having come over as an appealing, charming and intelligent character, and never having indulged in undignified stunts. He feels the media always trivializes him and is more concerned with the minutiae of his private life rather than his work and concerns. And like other public men, he complains of being misrepresented. He finally gave up the ghost after the showing of a favourable, even obsequious, two-part television documentary on him, when he realized that all anyone had remembered of it was his light-hearted aside that he talked to his plants. He has become withdrawn, to the extent that he will no longer agree to interviews with authors attempting a serious appraisal of his work.

But if he has closed the shutters on questions about himself, he becomes ever more voluble and contentious on the public platform upon matters which concern him. The question is whether in doing so he strays into the political minefield which the Crown is supposed so assiduously to avoid if it is to continue to reign with the support of the people. To understand that it is necessary to understand the essential difference in the position of the monarch and that of her Heir Apparent. Each plays an important role in the functioning of the Crown, but these roles are quite different.

There is only one sovereign. By convention – for the job description of monarchy is nowhere officially written down – she strictly avoids the expression of political opinions which could in any way be contrived as contentious. She is there to symbolize continuity beyond the span of elected governments, and to personify the nation's common ethos. Mostly she has been scrupulous in her political silence, except on one occasion in 1986 when she allowed her then press secretary, Michael Shea, to let it be known to *The Sunday Times* that she felt Margaret Thatcher was an unfeeling Prime Minister who was leading the nation into a dangerous division of haves and have-nots. The inspiration for the leak was strongly suspected at the time to be Prince Philip, but it almost certainly was an accurate reflection of the Queen's own views; she is by upbringing and inclination an old-fashioned patrician Tory of the pre-Thatcherite kind that believed in one nation in which the rich looked after the poor.

She also has sympathy, no doubt, with a moderate Labour outlook, and it has always been claimed, and never denied, that she warmed particularly to her Labour Prime Ministers Harold Wilson and James Callaghan. It would, of course, be in the interests of one nation for the pinnacle of High Toryism to display at least a working rapport with the socialist camp. In spite of her lack of formal education she is sharp, perceptive and with an experience of the nation's affairs no mere politician can match; Americans would call her pretty damn smart.

The position of the Prince of Wales is quite different. Unlike the Queen, whose function is one either of ceremonial or of strictly private consultation with her ministers and advisers, his role is almost entirely public. Unless he is acting for the Queen in her absence abroad, he has no formal part to play in the affairs of State, and to a large degree it is up to each individual heir what he does with himself during his sometimes lengthy wait for the Crown. Since Crown princes ceased to be a focus for the Parliamentary Opposition, they have become variously playboys, full-time sailors, or social workers; the only unwritten stipulation – which has not been universally observed – is that they should not bring the Crown into disrepute, nor nail it by association to any particular political faction.

Prince Charles avoids politics, although his detractors claim that he treads too close to the political arena. To associate himself with an obviously Tory or anti-Tory view would immediately limit his freedom of expression and his credibility, and would by association tarnish the shining

248

detachment of the Crown. He would not wish the latter; he has an enormous and utterly unwavering respect for his mother. His pronouncements on inner cities are not party political; they spring from a deeper philosophical well. It is noticeable that, apart from two anodyne speeches early in his full-time career as Crown prince, he has declined to use his seat in the House of Lords as a platform for his crusades.

Instead of political attachment, Charles has a strong and positive personal commitment which is entirely his own. Privately, his politics lie somewhere between the Social Democrats and the wetter wings of the Tory party; he is certainly no adherent of Thatcherism, its relentless meritocracy and unbridled *laissez faire* capitalism, although there are some elements of the New Conservatism that he undoubtedly shares.

He has, in his own sometimes vague and ethereal way, become a focus for an opposing view, but for an alternative view of present-day society rather than for the narrow factional interests of Parliamentary Opposition, some of which would indeed like to abolish the post he is destined to inherit.

His views can occasionally appear disjointed, his thoughts random and his outlook dreamlike. But his overriding and unifying philosophy is that our modern technological civilization pays too little attention to the spiritual dimension of life. In our headlong rush to make a better microchip for which the world will beat a path to our door, we have forgotten all that is best and noblest in our cultural and religious heritage, and are destroying the earth in the process.

He told an American audience at the 350th anniversary celebrations of Harvard University: 'While we have been right to demand the kind of technical education relevant to the needs of the twentieth century it would appear that we may have forgotten that when all is said and done a good man, as the Greeks would say, is a nobler work than a good technologist. We should never lose sight of the fact that to avert disaster we have not only to teach men to make things, but also to produce people who have complete moral control over the things they make. Never has this been more essential and urgent than at this moment in man's development. Never has it been more important to recognize the imbalance that has seeped into our lives and deprived us of a sense of meaning because the emphasis has been too one-sided and has concentrated on the development of the intellect to the detriment of the spirit.'

And he went on: 'Surely it is important that in the headlong rush of mankind to conquer space, to compete with nature to harness the fragile environment, we do not let our children slip away into a world dominated entirely by sophisticated technology, but rather teach them that to live in this world is not an easy matter without standards to live by.'

His exploration of the spiritual against the technological has manifested itself in many ways. He believes in the conservation of the countryside, because technology and greed have destroyed so much of it, from the wild flower meadows of the West Country to the forests of the Amazon, whose rapid shrinkage in the cause of profit he largely blames for upsetting the weather patterns and bringing drought and famine to Ethiopia. He is an immense admirer of Bob Geldof, and vice versa. He has expressed an interest in the paranormal, and an admiration for one of its most eminent explorers, the late Arthur Koestler. He has supported alternative medicine, partly through a long tradition of royal faith in homeopathy, and partly through a belief that the patient's state of mind is as much a key to healing as are powerful drugs.

It manifests itself too in a belief in the human dimension of life, and things that operate on a human scale. He likes individualism, and supports it against the might of bureaucracy, and against experts who think they know what is good for people better than the people themselves. He is a staunch believer in the philosophy that small is beautiful, because in the big the individual loses his soul. He dislikes the monumental brutalism of high-rise building, because it offends his sense of classical tradition and destroys the human scale of cities.

The inner cities are an area in which he feels his small-scale individualist approach can be advanced without becoming a divisive political issue; he is certainly not in a position to head any large-scale, corporatist approach, because then he would have to be the chairman of a municipal authority, or a capitalist property developer. He advocates community architecture, because it gives tenants a say in the kind of houses they live in, and through various trusts he promotes small-scale job creation, because it fits his individualist philosophy and because it is something which, in his position, he is actually able to do.

He enjoys the luxury of not being a politician who has to grapple head-on with the country's social problems; he can, if he so wishes, turn on his heel and walk away from any of his concerns at a moment's notice. But his position of privilege brings with it the frustration of relative powerlessness. Recently he crossed swords with the Ministry of Defence; always concerned for the fate of ethnic minorities, he remarked to a group of senior Army officers over dinner that there were never any black Guardsmen on duty outside Buckingham Palace. Something, he said, should be done about the obvious racial imbalance of the elite Brigade of Guards; perhaps the formation of an all-black Guards unit. No such thing happened; some months later one token black Guardsman was admitted to the ranks.

Should he be airing views about contentious subjects at all? As he has said himself, 'I don't have to do this, you know.' Viscount Whitelaw, the former Deputy Prime Minister, said in a recent magazine interview, 'I think he can raise questions, but not propose solutions.'

On the subject of inner cities, he keeps before the public mind a major issue which politicians might be tempted to neglect, or to turn to narrow party advantage. It is a public cause of high concern, and the general principle that something must be done about it is shared by all major political parties; the only difference between them is how, and how urgently. He tries to address the subject intelligently

– his background research, initially dangerously sketchy, is improving as his knowledge grows – humanely, and always with the common man in mind.

It is something of a paradox that one of his guiding lights should be the German Jew, Kurt Hahn, whose educational philosophy was designed to breed a ruling caste for the rudderless society of Weimar Germany. Charles's appeal is at its narrowest when he prescribes doses of character-forming adventure as a pick-me-up to the ills of listlessness and unemployment among the young. It smacks a little too much of elitism, of benefiting only those who pass the commando-style entrance tests, although several thousand youngsters who sailed in Operations Drake and Raleigh would no doubt disagree.

He walks a tightrope, from which he can so easily tumble, on the one side into the desert of meaningless platitude and on the other into the shark-infested waters of party political debate. On the whole he has kept his balance with great skill, and those who think he is about to lose his footing should remember that ultimately he represents nobody's point of view but his own. Yet he has won sufficient popular support and affection for his various stances, especially with the ordinary man, for him to be less racked by insecurity and self-doubt than he clearly is.

Charles represents the future, and his interests and causes are therefore understandably directed chiefly at the young. He is there to represent and encourage what is good in our contemporary culture, and what carries hope for the eventual reign of King Charles III. But he never speculates about his own reign-to-be, because that implies criticism of the present reign; he was furious with the architect Rod Hackney who claimed that Charles, voicing concern that he would inherit a divided nation, had used the phrase 'When I am King'. Charles denied that he had said such a thing, or ever would; it implied that his mother would one day die, which she surely will, but it is *lèse-majesté* for the heir to remind the nation of that inevitability.

Nor will he entertain any suggestion of his mother's abdication, an option occasionally raised in opinion polls and favoured by those who, whilst retaining admiration and respect for Elizabeth II, would like to see Charles in the job while he is still young, energetic and attractive. Anyone who cares to wager what the Queen will do at some future date would be better advised to put his money on a rank outsider in next year's Derby, but abdication is against all tradition, against the Queen's nature, and against her Coronation vows; for her it would be a more fundamental breach of promises made in the name of God than would be divorce from her husband. Even a groundswell of popular opinion calling for her retirement in favour of Charles would be unlikely to change her mind. Whilst it must be admitted that almost the only certainty about the future is that predictions of it will be wrong, and whilst nothing is impossible, Charles certainly neither hopes nor expects to succeed to his destiny until he is into his sixties. His reign will be relatively brief, and all other things being equal, it is Prince William who is likely to occupy the throne for a substantial part of the twenty-first century.

That Charles should succeed at all presupposes two things; that the monarchy continues to exist in something approaching its present form and that he has the backing of the nation at large to be its representative.

Any monarch now who ascends the throne without the backing of his kingdom would be exceedingly foolish, and would run the grave risk of destroying the institution. Monarchy is neither mystical nor indispensable; it is merely useful, although at present unquestionably effective and popular.

The Stuart kings discovered that as individuals they did not rule by Divine Right; no more does the institution exist by some Almighty will. Its standing is currently high, not solely through the calibre of its present occupant, but through the decline in esteem of one of the other estates of the realm. The House of Commons has had its stature eroded by the gradual shift of real power and decision-making into the Cabinet, and because its proceedings are now broadcast for all to hear and see it is perceived to be peopled by a loutish and unseemly rabble. Against that the Crown is seen to have preserved its position and its dignity.

Because the Crown fills what would otherwise be a power vacuum, there are inevitably those who would prefer to occupy that space themselves. Opposition to the monarchy as an institution is currently small in Britain, but it does exist. The socialist left has a religious objection to the privilege and undemocratic plutocracy that monarchy represents, but abolishing the Queen is too much a vote-loser ever to have surfaced as serious Labour Party policy. The now-retired anti-monarchist MP William Hamilton was for much of his career a lone voice in his campaign against the royal family.

His principal objection was its cost to the taxpayer, which was not perhaps the most effective approach; even at a total annual cost of about £40 million, which includes maintenance of the State-owned palaces, the royal yacht and the Queen's Flight, the institution is something of a bargain, and, if nothing else, an enormous generator of tourist revenue.

The intellectual left has floated the notion that the best hope of abolishing the monarchy, or at least changing it out of all recognition to the demotic position of the bicycle-riding Danish and Swedish sovereigns, may be Prince Charles himself. An anti-royal feature in a 1987 issue of the weekly *New Statesman*, which went almost unnoticed, made an interesting assertion: 'We have a succession crisis in the making. The Crown prince, Charles, is a man with too much sensitivity and intelligence – to say nothing of his eccentricities – to take for granted the huge pretence that the plutocratic monarchist carbuncle on the face of the nation should have a socially useful or even acceptable role in a modern democracy which faces sharp divisions in the years ahead.'

The article concluded: 'Queen Elizabeth plods on through her royal engagements, meeting her people and other people's peoples, hoping her consort does not insult too many of them, doubtful whether her son is shrewd or ruthless enough to preserve what John Pearson (in *The Ultimate Family*) calls "the supreme achievement of the Royal House of Mountbatten-Windsor, the way it has learned to use the modern media to perpetuate itself."

'But the succession *must* come: and with it, perhaps, the best hope this country will have for the beginnings of a withdrawal from the thraldom of royalty.'

Curiously, a parallel argument can sometimes be heard expressed in privacy at the opposite end of the political spectrum. There are some dyed-in-the-wool conservative aristocrats who believe that the best guarantee of the monarchy continuing exactly as it is – and their own privileged lives therefore remaining undisturbed – lies not with Charles but with his younger brother Prince Andrew, Duke of York, a much more bluff, straightforward character who, not being gifted with Charles's sensitivity and not under quite such an obligation to find himself a useful role in life, is not racked by Charles's questioning conscience and self-doubt. Should Charles decline the throne, there would now be some constitutional embarrassment, although presumably not insuperable difficulty, in offering it to Andrew, who has slipped to fourth in line of succession.

Politicians of any persuasion who regard Charles as a foil for their own purposes are making a serious mistake. Certainly he has sometimes shown himself less than fully streetwise in political matters, as when he wanted to say mass with the Pope, but both his mother and grandfather were infinitely wetter behind the ears when they first had greatness thrust upon them.

Most importantly, beneath all Prince Charles's bleeding-heart liberal conscience, his eccentricities and his anguish about whether he is doing anything useful at all, he is an absolute traditionalist, with duty written through him like a stick of rock.

He is not really a Social Democrat at all; he is an old-fashioned Whig. That party, which held power for most of the first half of the eighteenth century, drew its support from the great English aristocratic landowning families, the new entrepreneurial business class created by the Industrial Revolution, and the Nonconformist element in the church. They advocated industrial progress, religious toleration, and were stoutly behind the Bill of Rights of 1688, and of parliamentary reform in 1832. They believed in rule by the privileged, but they also believed in a benevolent paternalism towards the working man. Their opponents were the Tories, the party of the local squire and the country parson, the party of letting things be.

Times have changed; the Whigs and Tories do not have their modern equivalents. Charles is out on a limb, because no present-day political party reflects his view of the world. The modern Conservative Party is too wedded to meritocracy and to every man for himself, the Labour Party still too rooted in the idea of the corporate state. The political centre in Britain, to which Charles might have felt himself most allied, lacks both roots and a sense of direction.

Social democracy with all its sweet reasonableness was popular with the electors in the privacy of the ballot box, but it failed when faced with the basic question of which side of the fence it sat on; was it, or was it not, for example, in favour of the nuclear defence of Europe? Political movements stand no chance unless their message is perfectly clear. Charles is a muddled thinker; there is no current faction in British politics which reflects his odd combination of aristocratic paternalism, public school do-goodery, and desire to return to the common man the spiritual dimension of life. His view of the world is eccentric, because he sees the world from a unique viewpoint.

His life is governed more by negatives than positives. He cannot be overtly political, because his family have survived through the twentieth century by keeping their heads below the factional parapet. He cannot misbehave, because two Princes of Wales within the last century did so and disturbed the foundations of the institution he was born to preserve. And he cannot actually achieve very much in any direction, because for all his high-born position he represents no one but himself. He is a chained crusader in search of a cause. He thinks he has found one, in reminding us all that there is more to life than technology. His cause is sometimes disjointed and ill-expressed, but he should not be dismayed that there is no current political movement which exactly mirrors it. He should enjoy the luxury of not having to win votes, and press on.

Yet in the long term he should not be judged by his concerns and interests as Prince of Wales. When he ascends the throne all previous bets are off, all previous views are silenced; he becomes transmogrified into the ceremonial Head of State, whose first duty is to ensure that he is not the last. He is not a revolutionary, merely a man anxious to do something useful while he awaits the inevitable, in the knowledge that then he will be truly gagged and bound by his office. He has similarities with his penfriend Pope John Paul II, whose public image is of a great peacemaker, reformer and media star, but who within the church he leads is as conservative a pontiff as it has been guided by for many a year.

By exhibiting so much social concern, and by appearing to take so little for granted, Charles is continuing the Windsor family talent for moulding itself to the times through which it lives. But he accepts his destiny and, given advisers of perception and quality – with whom he has not always been surrounded, it must be said – he can show the Crown to be an institution that is not only durable, but useful.

King Charles III is likely to disappoint the intellectual left and the aristocratic right. He has not given us many grounds for thinking that he will disappoint the rest of us.

INDEX

INDEX

James Callaghan

Time and Chance

James Callaghan's career has been unique: no other British politician has held the four great posts of Chancellor of the Exchequer, Home Secretary, Foreign Secretary and Prime Minister. In these long-awaited memoirs he writes openly of the issues and crises of the times, and conveys vividly what it is to be in the front rank of politics in a modern democracy.

He describes his relationship with the trade unions and the struggle to establish and maintain an incomes policy; the problems of law and order; the long, complex negotiations over the Common Market and arms control, and the constant battle – ultimately in vain – to prevent the devaluation of sterling. Personalities loom large, with incisive portraits of friends and rivals, Harold Wilson, Henry Kissinger, Presidents Ford and Carter among them.

Time and Chance is a compelling account of life in high office, where international conflicts vie for attention with the bubbling cauldron of internal party politics.

'An accurately researched, engagingly and modestly presented account of one of the great political careers of the second half of this century.' Roy Jenkins – *Observer*.

FONTANA PAPERBACKS

Keep Going For It!

Living the Life of an Entrepreneur

Victor Kiam is going for it again! Just in case you thought it might be time to take it easy, the king of entrepreneurs has put together a second colourful cocktail of advice and anecdote to keep you up and running with the best of them.

Victor Kiam is know to millions as 'the man who bought the company' – the man who liked the Remington shaver so much that he bought the entire corporation that made it. He took a loss-maker and made it profitable – then wrote *Going For It!*, the bestseller that explained how it was done. End of story? By no means, Victor Kiam is an entrepreneur, a man who knows that if you stop developing you're not just standing still – you're going backwards.

In *Keep Going For It!* Victor Kiam explains how to succeed as an entrepreneur – and then keep on succeeding. Whether your pitch is a market stall or a conglomerate's boardroom the principle is the same – recognize your potential, maximize that potential and keep on maximizing that potential. Just what should be done when it seems every tangible asset's been exhausted and a project still won't rise off the ground? What happens when it seems that every potential buyer for your brilliant new idea just can't see past the first trifling hurdle? What can be done when a new scheme falls flat – even crashes into failure? Who should win when your home life and your business life are set on a collision course? *Keep Going For It!* offers hardnosed solutions to each of the above – and more – with specific examples drawn from a lifetime of successful risk-taking.

If you're a true entrepreneur then business is *the* great adventure – but only if you *Keep Going For It!*

Sally Moore

Lucan: Not Guilty

On the night of 7 November 1974 Sandra Rivett, nanny to the children of Lord and Lady Lucan, was brutally murdered in their Belgravia home.

Lady Lucan was also attacked, and identified her assailant as her estranged husband, the 7th Earl of Lucan, a stylish professional gambler.

Lord Lucan disappeared that night and has been hunted, dead or alive, ever since. Seven months later, an inquest jury branded him guilty of murder. But was he – is he – innocent?

In *Lucan: Not Guilty* Sally Moore throws startling new light on the world's most baffling high society murder case. Meticulously documented and compulsively readable, it tells the fascinating inside story of a crime which has become the ultimate whodunnit.

'This enthralling book . . . is painstakingly researched' – *The Times*

'Her tale is full of mysteries . . . fine detective work' – *Literary Review*

FONTANA PAPERBACKS

Fontana Paperbacks: Non-fiction

Fontana is a leading paperback publisher of non-fiction, both popular and academic.

- ☐ Street Fighting Years *Tariq Ali* £3.95
- ☐ The Boys and the Butterflies *James Birdsall* £3.95
- ☐ Time and Chance *James Callaghan* £5.95
- ☐ Jane Fonda *Michael Freedland* £3.95
- ☐ Perestroika *Mikhail Gorbachev* £3.95
- ☐ The Real Charles *Alan Hamilton* £3.95
- ☐ Going For It! *Victor Kiam* £3.95
- ☐ Keep Going For It! *Victor Kiam* £3.50
- ☐ In the Name of the Working Class *Sandor Kopacsi* £3.95
- ☐ Lucan: Not Guilty *Sally Moore* £3.95
- ☐ Yamani *Jeffrey Robinson* £3.95
- ☐ Don't Ask the Price *Marcus Sieff* £3.95
- ☐ Nor Iron Bars a Cage *Penelope Tremayne* £3.95
- ☐ Just Williams *Kenneth Williams* £2.95

You can buy Fontana paperbacks at your local bookshop or newsagent. Or you can order them from Fontana Paperbacks, Cash Sales Department, Box 29, Douglas, Isle of Man. Please send a cheque, postal or money order (not currency) worth the purchase price plus 22p per book for postage (maximum postage required is £3).

NAME (Block letters) _____

ADDRESS _____

_____

_____